T0225860

SAS Stored Processes

A Practical Guide to
Developing Web Applications

Philip Mason

Apress®

SAS Stored Processes: A Practical Guide to Developing Web Applications

Philip Mason
Wallingford, UK

ISBN-13 (pbk): 978-1-4842-5924-5   ISBN-13 (electronic): 978-1-4842-5925-2
https://doi.org/10.1007/978-1-4842-5925-2

Copyright © 2020 by Philip Mason

This work is subject to copyright. All rights are reserved by the Publisher, whether the whole or part of the material is concerned, specifically the rights of translation, reprinting, reuse of illustrations, recitation, broadcasting, reproduction on microfilms or in any other physical way, and transmission or information storage and retrieval, electronic adaptation, computer software, or by similar or dissimilar methodology now known or hereafter developed.

Trademarked names, logos, and images may appear in this book. Rather than use a trademark symbol with every occurrence of a trademarked name, logo, or image we use the names, logos, and images only in an editorial fashion and to the benefit of the trademark owner, with no intention of infringement of the trademark.

The use in this publication of trade names, trademarks, service marks, and similar terms, even if they are not identified as such, is not to be taken as an expression of opinion as to whether or not they are subject to proprietary rights.

While the advice and information in this book are believed to be true and accurate at the date of publication, neither the authors nor the editors nor the publisher can accept any legal responsibility for any errors or omissions that may be made. The publisher makes no warranty, express or implied, with respect to the material contained herein.

Managing Director, Apress Media LLC: Welmoed Spahr
Acquisitions Editor: Susan McDermott
Development Editor: Laura Berendson
Coordinating Editor: Rita Fernando

Cover designed by eStudioCalamar

Distributed to the book trade worldwide by Springer Science+Business Media New York, 1 New York Plaza, New York, NY 10004. Phone 1-800-SPRINGER, fax (201) 348-4505, e-mail orders-ny@springer-sbm.com, or visit www.springeronline.com. Apress Media, LLC is a California LLC and the sole member (owner) is Springer Science + Business Media Finance Inc (SSBM Finance Inc). SSBM Finance Inc is a **Delaware** corporation.

For information on translations, please e-mail rights@apress.com, or visit http://www.apress.com/rights-permissions.

Apress titles may be purchased in bulk for academic, corporate, or promotional use. eBook versions and licenses are also available for most titles. For more information, reference our Print and eBook Bulk Sales web page at http://www.apress.com/bulk-sales.

Any source code or other supplementary material referenced by the author in this book is available to readers on GitHub via the book's product page, located at www.apress.com/9781484259245. For more detailed information, please visit http://www.apress.com/source-code.

Printed on acid-free paper

Table of Contents

About the Author ix

About the Technical Reviewer xi

Chapter 1: Introduction 1

Background 1

What's a Stored Process? 3

Benefits of Stored Processes 6

Other Key Features of Stored Processes 7

Skills Needed 8

SAS Products Required 9

Summary 9

Chapter 2: Developing Applications 11

Development Models 11

Freestyle Approach 11

V-Model 12

Agile 13

Architectural Concepts 14

Useful Documents to Produce 15

Source Control Systems 16

Environments for Developing Web Applications 18

Ways to Develop with SAS 19

Commonly Used SAS Tools 19

Write Your Own Tools in SAS 20

Simple Techniques for Building Applications with Stored Processes 21

Useful Tools for Building Web Applications 22

    Lint Tools 22

    IDE Tools 23

Using a JavaScript IDE 24

    JavaScript Debuggers 24

Code Comparison Tools 26

Summary 29

Chapter 3: HTML 31

Importance of Using HTML5 31

HTML Basics 32

    FORM Tag 34

    Ways to Generate HTML 36

    General Techniques to Add HTML to a Web Page 44

Making a Stored Process Generate Its Own HTML Menu 54

    Form Attributes 57

Persistence – How to Pass Data Between Stored Processes 59

    Storage 60

    Cookies 60

    Files or Tables 62

    URL 62

Where to Put HTML Code, JavaScript Libraries, Images, and More? 62

Summary 64

Chapter 4: JavaScript 65

Basic Example of a JavaScript Program 66

Writing and Testing 67

Debugging JavaScript 68

Using JavaScript with HTML 69

    Basic DOM 70

Using Stored Processes to Generate Pure JavaScript 71

    How Data Is Stored and Used 72

    How SAS Stored Processes Can Feed Data to Objects 72

More About Where to Put Files on Your Web Server 73

    Directories 74

    Relative Paths 74

    Specifying Libraries 75

Building Interactivity with JavaScript 76

    Pop-Up Windows 76

    Validating Form Fields 77

    Linking to One or More Other URLs 79

Summary 80

Chapter 5: JavaScript Libraries **81**

Benefits of a Library 81

Choosing a JavaScript Library to Use As a Framework 82

Recommended Libraries 83

    Content Delivery Networks (CDNs) 84

    jQuery 85

Getting Started 86

    Selecting Elements in jQuery 88

Fundamental jQuery Techniques 93

    Actions 94

Summary 96

Chapter 6: Data **99**

Dynamic Data 99

    Using Stored Processes to Create Dynamic Data 100

How SAS Stored Processes Can Feed Data to Objects 101

Static Data 104

    CSV 105

    XML 111

    JSON 115

Summary 124

Chapter 7: Stored Processes **125**

Converting a SAS Program into a Stored Process... 125

Creating a Stored Process 129

    Creating a Stored Process with Management Console 130

    Using Enterprise Guide to Make a Stored Process 147

    Adding Dependencies... 190

    Using Input Streams and Output Prompts 196

Summary... 202

Chapter 8: SAS Stored Process Web Application **203**

Index Page 203

Sample Stored Processes 206

Reserved Macro Parameters... 207

    Macro Variables Used with %stpbegin 207

    Automatic Macro Variables in Stored Processes Run via SAS Stored
    Process Web Application 213

    How to Use Macro Variables.. 215

    Step-by-Step Guide to Building a Web Application Using Stored Processes........ 216

A Note About Authentication 234

    Creating an HTML Menu for Our Stored Process... 234

    Step 8: Use HTML Forms to Run Stored Processes 236

Uploading Files with a Stored Process 246

    Example: Uploading Three Files... 249

    Passing Multiple Parameters of the Same Name 252

How to Use Sessions... 256

    Sessions with Graphs 259

Logs That Record Information About Stored Processes 261

    Stored Process Server Logs 261

    Workspace Server Logs... 262

    Pooled Workspace Server Logs... 262

    Metadata Server Logs 264

    Object Spawner Logs... 266

Linking Stored Processes 266

    Stored Process Example.. 267

Loading a Stored Process into Part of a Web Page.................................... 271

Other Recommended JavaScript Libraries 272

    Grids 272

    Highcharts 276

    D3 278

Summary... 280

Chapter 9: SAS Procedures... 283

PROC STP... 283

PROC JSON 289

PROC STREAM.. 296

    Streaming with a Data Step.. 297

    Streaming with PROC STREAM.. 298

PROC HTTP... 308

    Example Accessing a Web Page 308

    Example Using a Web Service 309

PROC EXPORT.. 312

    Use Code with a Macro Variable for the Table Name.............................. 313

    Call Stored Process Passing Parameter for Table................................... 313

    Use Code in JavaScript to Feed Objects... 313

PROC IMPORT... 313

Summary... 317

Index... 319

About the Author

Philip Mason is a SAS expert with 35 years' experience in many different industries. He has worked extensively with SAS his entire career and has shared his expertise with others. The last few years he's been working on building web applications using SAS and other technologies. For most of the last decade, Phil has enjoyed working around SAS architecture; mentoring and training people in SAS; working with big data, business intelligence, and analytics; and tuning and building web applications using SAS Stored Processes, HTML, and JavaScript. He's the author of several books on SAS.

About the Technical Reviewer

Allan Bowe is a SAS geek with a passion for HTML5 apps on SAS. Allan has made a number of contributions to the SAS community such as SASjs (an adapter for bidirectional communication between HTML5 and SAS), sasjs-cli (a command-line tool for managing SAS project compilation, build, and deployment), and macrocore (a SAS macro library for building SAS apps on both SAS 9 and Viya).

When not building web apps, Allan is working on Data Controller, a commercial data capture, data quality, and data governance web app for both SAS 9 and Viya.

CHAPTER 1

Introduction

SAS has been utilized by programmers for more than four decades. To keep up with the ability to retrieve, edit, modify, and report on nearly any type of data from anywhere, SAS has built SAS Stored Processes. Although you can find information about Stored Processes in the SAS documentation on the SAS site, this book focuses on helping programmers utilize the SAS Stored Process Web Application to create amazing tools for your end users.

Background

When I started using SAS in 1985 on IBM mainframes, I was using SAS 82.5 – in the days before SAS started renumbering its products into the series we know today. We used terminals connected to the mainframe and could write a program that was either run interactively or saved and run in batch. The output produced was basic by today's standards and was effectively static output that was printed out and handed to users. If changes were needed, we would edit the programs and re-run them.

Obviously, SAS has evolved over the decades, adding more and more features that are useful in processing data into information and delivering it to users. Now you can access data anywhere, process it, and display it in almost any way. The following are just a few of the innovations in SAS over the years that have occurred since I started using SAS:

- SAS/AF lets us produce applications which run in the SAS environment and are very flexible. There are now many people porting their old AF applications to Stored Processes running in a web browser.

- SAS/IntrNet enables a web browser to prompt users for information before using that to customize results of programs. Changing these old programs to Stored Processes is very easy.

© Philip Mason 2020
P. Mason, *SAS Stored Processes*, https://doi.org/10.1007/978-1-4842-5925-2_1

- ODS lets us easily provide output in a wide range of formats using the same program. For instance, we could produce HTML, RTF, and PDF from one report. This is all very helpful when using Stored Processes.

- SAS/ACCESS, together with Filename and Libname engines, lets us read and write lots of different data formats whether Oracle database, EXCEL spreadsheets, XML files, or many others. This enables Stored Processes to read and write to almost any supported system or file format.

- SAS Visual Analytics provides a complete platform for analytics visualization, enabling you to identify patterns and relationships in data that weren't initially evident. Interactive, self-service BI and reporting capabilities are combined with out-of-the-box advanced analytics so everyone can discover insights from any size and type of data, including text. Stored Processes can be used directly from VA or included in reports. You can also link to a URL, which can be running a Stored Process.

Since SAS 8.2 came out in 2001, web applications could be used through SAS. Originally, HTML was generated from a data step, which could then be used through a web browser. Then SAS/IntrNet came along which enabled the creation of more flexible web apps. But now SAS has the SAS Stored Process Web Application – a powerful way to deliver content to a web browser. The Stored Process Web Application runs a Stored Process on behalf of a user and can deliver the output to the web browser. Stored Processes can be used in this way to build web applications. They can produce all the HTML and JavaScript needed to make a web application or just be used to produce some data needed for a table displayed.

Some of these technologies have lasted many years and are still just as useful today as they were 20 years ago. Some of the technologies are hardly used any more (such as SAS/AF), but SAS has provided new and improved technologies in their place. Never before have there been so many ways to turn data into information and build applications with SAS.

This book will show you how to use the web technologies that you frequently see used in impressive websites. By using Stored Processes, you will be able to build applications that exploit CSS, JavaScript, and HTML libraries, which will enable you to build powerful and impressive web applications using SAS as the back end. In the last few years, some SAS users around the world have started to do this with amazing results. This kind of approach is still very uncommon with SAS users around the world. People who have SAS skills usually don't have web development skills and vice versa. Occasionally, people have both skills but are unaware of how to connect them with the SAS Stored Process Web Application. This book lays out the skills needed to connect all of this together.

What's a Stored Process?

A Stored Process lets you write SAS that is stored on a server and use it from many places expanding on the utility of the SAS Software. A Stored Process can be executed as required by requesting applications.

Stored Processes were introduced in SAS 9 in 2002 and are essentially just a SAS program with some metadata associated with it. Metadata is generally defined as "data about data." Stored Processes are similar to the concept of a SAS macro, in that a Stored Process can also have a range of parameters associated with it; however, there is much more to a Stored Process in SAS.

Virtually, any SAS program can be a Stored Process. "Just add metadata" and you can turn your SAS program into a Stored Process! As long as you define at least a few key things, such as where it will run and where the code is stored, most other things will default nicely for you. And Stored Processes can always be changed later if you want to alter any defaults, add parameters, and so on.

There are two parts to a Stored Process:

1. The SAS code, which is run when the Stored Process is executed. This might be stored within the metadata or stored elsewhere on a disk as shown in Figures 1-1 and 1-2.

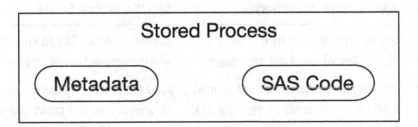

Figure 1-1. *Stored Process with code stored in metadata*

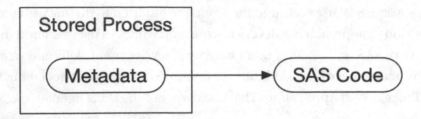

Figure 1-2. *Stored Process with SAS code stored on disk*

2. The metadata for the Stored Process which holds information about these:

    1. Which server it will run on, which can be either a Stored Process server or Workspace server

    2. Which users are allowed to run it, as well as which users can change the metadata for the Stored Process

    3. What parameters can be used, including any ranges, required parameters, and default values

Web applications are a great way to provide information and functionality to users. Since they run in a web browser, it means that there is no software to be installed, which makes it easy for anyone to use them. Running from a web browser means that any devices which are able to browse the Web can initiate something to run on the web application. So, whether you want to use your web app on a mainframe, PC, Mac, or tablet, you will be able to. Remember the web app runs on a server, but you interact with it through your client. See Table 1-1 for a comparison between stored processes and workspace servers.

Table 1-1. *Feature comparison for Stored Process vs. Workspace servers*

Feature	SAS Stored Process Server	SAS Workspace Server
Server	Started up once and then used to run Stored Processes of different users	Started up when Stored Process is run and then closed down when complete
Startup time	The first time a server is used, it must start up, but then will be very fast as it is already running	Always starts a new server, so depending on your installation could take very little time up to 10 or 20 seconds

(continued)

Table 1-1. (*continued*)

Feature	SAS Stored Process Server	SAS Workspace Server
User ID	When a SAS Stored Process is run on a SAS Stored Process server, it is run on behalf of a user by a special user id. If you have configured SAS in the default way, then Stored Processes will usually be run under the `sassrv` user-id. So, if a SAS metadata user called pmason tried to run a Stored Process, it would check whether that SAS metadata user was allowed to run that Stored Process, and if so, it would be run using the `sassrv` user-id. This is an important fact to be aware of when designing applications, particularly for UNIX systems which are very fussy about permissions	When a Stored Process is run on a Workspace server, it is executed under the account associated with that SAS metadata user

Stored Processes can produce output which can be sent directly to the web browser. This is called streamed output. There is a special `fileref` (`_webout`) where the Stored Process execution context can use to steam output directly to the client. In a web browser, the execution context would be the Stored Process Web Application, and it would take anything written to it and send it to the client. This is enormously flexible and powerful. It means that anything you can produce from SAS using ODS, or even a data step, can be written to a web browser.

Stored Processes can run on SAS Stored Process servers or SAS Workspace servers; however, many customers find it helpful to use Stored Process servers since they will typically get started faster since they are shared. A Stored Process server will run under the sassrv user account (by default); however, if running on a Workspace server, it will run under the user's account. Some customers find it useful to run on a Workspace server for security reasons. It is useful to be aware of how the servers are configured and how many multibridge connections are available of each of the defined servers. This can help in choosing the best one to use.

Benefits of Stored Processes

A Stored Process basically gives your SAS program the ability to run in many more places than before – not only within a SAS environment but also in other applications and all kinds of other places. The following are some reasons for using a Stored Process:

- Centralized code on server providing "one version of the truth."

- The user can be prompted to enter various parameters.

- Parameters can be passed to the Stored Process so that it can be written in a very generic way.

- Code can be run on a server or grid to provide the best available environment to run the code.

- Code can be run in many places:

    - Web browser

    - Microsoft Office: Excel, Word, and PowerPoint

    - Many SAS clients

    - Windows programs using .Net connection provided

    - Many programs using Java connection provided

    - Web services

    - Accept user input from browser or via parameters on URL

    - Produce output in web browser

- **Easy to use** – You can use a wizard in Enterprise Guide to create a SAS program and then use a wizard to create a Stored Process from it.

- Logically separates the SAS code (what it does) from the metadata (who can run it, where it runs, etc.).

- Use the power of ODS destinations.

    - Create files such as PDF, Excel, PowerPoint, and Word.

    - Render files produced using various applications such as MS Word, MS Excel, PDF Viewer, and so on.

- Integrate output produced into other applications written in a range of technologies such as HTML, Java, C++, and so on.

- Produce JSON or XML files to represent data in the form required by other objects or applications.

- Use Proc HTTP or Proc STP to run a Stored Process with the Stored Process Web Application, allowing you to run a Stored Process within a Stored Process.

- Embed URL calls in emails, Word documents, or PowerPoints, so user can click a link to run Stored Process and produce some content.

- Output produced by a call can be modified in various ways by passing parameters to it, such as _odsdest or _xpixels.

- Can schedule URLs to run in windows scheduler, which could produce a package and email it to someone, for example.

- Can run from Excel, Word, PowerPoint, and many other applications, even without the Microsoft Office Add-in. It just has to be an application capable of using a URL as input.

- Integrates with many other SAS clients such as the BI Dashboard, Portal, Web Report Studio, Enterprise Miner, Visual Analytics, Visual Statistics, and even JMP.

- Integrates with many other applications such as Tableau by producing an output like a CSV and then automatically downloading it to client and into application.[1]

Other Key Features of Stored Processes

The key thing that makes a SAS program a Stored Process is some metadata, which is defined and points to (or includes) the SAS code. If you compare a Stored Process and some SAS code that effectively are doing the same thing, you will find that the Stored Process can be run from many more places and be used in a far more flexible way. For

---

[1]Using HTTP headers and Open With.

instance, running the Stored Process via the Office Add-in could bring results into Excel, or running it with BI Dashboard could populate part of a screen.

If your Stored Process is producing ODS output, then you need to use ODS statements. SAS has provided some great autocall macros you can use to take care of this. You simply put **%stpbegin** at the start of your Stored Process and **%stpend** at the end. There are lots of optional macro variables which can be set to alter the behavior of ODS if you use these standard macros. Or you could just code your own custom ODS statements if you want; however, if you don't use the standard stpbegin and stpend macros provided by SAS, you might find that the Stored Process doesn't run as you expect.

Your Stored Process doesn't have to produce any output. It might just produce a table in a database, copy a file, or carry out some other operation in the background. Of course, generally you will want to provide some kind of output so that you know whether the process worked or not. Your Stored Process might produce a report of some sort in HTML for display in a browser, or a PDF file, or some CSV data to be loaded by a Python program. The possibilities are endless.

The most important `fileref` to know for the Stored Process programmer is `_webout`. It is automatically available when running a Stored Process through the Stored Process Web Application. Writing to this allows you to write directly to the web browser, which provides you with a very powerful technique that we will explore later.

You can run Stored Processes from lots of different places within SAS, but also outside of SAS which can provide a great way to call SAS code from other applications.

Skills Needed

The Stored Process Web Application and/or the Stored Process service API can be used to implement web apps. An advantage of using the Stored Process Web Application is that you only need HTML and SAS skills in order to build a web application. However, if you use the Stored Process service API, then you will need Java skills in order to build your web application in Java which then calls Stored Processes via the Stored Process service API.

SAS Products Required

To use Stored Processes in SAS, you will need the following products as a minimum:

- SAS Core

- SAS Integration Technologies

SAS runs across many kinds of hardware and is supported by many operating systems. For example, you could be running PC SAS on a Windows laptop or using SAS Studio from a web browser on your iPhone. However, if you want to run Stored Processes, you will need a server somewhere that you can connect to and run those Stored Processes, returning the output to you. That server needs to have the appropriate parts of SAS installed on it to enable Stored Processes to run.

The standard way to develop Stored Processes provided by SAS is Enterprise Guide which requires Windows, as it doesn't run on other platforms. JMP is a powerful tool that runs on Windows or Mac and can access SAS in a number of ways, including the running of Stored Processes.

If using the Stored Process Web Application, all you need is a browser, which could be run on PC, Mac, Linux, mobile phone, or tablet.

Summary

We have been introduced to SAS Stored Processes in this chapter and learned some things about them:

- A stored process is basically a SAS program with some metadata that says who can run it, where it runs, and what parameters are used.

- You can use stored processes to build web applications and leverage your SAS infrastructure.

- Stored processes run either on a Stored Process server or a Workspace server.

- Stored processes work with Microsoft products, Java applications, and .Net applications and even act as web services too.

- The `_webout fileref` can be used to write directly back to the client using the stored process.

- Most SAS programmers can use stored processes quite easily without much extra learning involved.

- Most big SAS installations have the required software available without needing to purchase anything extra.

CHAPTER 2

Developing Applications

When developing applications with SAS, it is wise to keep in mind some principles and best practices to follow. If you follow these principles, then they will help to avoid many of the common problems and pitfalls that developers are confronted with. These things are much easier to implement at the start of a project rather than part way through and will provide a lot of benefits for the investment of time and effort.

This chapter is aimed at the project manager or architect of a project, as they tend to be the person who thinks about the project as a whole. Sometimes this will be the programmer, especially for small projects. There are advantages to following these principles even with small projects, but the benefits grow as the size of the project grows in size.

Development Models

There are many ways to carry out development. I will briefly outline some of these now.

Freestyle Approach

The freestyle approach is how many untrained people develop things. It basically involves just diving in and starting to code with no planning at all. Of course, you need some idea of what you are trying to build, but that can be a sketch on the back of an envelope or a vague idea in your head. Many great systems have started this way, and often it is a valid way to innovate new solutions. However, typically it's not the best way to develop a big system or application especially when more than one person is involved in the team.

For many years, the most popular model for larger developments was the System Development Life Cycle (SDLC) pictured in Figure 2-1. When you look at this, it makes a lot of logical sense and in fact is pretty much the process any sensible developer would go through if doing it freestyle.

© Philip Mason 2020
P. Mason, *SAS Stored Processes*, https://doi.org/10.1007/978-1-4842-5925-2_2

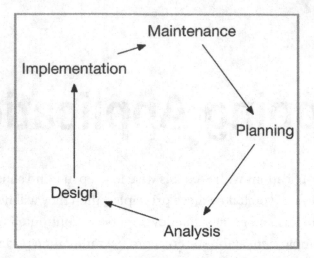

Figure 2-1. *SDLC/Waterfall*

This model can run into some problems when the stages become very prescriptive and lots of rules and guidelines are defined in an attempt to achieve best practice. I have seen companies where there are many long documents that must be delivered at each stage of this process which can mean that a small development that might take a day to write code for ends up taking four weeks to complete once all the documents, meetings, and stages have been done. This model is sometimes called the Waterfall model, as the diagram can be drawn as a waterfall from "Planning" to "Maintenance." Sometimes "Planning" and "Analysis" are replaced by "Requirements," and a "Verification" step is added after "Implementation."

V-Model

The V-model of software development is an extension to the SDLC model. Each phase on the left of Figure 2-2 has a corresponding phase on the right which is for validation. For instance, the "Concepts of Operations" is validated by the "Operation & Maintenance."

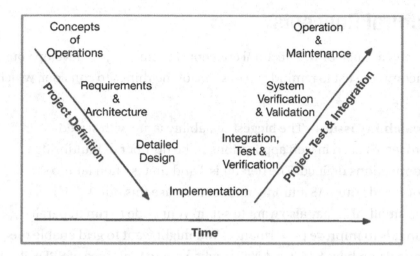

Figure 2-2. *V-model*

One common problem with this model is that it doesn't fit the needs of all people in the project. It's a nice way for a project manager to look at a project, but not the best way for a developer. And it is fairly inflexible although still probably a lot better than SDLC.

Agile

The Agile approach to development has shorter cycles of development and delivery so we get results quicker which users can see, which in turn affects further development. It is quite similar to another model called Rapid Application Development, which has been around for many more years. Agile welcomes changes in requirements, which other models don't because it means returning to an earlier phase of the process. Agile has many iterations of development, testing, and delivery, so users get things in weeks rather than months. Developers and clients work together closely on an almost daily basis. This model is sometimes preferred by developers and clients but is harder to manage for project managers.

Architectural Concepts

It is wise to keep a range of architectural concepts in mind as you develop your software. This is an incomplete list to remind you of some of the things to consider, which can lead to a better design:

- **Scalability issues** – The biggest scalability issue with stored processes used in web applications is the number of multibridge connections defined. The default is 3 and that is often far too small. You need your SAS administrator to increase this number if it is too small. You may also want to set up your code to run in parallel threads to improve performance. You might want to grid enable the code if you have SAS/Grid. You might want to make use of SPDS if you have that, since it can help improve performance on your tables removing the need for sorting (for example).

- **CRUD issues (Create Read Update Delete)** – This is often a consideration if you are developing web applications and want to create tables, update records, or delete things. It's easy to read data, but there are various issues around these other things. It is more difficult to use SAS tables with CRUD than using some other database systems such as MySQL or Postgres.

- **Browser differences** – If you're developing web applications, then you need to look at how you support different browsers. You can detect the browser you are using and potentially write special code to handle its differences or make use of a JavaScript framework which will handle many of these issues automatically.

- **Complexity of code vs. ability to support it** – You can sometimes write complex code and reduce the number of lines needed. However, you can usually achieve a similar level of performance by using a simpler technique that perhaps has more lines. But if things are easier for a future maintainer of your code to understand, then you are wise to choose the simpler code.

- **Platform differences** – Will your application only ever run on a laptop? What if it runs on a huge monitor with many times the resolution of a laptop? Maybe you want to detect that and change the way you are producing the user interface. What if it runs on a mobile phone or tablet? Perhaps you want to detect that and change things. It is useful to be aware of various development frameworks that handle different platforms, such as Bootstrap. Many of those systems allow setting up things on screen with a grid system and defining different layouts for different sized devices so that you can write one piece of code for mobile phones, laptops, and large screen devices.

Useful Documents to Produce

It's best not to go overboard with the production of documents for your development. However, there are some documents that are usually advisable to create; even if on a small development, you include them all in one:

- **Requirements Documentation** – Identifies what the system should look like and be capable of.

- **Architecture/Design Documentation** – Describes how the software components are designed and should have sufficient information for programmer(s) to develop the programs.

- **Technical Documentation** – Documents the code, algorithms, user interfaces, APIs, and so on. It is a document written by the programmer(s) for other programmer(s) who might come along later and need to understand and maintain the code.

- **End-User Documentation** – Describes how the software works for those people that will use it. That could be end users, system administrators, and support.

- **Marketing/Training Material** – Useful to provide to potential users of the software to show the benefits.

15

Source Control Systems

Source control systems are used to track changes to files, maintain different versions of the same files, and allow multiple people to collaborate during the development phase. These systems are sometimes called version control systems or revision control systems too. The main idea is that the system manages source code and maintains a number of versions and history.

If you have access to Data Integration Studio, this can handle source control for you – so look no further. You will still need to do some additional configuration beyond the default, such as setting up a SVN, CVS, or Git server. However, if you don't have DI Studio, then read on.

Using source control is extremely beneficial, because as we develop programs, the system maintains previous versions. We can return to an old version if we need to. We can compare the current version of the code to old versions to see what has changed. The system can keep track of who has changed parts of the code. It can manage the code so that only one person at a time is updating it.

Some important features that you should look for when choosing source control systems are

- **Concurrent development** – A source control system should provide tools to allow multiple developers to work on source code at the same time. This might provide a mechanism for merging code together in a controlled way.

- **Tracking changes** – It should provide a mechanism to see what changes have been made by people, even when code is merged back together.

- **Locking or branches** – Locking applies to some source control systems that manage code by locking it for use by one person at a time. Other systems take an alternate approach of keeping multiple copies of code, such as in different branches, which can then be merged together. A system using locking can handle locking of modules and checking code in and out. If a team member wanted to make changes to the code, they could check it out. That would lock the code so that others could not make changes to it until it was finished with and checked back in. The benefits of this grow as the size of a team increases, in that the more people trying to work together on code, the easier a system like this makes it.

- **Archive and backup** – A system can also handle archiving and backing up of code. Archiving tends to happen for code that is not currently in use and therefore is copied away to an archive area so that it can be retrieved if it is needed in future. Backups are taken regularly with the aim of being used if code is lost or recent changes lost. It is for current code that is in use but which we want another copy kept as insurance.

- **Release management** – Release management is concerned with releasing versions of code into different environments and can be helped or managed with a source control system. Often an application is made up of a number of programs which many people might be working on together. Many of these pieces of code may form modules within an application. A collection of these are usually bundled up into a release. It might be the entire application code or a collection of modules from the application. When a release happens, you would usually increment the version of your application (e.g., Data_explorer v1.11). Usually you would increment by an integer for a major release and increment decimals for minor releases. A good source control system that manages releases would be able to issue a release, perhaps by packaging up the new bits and passing them to another environment. It could also roll back a release by packaging up a previous release and delivering that to replace a current release that might have problems.

There are many source control systems available with these features and more are coming out year by year. Some of the common ones that have been around for many years are Subversion (SVN), Git, Team Foundation Server (TFS), and Concurrent Versions System (CVS). There are newer systems like GitHub for which SAS now provides some integration. This is a fantastic system to use with SAS development, and I suggest you search the SAS Global Forum proceedings online for papers from users describing how to use this.

You may have a source control system that you have to use because it is the company standard or already in use. If you do get to choose, look for one that has a client for your operating system that supports it and makes it easier to use. For example, GitHub has a desktop version that can be downloaded for Windows or macOS.

Environments for Developing Web Applications

A development environment is the software that allows you to write, test, and edit a program. You can develop in a single environment, but it is advisable to use at least two environments. If you do develop in a single environment and then people use your application from that environment, then when you have to fix a problem and make an enhancement, you are doing it with the live code, which is likely to cause problems to your users. One mistake and the application stops working.

You should develop in one development environment and then deliver the developed code to production in another development environment. This allows you to have the current release of your program running in production while you are changing the development version and getting it ready to become the new production version.

If you are able to have three environments, then that allows you to have a Development, Test, and Production environment. You then develop in Development and, when something is ready, deliver it to Test for testing and user acceptance. Once that is done, it can be moved to Production.

Sometimes people will have a Personal Development Environment (PDEV) as well as a Common Development Environment (CDEV). Then they can do things in PDEV without affecting anyone else, and once they are happy with that code, they can move it to CDEV.

Some larger companies have even more environments:

- Common Development (CDEV)

- Personal Development (PDEV)

- Component Integration Testing (CIT)

- System Integration Testing (SIT)

- User Acceptance Testing (UAT)

- Production (PROD)

This allows different kinds of testing to be done in different environments. Figure 2-3 shows what the flow of development would be in a multiple environment system.

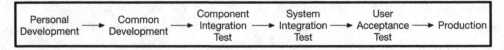

Figure 2-3. *Multiple environment system flow of development*

Ways to Develop with SAS

SAS provides lots of different tools for developing applications. Each has some advantages and disadvantages. It's important to know what release of the software you are using too, as that can make a difference as to what useful features you may or may not have. For instance, at the time of writing, the latest version of Enterprise Guide has a data step debugger built into it, whereas prior versions do not.

Commonly Used SAS Tools

Commonly used SAS tools include the following:

- PC SAS, in which we can write SAS code of all kinds, but if creating Stored Processes, we need to also use SAS Management Console.

- Enterprise Guide, which can create most kinds of SAS code including SAS Stored Processes. It spawns a SAS Workspace server to run SAS code from it.

- SAS Studio, which is similar to Enterprise Guide but only requires a web browser to use. It doesn't allow creation of Stored Processes via any kind of wizard, but you can create them programmatically with standard SAS code. That code would need to make metadata calls in order to create them, perhaps using some open source macros available for that purpose.

- Data Integration Studio provides a controlled way to create SAS programs using a collection of transformations and custom SAS code. It includes the ability to check out and check in code so that teams of people can work on large systems together.

- Office Add-in provides a SAS program window from the add-in toolbar which lets you write SAS code and execute it on the sever. The results are brought back and displayed in the Word, EXCEL, or PowerPoint. You can also view the SAS log.

There are lots of other less common SAS tools that can be used for developing, but I will be focusing on the ones mentioned already.

Most people will create Stored Processes with Enterprise Guide, and it is the way that SAS documentation says to create them. Doing this will use a system account for the stored process though, and it has inherent dangers associated with that. Currently, you must either use Enterprise Guide or Management Console to create Stored Processes as there is no other simple way provided by SAS to do so. There are metadata functions that can be used from Base SAS to create a stored process, and there are even some macros available that make that easy to do. I recommend taking a look at them.[1] One nice thing that Enterprise Guide does for you is to take you through a wizard to help you make the Stored Process. It also will do things like add the stpbegin and stpend macros around your SAS code by default so that ODS will work in the various clients you use your Stored Process with. If you are new to Stored Processes, then use Enterprise Guide to create them until you find a reason to use another method.

Write Your Own Tools in SAS

As we will see in this book, we can write our own tools. You will be able to create bespoke tools that you need with the features you want and without features that are not required. You can leverage the skills you have with SAS to make your tools without needing knowledge of other languages. They can be SAS macros that we can provide parameters to choose what we want them to do. Or we can build Stored Processes which are far more flexible. I have created Stored Process tools like this which run through the web browser and give me functions like

- Scheduling SAS programs to run

- Analyzing directories of SAS and Enterprise Guide projects, producing reports summarizing each of the programs

- Displaying the output and logs from scheduled jobs, allowing them to be viewed

- Displaying the logs or Stored Processes that have run recently or are currently running

---

[1]You can create a stored process from a SAS program with the code located here: https://github.com/macropeople/macrocore/blob/master/meta/mm_createstp.sas

Simple Techniques for Building Applications with Stored Processes

I have made many a prototype application using one or more Stored Processes in a matter of hours. You can use some simple techniques to do this kind of thing:

- Enterprise Guide can generate a web page automatically via a wizard in older versions. For some reason, this was removed in newer versions of EG.

  - If you have a macro that does something (like produce a report from some parameter choices), then this can be simply turned into a Stored Process. Just make a Stored Process and put the macro invocation into it, along with either the macro code or option to point to an autocall library that has it. You will be able to define a prompt for each macro parameter and use those values to invoke the macro. Run this through the SAS Stored Process Web Application and you have an application based on your macro.

- Stored Processes, which create their own interactive elements, are a great way to build applications. For instance, you can make a Stored Process that produces selection lists, radio buttons, and so on based on SAS data. This lets you build a form with selections you can choose from which can then be defined to call another Stored Process to make use of those selections.

- It's easy to generate HTML with hyperlinks to other HTML from a Stored Process.

- You can implement drill-down by making your Stored Process generate HTML links that link to the Stored Process that produced them, but passed a parameter value in with the call, thereby implementing drill-down. For example, make a graph that has bars with drill-down links that call the same Stored Process but add the info for passing the bar value clicked.

- Make menus by a Stored Process generating forms with HTML, which then call other Stored Processes.

- JavaServer Pages (JSP) can be created in a particular location with the same name as a Stored Process. If you then invoke the Stored Process with a certain _action parameter value, then the JSP will be displayed, rather than the Stored Process being run. This allows a flexible program to be written to prompt the user for parameters before running the actual Stored Process. You can "hack" this process by simply putting an HTML file in the JSP directory, with a JSP file type, and your HTML will then be displayed in the same way.

Useful Tools for Building Web Applications

Here is a range of mostly free tools that can be used to make the process of building web applications with SAS much easier. I will outline some of these tools and describe how they are useful. Tools come and go though, so some things I mention might not be available in future or there may be better tools around. Hopefully, being aware of the kind of tools on offer will enable you to search for others that superseded these ones.

Lint Tools

Lint was originally a tool on UNIX systems that flagged suspicious or non-portable code in C programs. However, people have extended this functionality to other languages and provided more functionality. Some tools will not only look for a range of errors in your code, but also lay out the code in a more standard way. Some tools will uppercase tags and attributes used, highlight unmatched parentheses, wrap long lines, and so on. So, it can take some very hard to read code and make it far easier to make sense of. Here are some useful tools for web application development:

- JavaScript Lint – `www.JavaScriptlint.com/` or `http://www.jslint.com/`

- HTML Tidy – `https://infohound.net/tidy/`

- CSS Lint – `http://csslint.net/`

- JSON Lint – `https://jsonlint.com/`

- CSV Lint – `https://csvlint.io/`

The JavaScript Lint tool will look for these common mistakes, as well as many uncommon ones:

- Missing semi-colons at the end of a line

- Curly braces without an *if, for, while,* and so on

- Code that is never run because of a *return, throw, continue, or break*

- Case statements in a switch that do not have a *break* statement

- Leading and trailing decimal points on a number

- A leading zero that turns a number into octal (base 8)

- Comments within comments

- Ambiguity whether two adjacent lines are part of the same statement

- Statements that don't do anything

IDE Tools

An IDE is an Interactive Development Environment. These are tools that aid you in developing in one or more particular languages. They provide some or all of these features: a source code editor with code completion, tools to automate building the code, a debugger, compiler, interpreter, version control system, extensive help on the language, and so on. Some IDEs worth looking at include

- NetBeans from Oracle; there are many versions of this and it's best to just download the HTML5/JavaScript version (`https://netbeans.org/`).

- Brackets is an open source code editor with live preview of changes and support for preprocessors (`http://brackets.io/`).

- Atom from GitHub is described as a hackable text editor, which means it can be customized extensively (`https://atom.io/`).

- Visual Studio Code from Microsoft supports debugging, syntax highlighting, code completion, snippets, and more (`https://code.visualstudio.com/`).

- Notepad++ deserves a mention, though it doesn't have fancy tools built into it. It is like a standard text editor on steroids and is my number one choice for editing all kinds of programs whenever possible. It does have syntax highlighting built in and can do great things like edit hundreds of files simultaneously and find text across them all very quickly (`https://notepad-plus-plus.org/`).

Using a JavaScript IDE

An IDE is an Interactive Development Environment. You can use JavaScript IDEs for developing HTML and JavaScript code. IDEs often have useful features like syntax highlighting, debuggers, preview windows, and so on. Many good ones are free including Notepad++ and Microsoft Visual Studio Code, which both run on Mac, Windows, and Linux.

It is sometimes useful to build some HTML and JavaScript code in an IDE and then look at moving it onto the SAS web server and integrating into a Stored Process.

JavaScript Debuggers

JavaScript debuggers are very useful for running your JavaScript and debugging any errors you have. You can also trace variables reporting their values when they change, which can be helpful in understanding how your JavaScript code runs. You can set breakpoints too, so that the code will run up to a certain point and then pause so you can look at the values of variables. Many web browsers have debuggers built in, so there is no need to buy or download one.

Most developers will have their favorite development tools in their favorite browser. For me, it has changed over time and was Firefox for many years, but more recently, I have found Chrome to be great. These two browsers are great because they work on many operating systems too. Internet Explorer only works on Windows, unless you make use of an emulator such as browserstack.com which lets you test you web page on lots of different browsers and platforms. I find that most browsers have much the same capabilities now, all of which are sufficient for helping to build web applications:

- Microsoft Internet Explorer has built-in developer tools (Figure 2-4) that can be accessed by pressing F12 or using Tools/Developer Tools/Console (`https://msdn.microsoft.com/en-us/library/gg589507(v=vs.85).aspx`).

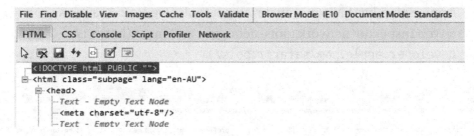

Figure 2-4. *Internet Explorer developer tools*

- Firefox has developer tools too (Figure 2-5) that can be accessed using the Tools/Web Developer menu. There is a debugger, web console, performance tools, and more (`https://developer.mozilla.org/en-US/docs/Tools`).

Figure 2-5. *Firefox developer tools*

- Google Chrome has built-in developer tools (Figure 2-6) which are accessed using the Tools/Developer Tools menu. It also has a web console, debugger, and other tools (`https://developer.chrome.com/devtools`).

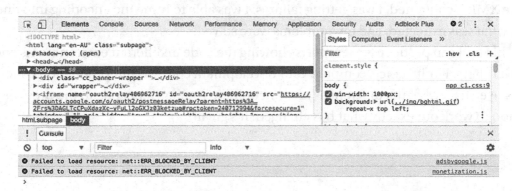

Figure 2-6. *Chrome developer tools*

25

- Apple Safari has built-in web developer tools (Figure 2-7) such as a Web Inspector, network tools, debugger, and more (`https://developer.apple.com/safari/tools/`).

Figure 2-7. *Safari developer tools*

Code Comparison Tools

I have saved many hours of time and done things that were almost impossible to do another way by using code comparison tools such as Beyond Compare (you've got to buy this one if you are using Microsoft Windows) and WinMerge (free and open source). My favorite of all time is Beyond Compare, even though it only runs on Windows and Mac. It will give you a fantastic side-by-side comparison of two directories or files. You can ignore unimportant differences (e.g., different numbers of spaces), show just things that are different, produce reports of the differences, and much more.

Recently, Beyond Compare helped me solve a problem where it showed me that two files were exactly the same, except one was twice the size of the other. Looking at the top of the display, I could see that one file was encoded in ASCII, whereas the other was Unicode. This also meant that when I uploaded one of the files to UNIX and tried to read in the XML it contained, I was getting failures. I was able to bring the encoding into line with what was expected, and my problems were solved.

This tool can produce great reports showing the code in different environments and how it differs. For instance, compare your development code to your production code and see exactly what the differences are. Or compare your current code to the previous version to work out exactly what has changed. It's great!

These tools can compare two files and report the differences:

- Beyond Compare from Scooter Software is the best tool in this category and does everything the others do. As well as comparing files and directories, you can generate reports of differences, use right-click menus through system integration, ignore unimportant differences, and much more (`www.scootersoftware.com/`).

In the sample screenshot (Figure 2-8), you can see me comparing two SAS programs. It shows me a map in the top left of where the differences are; I have selected to see the differences in context, and it is very clear what they are; when I select a line, it even shows me the line comparison at the bottom.

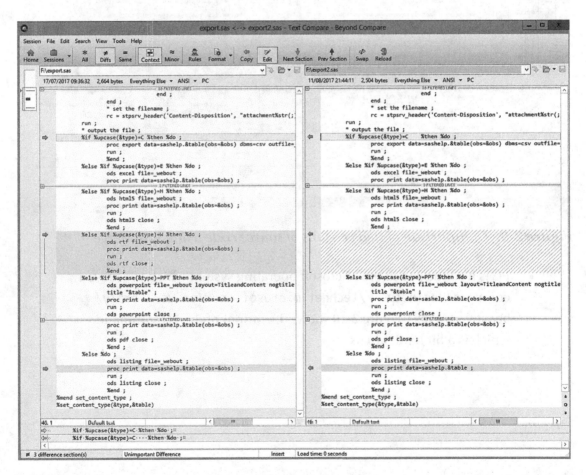

Figure 2-8. *Comparison of two versions of source code using Beyond Compare*

- WinMerge is a free, open source file and directory comparison/
  synchronization tool. It does much of what Beyond Compare does,
  and being free may be a better choice for you (`http://winmerge.`
  `org/?lang=en`).

Figure 2-9 shows the same two SAS programs being compared using WinMerge.

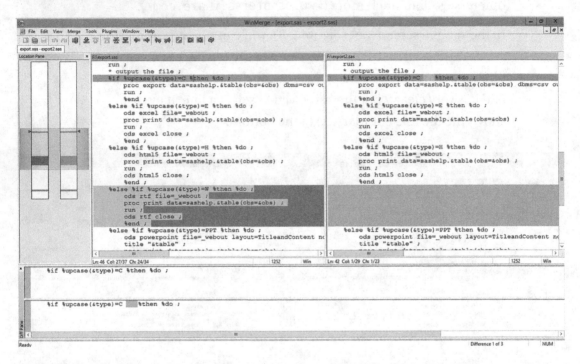

Figure 2-9. *Comparison of two versions of source code using WinMerge*

- FC is a command in the Microsoft operating system which will let you
  compare files (`https://technet.microsoft.com/en-us/library/`
  `bb490904.aspx`). Figure 2-10 shows the output of the FC command,
  which is a bit harder to use.

```
F:\>fc export.sas export2.sas
Comparing files export.sas and EXPORT2.SAS
***** export.sas
        * output the file ;
        %if %upcase(&type)=C %then %do ;
                proc export data=sashelp.&table(obs=&obs) dbms=csv outfile=_webo
ut replace ;
***** EXPORT2.SAS
        * output the file ;
        %if %upcase(&type)=C       %then %do ;
                proc export data=sashelp.&table(obs=&obs) dbms=csv outfile=_webo
ut replace ;
*****

***** export.sas
                %end ;
        %else %if %upcase(&type)=W %then %do ;
                ods rtf file=_webout ;
                proc print data=sashelp.&table(obs=&obs) ;
***** EXPORT2.SAS
                %end ;
        %else %if %upcase(&type)=PPT %then %do ;
                ods powerpoint file=_webout layout=TitleandContent nogtitle nogf
ootnote;
                title "&table" ;
                proc print data=sashelp.&table(obs=&obs) ;
*****

***** export.sas
                run ;
                ods rtf close ;
                %end ;
        %else %if %upcase(&type)=PPT %then %do ;
                ods powerpoint file=_webout layout=TitleandContent nogtitle nogf
ootnote;
                title "&table" ;
***** EXPORT2.SAS
                run ;
                ods powerpoint close ;
                %end ;
        %else %if %upcase(&type)=PDF %then %do ;
                ods pdf file=_webout ;
                title "&table" ;
*****

***** export.sas
                run ;
                ods powerpoint close ;
                %end ;
        %else %if %upcase(&type)=PDF %then %do ;
                ods pdf file=_webout ;
                title "&table" ;
                proc print data=sashelp.&table(obs=&obs) ;
```

Figure 2-10. *Comparing two files using the FC command*

- DIFF and DIFF3 are utilities built into most UNIX operating systems which let you compare files. Their output is similar to the Microsoft FC command, however perhaps a bit easier to use. You can read more about them here: www.computerhope.com/unix/udiff.htm.

Summary

In this chapter, we have learned some more general concepts about developing applications, which are very useful when developing SAS Stored Process–based applications:

- Freestyle approach to development has many disadvantages which other approaches overcome.

- SDLC and the Waterfall model are commonly used methodologies which are quite useful.

- The V-model is a development of the Waterfall model and has some advantages over it.

- Agile development has become very popular in software development in recent years, and I would recommend this.

- When planning for development, you should consider the architectural aspects, especially from a SAS architecture standpoint.

- Make sure you have the most useful documents required for a development project.

- Consider your toolkit such as IDE, source control, debuggers, code comparison, automation tools, deployment tools, and so on.

CHAPTER 3

HTML

If you are a web developer or have some experience doing web development, you can probably skip this chapter. It is intended to introduce the world of web development to SAS programmers.

Importance of Using HTML5

There have been many versions of HTML over the years, and the latest evolution is HTML5. Current browsers support HTML5 well, but if you were using an old browser such as Internet Explorer 6, you might find that parts of it are not supported, in which case there might be some reasons for using HTML4. But HTML5 has been enhanced and offers many advantages over older versions. Some of these advantages are

- HTML5 uses a new W3 specification called ARIA which is used to assign specific roles to elements on HTML on a page. For example, headers are tagged where you put your header for the page. This makes it easy for screen readers to interpret a page making it more accessible to all.

- The Canvas tag (`<canvas>`) allows us to produce all kinds of graphics and animations in the browser. This is a hugely powerful feature which has already been the subject of several books.

- Responsive design is easier. The device type is detected, and the output display is changed to suit the device.

- Cleaner code can be written with less reliance on div tags, and it is easier to read if you use the more meaningful tags available. This increases maintainability and makes it easier to understand.

- Audio and video are handled via their own tags, though I don't tend to use much of that in my reporting.

© Philip Mason 2020
P. Mason, *SAS Stored Processes*, https://doi.org/10.1007/978-1-4842-5925-2_3

HTML Basics

Teaching HTML is outside the scope of this book, but I advise you to look at some of the excellent resources for learning about web development and HTML on www.w3schools.com/. It is worth making sure you understand forms really well by using a tutorial such as this: www.w3schools.com/html/html_forms.asp. You can also learn CSS and JavaScript on this site. I will go through some basics of HTML briefly here and spend a little time looking at some of the more useful parts that can be used with Stored Processes in building web applications.

The HTML document shown in Figure 3-1 produces the output on your web page (see Figure 3-2).

```
<html>
<head>
</head>
<body>
<h1>My heading</h1>
<h2>Sub heading</h2>
<p>Paragraph</p>
</body>
</html>
```

Figure 3-1. *Example of some simple HTML code*

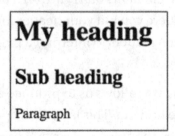

My heading

Sub heading

Paragraph

Figure 3-2. *This is what is shown in browser from the HTML code in Figure 3-1*

Notice that tags in Figure 3-1 are enclosed in angle brackets "<" and ">". There is usually an open tag (e.g., <HTML>) and then a corresponding closing tag (e.g., </HTML>). Note the closing tag has the same name as the starting tag but is preceded with a "/". Tags can optionally have parameters specified on them by specifying name=value pairs (e.g., parameter names are in **bold**, name of tag is <u>**underlined**</u>):

<<u>**input**</u> **type**="submit" **name**="button name" **value**="button value">.

The general structure of an HTML program is that there is a head section and a body section. The head section is a container for metadata in which things like styles, character sets, links, and JavaScript libraries are defined. Effectively this is for setting up the environment of the page. The body section is where the content is defined, such as a text, hyperlinks, tables, lists, figures, and so on.

A typical head section might contain a link to load the jQuery library for use. It would look like this:

```
<head>
<script src="jquery-3.2.1.min.js"></script>
</head>
```

Or you might define some CSS in your head section so that you can define how your text looks, for example:

```
<head>
<style>
h1 {     text-decoration: overline;}
h2 {     text-decoration: line-through;}
h3 {     text-decoration: underline;}
</style>
</head>
```

The body section has the content for the page, for example:

```
<body>
<h1>This is heading 1</h1>
<h2>This is heading 2</h2>
<h3>This is heading 3</h3>
</body>
```

Using the CSS in the head section with the heading tags in the body section gives us a page that looks like Figure 3-3.

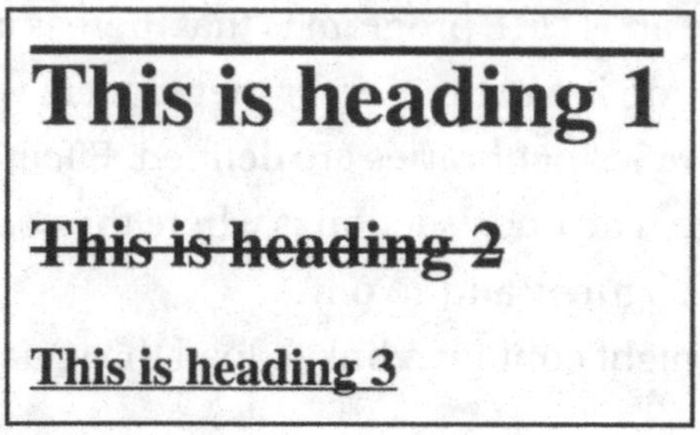

> **This is heading 1**
>
> ~~This is heading 2~~
>
> **This is heading 3**

Figure 3-3. *This is what is displayed in browser from the HTML and CSS specified*

FORM Tag

The FORM tag is probably the most useful thing in HTML for building web applications. With it, we can build a form that prompts a user for information and will then pass the values entered back to the application for processing. Forms start with the <FORM> tag and end with the </FORM> tag. Prompts include

- Get input from the user by using an <input> tag.

- Specifying name on the <input> tag defines the name of the parameter that will be passed on the URL, which will then appear as a macro variable available to be used by our SAS code (e.g., <input name="country">).

- Specify type on the <input> tag to choose between several available types. By default, you don't need to specify it and the type will be text. But there are several other useful types to know about:

  - **Button** displays a pushbutton which can be clicked. This is often combined with some JavaScript code to carry out some special actions when pressed on. You can do this by using the onclick parameter.

  - **Checkbox** shows check box(es) which allow choosing multiple options for a parameter. This is similar to radio, though radio only allows choosing one value.

  - **Color** allows choosing a color using the systems color picker.

  - **Date** allows choosing a date using standard date picker.

- **Datetime-local** allows choosing a date and time.

- **Email** allows entering a valid email address.

- **File** shows button to use file picker to get a filename.

- **Hidden** doesn't display the field at all even though it is still there and will be added to the URL created.

- **Image** displays an image and when it is clicked acts like a submit but also sends the x and y coordinates of where the image was clicked. So you could have an image with various parts to it and be able to work out what part of the image was clicked.

- **Month** allows choosing a month.

- **Number** allows the entering a number and prevents entering anything other than a number.

- **Password** is like text, except it doesn't show the characters as the user types. It is perfect for passwords and other secret text.

- **Radio** shows radio buttons allowing the choice of one option.

- **Range** displays a slider and allows choosing a value using it. Remember that many of these types have associated parameters. Range also makes use of min, max, and value which define the range used and a starting value.

- **Reset** provides a pushbutton which if pressed will restore the fields on a form to their default values.

- **Search** displays a text entry box to specify something to search for. Some of these items produce useful effects when used on mobile devices and tablets. For instance, search gives you a specific keyboard with a search button.

- **Submit** provides a button to click which will then submit the URL that was created by the form.

- **Tel** allows entry of a telephone number. Mobile devices will give you a phone number entry keyboard.

- **Text** provides a box to enter some text in.

- **Time** allows entry of a time using time dialog.

- **Url** allows entry of a URL.

- **Week** allows entry of a week number using a date picker.

With all those input types, we already have something very functional that we can use when producing customer HTML from our Stored Process. But there are even more elements that can be used in forms that give us more abilities:

- **Select** lets us define drop-down lists of options to choose from.

- **Datalist** is very similar to Select, but it also lets you type into the box and displays a list of matching options in the drop-down list as you type.

- **Textarea** defines a multiple line box into which a lot of text can be entered.

Ways to Generate HTML

The simplest technique that can be used to enhance the output from your Stored Processes is to generate HTML which is then displayed in a web browser. Web browsers have been created specifically for displaying output of various kinds. There is lots of built-in functionality to display all kinds of text in various sizes and colors, as well as displaying all kinds of graphics. In addition, you can animate things and detect where the mouse is, and when it clicks in various ways, you can let the user interact with the output and change it. You can produce static output which displays but does not change, as well as dynamic output which changes in various ways. Web browsers can also display many other kinds of output that you may generate with SAS, such as RTF and PDF files.

Another aspect of using HTML to generate output is that you can generate it in flexible ways dependent on the platform you are delivering it to or add JavaScript or other scripting to make the HTML adapt for the platform. This means you can make sure your output displays in the best way on phones, tablets, computers, and so on.

There are several basic ways that you can use your Stored Process to generate HTML: basic ODS, custom HTML, PROC STREAM, or writing your own HTML. Let's examine each of these in turn.

Basic ODS

Stored Process can generate HTML, as it might do with a range of ODS HTML reports. In this model, we can make some enhancements to the HTML generated by inserting bit of custom HTML/JavaScript in various ways such as by modifying templates, inserting data _null_ steps to write bits to _webout, and adding links to titles/footnotes.

Custom HTML

Stored Process can generate custom HTML by using a data step that writes to _webout. In this technique, we can write anything directly to the browser just as though it was part of a standard web page. If you want to run this from a program in Enterprise Guide, just to see what is generated, then you could use a filename statement to create _webout and then look at what is written there.

The following code can be used as the source code for a stored process run through a web browser. We can create simple HTML in several ways:

- We can simply have code in a cards statement and write it out:

```
data _null_ ;
  input ;
  file _webout ;
  put _infile_ ;
  cards ;
<HTML>
<h1>Hello</h1>
</HTML>
;;
run ;
```

- We can have code in a cards statement with macro references and run it through a resolve function before writing it out:

```
data _null_ ;
  input ;
  line=resolve(_infile_) ;
  file _webout ;
  put line ;
  cards ;
```

```
%make_HTML
;;
run ;
```

- We can generate code at different times and stream it to the browser as needed:

```
data _null_ ;
  input ;
  file _webout ;
  put _infile_ ;
  cards ;
<HTML>
<BODY>
<h1>Summarizing customer data</h1>
;;
run ;

Proc summary data=big_file ;
  Class product group name ;
  Var paid ;
  Output out=big_file_summary sum= ;
Run ;

data _null_;
  input ;
  file _webout ;
  put _infile_ ;
  cards ;
<b>Summary has finished</b>
;;
run ;
```

A variation on this is to keep static code in one or more external files or in a parmcards statement which can then be read in using INPUT/PUT statements when required. These might have a static header with a company logo which you want at the top of every page, a static footer, standard libraries to load, and so on.

PROC STREAM

This is the preferred method if you have SAS 9.3 or later. It lets you write your HTML, JavaScript, CSS, and so on and include macro programs and variables. These will be resolved as the code is streamed to the browser. This allows an enormous amount of flexibility by specifying the HTML that you want to use with macro language mixed in with it. PROC STREAM will resolve the macro language as each line is copied to the file or web browser you are writing to.

Writing Your Own Custom HTML

When working with a web browser, you have the _webout fileref pre-allocated if you are using streaming output from your stored process. Anything written to _webout will be directed to the browser. The key thing to remember in writing your own HTML from a Stored Process is to write to the _webout fileref. If you have called the Stored Process from the SAS Stored Process Web Application, then anything written to _webout will be written to the environment you have called the Stored Process from. So, when calling from a web browser, _webout points to the web browser. If calling from an application like Excel, then output is written to that.

You need to be aware that these techniques that involve writing your own custom HTML work best with a web browser, since that offers the widest support for HTML, JavaScript, and CSS. In fact, how well it works will vary from web browser to web browser too. But if you are writing HTML and then delivering output to other clients, like Excel, then the techniques will work less well with less support for handling of HTML in various clients.

STPBEGIN and STPEND Macros

You need to be careful when using %stpbegin and %stpend. These do a range of things, but primarily they start and end ODS output. By default, Enterprise Guide will add them in before and after your code when you make a Stored Process. When you create the Stored Process, you can see that the Stored Process macros are selected by default as shown in Figure 3-4.

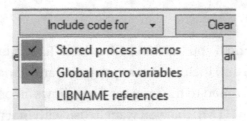

Figure 3-4. *Enterprise Guide's editor allows you to choose what to add to code automatically*

That is fine if you are doing something like using a procedure to produce some output such as a Proc Report. However, if you are trying to write some custom HTML, then as you try to write to the _WEBOUT fileref, you will find that it is already being used by ODS and is not available. This results in you generating the following error in your log for the Stored Process (Figure 3-5).

```
20          data _null_ ;
21          file _webout ;


22          put '<h1>Test of _webout</h1>' ;
23          run ;

ERROR: File is in use, _WEBOUT .
NOTE: The SAS System stopped processing this step because of errors.
NOTE: DATA statement used (Total process time):
      real time            0.03 seconds
      cpu time             0.01 seconds
```

Figure 3-5. *A common error you will see if you try to use _webout but are still including code for Stored Process macros automatically*

To avoid this error, you need to ensure that _webout is not in use when you want to write to it. One way is to deselect the Stored Process macros when you create your code. That means that they are not used, and so _webout is never allocated to ODS output. You can still allocate ODS to _webout yourself in your own code or call the %stpbegin and %stpend macros yourself at another point in you program. For example, you could use the following code shown in Figure 3-6.

SAS Code

```
data _null_ ;
  file _webout ;
  put '<h1>Hello</h1>' ;
run ;
%stpbegin
proc print data=sashelp.class ;
run ;
%stpend
```

Figure 3-6. *You can still use the Stored Process macros even if you don't include them in the source code automatically*

This results in the output in the web browser shown in Figure 3-7.

Hello

Obs	Name	Sex	Age	Height	Weight
1	Alfred	M	14	69.0	112.5
2	Alice	F	13	56.5	84.0
3	Barbara	F	13	65.3	98.0
4	Carol	F	14	62.8	102.5
5	Henry	M	14	63.5	102.5
6	James	M	12	57.3	83.0
7	Jane	F	12	59.8	84.5
8	Janet	F	15	62.5	112.5
9	Jeffrey	M	13	62.5	84.0
10	John	M	12	59.0	99.5
11	Joyce	F	11	51.3	50.5
12	Judy	F	14	64.3	90.0
13	Louise	F	12	56.3	77.0
14	Mary	F	15	66.5	112.0
15	Philip	M	16	72.0	150.0
16	Robert	M	12	64.8	128.0
17	Ronald	M	15	67.0	133.0
18	Thomas	M	11	57.5	85.0
19	William	M	15	66.5	112.0

Figure 3-7. *This HTML table is produced by the SAS code in Figure 3-6*

You can look at the HTML generated for this by viewing the source from your browser. This shows something like Figure 3-8 at the start.

```
1  <h1>Hello</h1>
2  <!DOCTYPE html PUBLIC "-//W3C//DTD HTML 4.01 Transitional//EN">
3  <html>
4  <head>
5  <meta name="Generator" content="SAS Software Version 9.4, see www.sas.com">
6  <meta http-equiv="Content-type" content="text/html">
7  <title>SAS Output</title>
8  <style type="text/css">
9  <!--
10 .aftercaption
11 {
12   background-color: #FAFBFE;
```

Figure 3-8. *This is some of the HTML code that the SAS code in Figure 3-6 generated, producing the table in Figure 3-7*

Beware Invalid Code   You can see the HTML code we wrote out from our data step, followed by some of the HTML generated by SAS. The HTML is not actually valid, and if you copy the source code into an online HTML validator, you will see the error messages clearly. The <h1> tag should be within a body section, inside an HTML section. So, we could adjust our code to write the required HTML around our <h1> tag, but then we need to do something to remove the other tags that stpbegin write out.

You will also notice that ODS generates quite a lot of complex HTML code which isn't necessarily required. The STPBEGIN and STPEND macros are quite flexible though so we can set some macro variables which will change the way that they behave. One of the most useful macro variables that can be changed is _RESULT. If we set that to a value of streamfragment,[1] then it causes the STPBEGIN macro to just produce the HTML code needed for the actual SAS output, rather than producing a full HTML program including CSS styles and so on. So, by modifying our program as shown in Listing 3-1, it results in a simpler form.

Listing 3-1. Use streamfragment to create minimal HTML

```
data _null_ ;
  file _webout ;
  put "<h1>Hello</h1>" ;
run ;
```

---

[1]This is not documented anywhere that I can find; however, I have been using it for many years, and it still works nicely. I suspect it is something that SAS may use internally but don't offer support to customers. So, use this at your own risk!

```
%let _result=streamfragment ;
%stpbegin
    proc print data=sashelp.class ;
run ;
%stpend
```

This produces a simplified output with the same content as before which looks like Figure 3-9.

Hello

Obs	Name	Sex	Age	Height	Weight
1	Alfred	M	14	69.0	112.5
2	Alice	F	13	56.5	84.0
3	Barbara	F	13	65.3	98.0
4	Carol	F	14	62.8	102.5
5	Henry	M	14	63.5	102.5
6	James	M	12	57.3	83.0
7	Jane	F	12	59.8	84.5
8	Janet	F	15	62.5	112.5
9	Jeffrey	M	13	62.5	84.0
10	John	M	12	59.0	99.5
11	Joyce	F	11	51.3	50.5
12	Judy	F	14	64.3	90.0
13	Louise	F	12	56.3	77.0
14	Mary	F	15	66.5	112.0
15	Philip	M	16	72.0	150.0
16	Robert	M	12	64.8	128.0
17	Ronald	M	15	67.0	133.0
18	Thomas	M	11	57.5	85.0
19	William	M	15	66.5	112.0

Figure 3-9. *Title and table produced by the code in Listing 3-1. This shows how we can combine some custom HTML with HTML produced by SAS's Output Delivery System*

However, the source code begins as shown in Listing 3-2.

Listing 3-2. Source code generated automatically by SAS

```
<h1>Hello</h1>
<div class="branch">
<a name="IDX"></a>
<div>
<div align="center">
<table class="table" cellspacing="0" cellpadding="5" rules="all"
frame="box" summary="Procedure Print: Data Set SASHELP.CLASS">
```

You will notice that there is no style information there, but now we just get right to the content. Our custom heading is written out and then the table produced by Proc Print. This is great since we can then produce various pieces of ODS HTML output with streamfragment, and just put them onto the web page we are making as we want to.

General Techniques to Add HTML to a Web Page

You can use the code in Listing 3-3 as a template to add HTML to a web page. You just need to put whatever HTML code that you want to put into the browser into the cards area.

Remember Whenever you are writing to _webout in a Stored Process, you have to ensure that the STPBEGIN and STPEND macro are not being used, unless you are specifically putting them in yourself and know what you are doing. So that means in the SAS code part of the Stored Process Manager, under "Include code for," you need to make sure that "Stored Process Macros" are not ticked. If you do forget to untick the option, you will get some errors, which you can read about here: http://support.sas.com/kb/13/599.html.

Listing 3-3. Writing HTML directly to browser via _webout

```
data _null_ ;
  input ;
  file _webout ;
  put _infile_ ;
  cards ;
```

```
<html>
<body>
<h1>Hello</h1>
It's the best practice to have properly formed HTML, like this.
</body>
</html>
;;
run ;
```

There is no reason why you can't have multiple data steps to write out your HTML as shown in Listing 3-4.

Listing 3-4. Writing HTML using multiple data steps

```
data _null_ ;
  file _webout ;
  input;
  put _infile_;
  cards;
<html>
<body>
;;
run;
data _null_;
  file _webout;
  set sashelp.class;
  put name ' is ' height ' centimetres high.<br>' ;
run ;
data _null_ ;
  file _webout ;
  input;
  put _infile_;
  cards;
</body>
</html>
;;
run ;
```

This code produces the output depicted in Listing 3-5, showing a collection of rather short people!

Listing 3-5. Shows lines of customized text produced from SAS code

```
Alfred is 69 centimetres high.
Alice is 56.5 centimetres high.
Barbara is 65.3 centimetres high.
Carol is 62.8 centimetres high.
Henry is 63.5 centimetres high.
James is 57.3 centimetres high.
Jane is 59.8 centimetres high.
Janet is 62.5 centimetres high.
Jeffrey is 62.5 centimetres high.
John is 59 centimetres high.
Joyce is 51.3 centimetres high.
Judy is 64.3 centimetres high.
Louise is 56.3 centimetres high.
Mary is 66.5 centimetres high.
Philip is 72 centimetres high.
Robert is 64.8 centimetres high.
Ronald is 67 centimetres high.
Thomas is 57.5 centimetres high.
William is 66.5 centimetres high.
```

Perhaps it's a good idea to have the units of measurement in these sample SAS tables.

Using this technique, you are able to have a lot of SAS code which will gradually build up the HTML that you want produced, thereby giving you precisely the result you are looking for. But there are some ways to extend the power of this technique by using macro language.

Macro Language

You might like to use macro variables in your custom HTML in order to add some flexibility. For instance, you can access the automatically generated macro variables, such as ones which tell you the userid, machine, date/time, and so on. You could use some macro variables that your SAS code generates in previous steps. You might also want to use macro variables with values that have been passed in as the Stored Process was run. These might have been some choices made by a user using parameters you have defined. Or it might just be some custom parameter(s) passed on the URL as the SAS Stored Process Web Application was called.

So, in order to do this, you might produce a program like the one shown in Listing 3-6.

Listing 3-6. Macro variables are not resolved in this code

```
data _null_ ;
 input;
 file _webout;
 put _infile_;
 cards;
<h1>Hello &sysuserid!</h1>
&message
;;
run ;
```

But when we run this, we get the output shown in Figure 3-10 in the web browser.

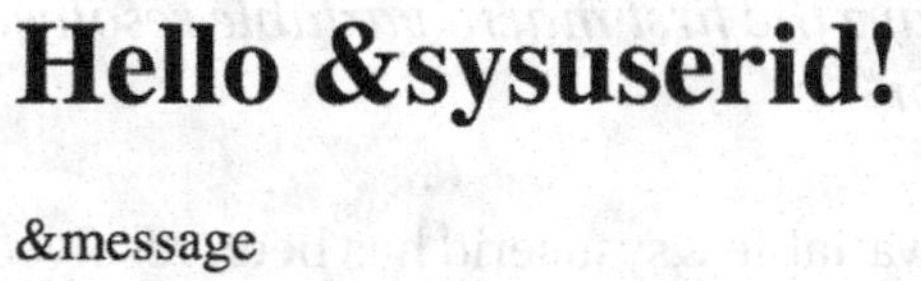

Hello &sysuserid!

&message

Figure 3-10. *Browser will display this, which is not what we want. We want the macro variables to be resolved, but they are not*

SAS has read the macro variables in and written them out to the web browser as is, without resolving their values. Fortunately, SAS provides us a fantastic little function called resolve. With resolve, you can give it some macro language, and it will return the resolved text. The macro language might be a simple macro variable but can also be a macro program. That provides a huge amount of potential power for the programmer. Modifying our code a little, as shown in Listing 3-7, we can get it to work as we want.

Listing 3-7. Macro variables are resolved in this code

```
data _null_ ;
  length line $ 60 ;
  input;
  file _webout;
  line=resolve(_infile_) ;
  put line;
  cards;
<h1>Hello &sysuserid!</h1>
&message
;;
run ;
```

Now our code reads a line in from the cards area, resolves any macro variables, and then writes it to the web browser. This results in this output shown in Figure 3-11.

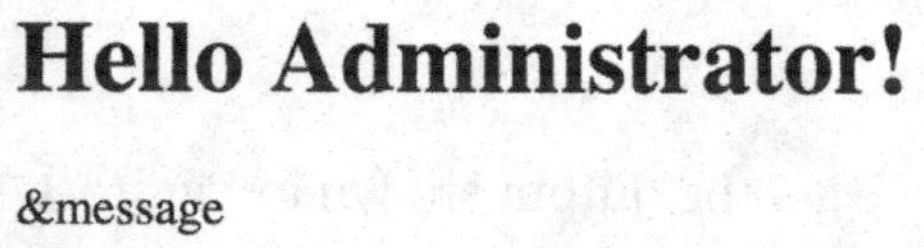

Hello Administrator!

&message

Figure 3-11. *Now we have the first macro variable resolved, showing the username "Administrator"*

The automatic macro variable &sysuserid has been resolved; however, the other variable &message has not been resolved, even though the resolve function was used, since there was no value defined for it. We could add this as a prompt for the Stored Process in order to create a default value for it or to prompt the user for one when invoked in certain ways. But we can invoke the Stored Process and provide a value for it using the SAS Stored Process Web Application by specifying the Stored Process using _ program and then the value of &message by specifying &message= in the URL. You could get most of the URL for this by going to the web application index page and right-clicking the Stored Process to copy the URL. But essentially, we just need to add **&message** to the end of the URL with a value for message. The ampersand indicated a parameter we are passing, and then we have an equal sign and its value. The first parameter in the URL mustn't have an ampersand, but must follow the question mark, which results in the output in Figure 3-12.

```
http://server-name/SASStoredProcess/do?_program=%2FUser+Folders%2Fphil%2FMy
+Folder%2Fmacros+resolved+from+data+step&message=Remember%20to%20get%20a%20
coffee
```

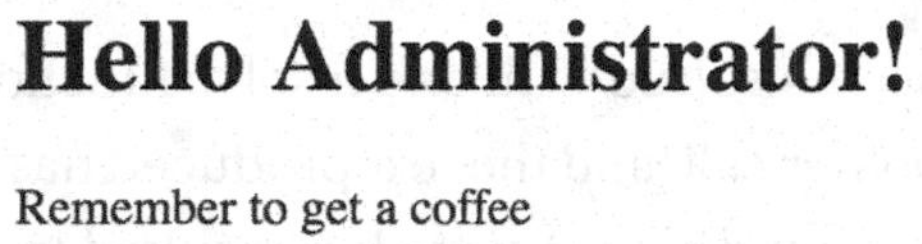

Hello Administrator!

Remember to get a coffee

Figure 3-12. *Having passed in a value for message, we see that value is displayed in the browser*

As I mentioned earlier, we can resolve any macro language in the resolve function, so if we wanted to use multiple macro variables on a line, then that would be OK. Also, if we wanted to use macro programs, then that too would be fine. So, for instance, we could use some code like the one shown in Listing 3-8.

Listing 3-8. SAS code to resolve macro program execution

```
%let first=Phil;
%let last=Mason;
%macro content;
  %do i=1 %to 10;
  Line &i<br>
  %end;
%mend content;
data _null_;
  file _webout;
  input;
  line=resolve(_infile_);
  put line;
  cards;
<h1>My name is &first &last</h1>
%content
;;
run;
```

The preceding SAS code would produce the HTML shown in Listing 3-9.

Listing 3-9. Result of resolving macro program execution

```
<h1>My name is Phil Mason</h1>
Line 1<br>   Line 2<br>   Line 3<br>   Line 4<br>   Line 5<br>   Line
6<br>   Line 7<br>   Line 8<br>   Line 9<br>   Line 10<br>
```

&first and &last have been resolved with one resolve function call. Then %content has been executed with another call, and the text produced has been streamed to the browser. Notice how my indenting in the macro has resulted in some extra spacing in the HTML produced. Notice how those spaces have been ignored when producing the output too, since the HTML ignores those spaces. Usually this kind of thing is not a problem, but it is worth keeping in mind as extra spaces can affect some things. That HTML produces the following output (Figure 3-13) in the web browser.

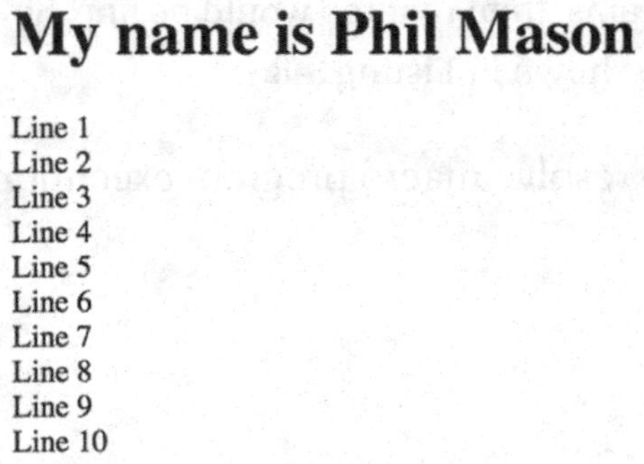

My name is Phil Mason

Line 1
Line 2
Line 3
Line 4
Line 5
Line 6
Line 7
Line 8
Line 9
Line 10

Figure 3-13. *HTML output*

I think the ability to call macro programs in the resolve function is very powerful. You could have quite a complex macro program which could open tables, use conditional logic, and generate all kinds of custom output.

There is a limitation with this technique though which involves the size of the input buffer. Since we are using cards and reading lines in with an input statement, each line will be read in to the input buffer and then any macro variables or programs will be replaced by text as they are resolved. But this all happens in the variable we are using, which is called line in my examples. We can expand the text up to the length of the variable being used, but then extra characters will be truncated which can cause all kinds of problems. We can mitigate against this issue by using a length statement and ensuring we have a nice long variable to use, but the problem can still hit us. SAS comes to the rescue with PROC STREAM though, which is not encumbered by any length limits.

HTML Forms

It's easy to make Stored Processes using parameters since SAS provides the prompting facility provided. This gives you a range of options that provide a huge amount of flexibility. But if you want even more flexibility, then that too is possible. You can still use the prompting facility as well, or you can just use the following technique in which we can add some custom prompting of our own.

The idea of this technique relies on calling a Stored Process via the SAS Stored Process Web Application which can be invoked with a URL. A custom URL can be built in HTML by using an HTML form. This is a fairly simple piece of HTML in which we define a basic URL and then let the user select some values for some parts of the URL which will be added to the end of it. For example, in Listing 3-10, we define a form to invoke a Google search using text entered by the user.

Listing 3-10. HTML form that will submit a search to Google

```
<html>
<form action="https://www.google.com/search?">
<input name="q">
<input type="submit">
</form>
</html>
```

When this is run, it produces what is shown in Figure 3-14 in the web browser.

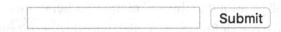

Figure 3-14. *Form displayed in browser*

This provides a box in which we can type a value for "q" and then click Submit. If we enter the input shown in Figure 3-15 and click Submit, then it produces the URL shown in Figure 3-16.

Figure 3-15. *Text entered in form*

Figure 3-16. *URL shown in web page after Submit is pressed*

So, you can see that it has taken the value of action and used the value we entered to add "q=sas" to the end of the URL. This searches Google for "sas" and returns the results in the browser.

Having looked at a simple pure HTML example calling Google, let's now take a simple example using SAS to get us going. We will use a simple Stored Process that can take one parameter. The HTML that we can use is shown in Listing 3-11.

Listing 3-11. Form to run a stored process and pass a parameter

```
<html>
<form action="https://d351tq92/SASStoredProcess/do?">
<input name="_program" value="/User Folders/phil/My Folder/test">
<input name="product_line" value="Children">
<input type="submit">
</form>
</html>
```

The action for the form is calling the SAS Stored Process Web Application, so it should be the first part of how you invoke that up to and including the question mark. Any extra parameters will be added to the end of the URL generated. The parameters are added in the sequence you define them, which usually doesn't matter unless using multiple parameters of the same name. **_program** is always needed since it defines that path through metadata to the Stored Process. In our example, we have a parameter called **product_line**, which we have given a default value of children. This HTML will produce what is shown in Figure 3-17 in the browser.

| /User Folders/phil/My Fold | Children | Submit |

Figure 3-17. *Form displaying stored process name and product_line prompts and Submit button*

Clicking the Submit button, it generates a URL like this:

http://d351tq92/SASStoredProcess/do?***_program***=%2FUser+Folders%2Fphil%2FMy+Folder%2Ftest***&product_line***=Children

Notice that the "&" was added to separate the first name/value parameter from the next one. This is always done automatically for you by the browser as it processes the form. Looking at this form displayed in the browser, we don't really want the _program field to be displayed as we don't want the user to be able to type over it, they don't need to see the value, and we might not want them to even know the value. We can use the hidden type in order to specify _program, but not show it (see Listing 3-12).

Listing 3-12. **Form to run stored process that will not display name of stored process**

```html
<html>
<form action="https://d351tq92/SASStoredProcess/do?">
<input name="_program" value="/User Folders/phil/My Folder/test"
type="hidden">
<input name="product_line" value="Children">
<input type="submit">
</form>
</html>
```

This produces the nicer looking screen in the browser (see Figure 3-18).

| Children | Submit |

Figure 3-18. *Form displaying product_line prompt and Submit button (stored process name not displayed)*

Making a Stored Process Generate Its Own HTML Menu

Now that we know how to make HTML menus with forms that can call Stored Processes, we can use another powerful technique to put our menu into our Stored Process. What we want to achieve is to be able to run a Stored Process which will firstly generate an HTML form-based menu. Once the user makes their selections, then it will call that Stored Process again to produce the output/report required.

In order to achieve this, we will need to detect when the Stored Process is called the first time to produce the menu and then when it is called the second time. The first time it is called, we won't have passed any parameters to it, so we could detect the absence of parameters which we expect to be present from the form. If we are missing some expected parameters, then we can generate a menu. If we detect those parameters, we know that the Stored Process has been called by the HTML form, and so we can run it to produce the output/report.

Listing 3-13 is a simple example of this.

Listing 3-13. Stored process code that first will prompt for a value and when called again will produce a report

```
%macro logic ;
%if %symexist(age) %then %do ;
    %stpbegin
    proc print data=sashelp.class ;
        where age=&age ;
    run ;
    %stpend
    %end ;
%else %do ;
    data _null_ ;
        file _webout ;
        set menu ;
        put line ;
    run ;
    %end ;
```

```
%mend logic ;
* put HTML into a table, since we can't use datalines in a macro ;
data menu ;
    input ;
    line=_infile_ ;
    datalines ;
    <html>
    <form action="http://d351tq92/SASStoredProcess/do?">
    <input name="_program" value="/User Folders/phil/My Folder/test12"
     type="hidden">
    <input name="age" value="14">
    <input type="submit">
    </form>
    </html>
    ;;
run ;
%logic
```

In this Stored Process, we read some lines of HTML into a table, since we can't do this inside a macro program. Then in the macro, if we find the age parameter, then we produce a report using the %stpbegin and %stpend macros to handle ODS. Otherwise, we write out the menu, allowing the user to choose a value for age. When they press Submit, the Stored Process is run again, passing the age value in. The menu looks like the box shown in Figure 3-19.

Figure 3-19. *First call of stored process prompts user for an age*

After pressing Submit, we have the report shown in the browser (see Figure 3-20).

Obs	Name	Sex	Age	Height	Weight
1	Alfred	M	14	69.0	112.5
4	Carol	F	14	62.8	102.5
5	Henry	M	14	63.5	102.5
12	Judy	F	14	64.3	90.0

Figure 3-20. *Second call of stored process produces a report using the age that was entered*

We could modify this code to generate a list of valid values for age and let the user select one from a list rather than entering one. This code would look like Listing 3-14.

Listing 3-14. Stored Process code to additionally produce a list of valid ages from which user can select one

```
%macro logic ;
%if %symexist(age) %then %do ;
    %stpbegin
    proc print data=sashelp.class ;
        where age=&age ;
    run ;
    %stpend
    %end ;
%else %do ;
    data _null_ ;
        file _webout ;
        set menu ;
        put line ;
    run ;
    %end ;
%mend logic ;
proc sql noprint ;
    select distinct "<option value="""|| put(age,2.)|| """>"||
        put(age,2.)|| "</option>"
        into :age_options separated by '' from sashelp.class ;
quit ;
```

```
* put HTML into a table, since we can't use datalines in a macro ;
data menu ;
    input ;
    line=resolve(_infile_) ;
    datalines ;
    <HTML>
    <form action="http://d351tq92/SASStoredProcess/do?">
    <input name="_program" value="/User Folders/phil/My Folder/test12"
    type="hidden">
    <select name="age">
    &age_options
    </select>
    <input type="submit">
    </form>
    </HTML>
    ;;
run ;
%logic
```

And the page displayed would look like Figure 3-21.

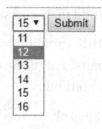

Figure 3-21. *User can now select a valid age*

Form Attributes

There are a range of other attributes that can be specified on the <form> tag. We have used action which defines the base URL to use when the form is submitted. This can be an absolute or a relative path (relative to the place the HTML is on the web server). But some of the other useful attributes are

- **Autocomplete**, which can turn autocomplete on or off for the form you are using. It can make it useful when you are using a menu over and over again.

- **Enctype** defines how the form data is encoded when it is sent to the server (if POST method is used). This usually comes in useful when you are sending files to the server from the form.

- **Name** defines the name of the form, which is useful if you want to refer to it with JavaScript.

- **Target** defines where to display the response that is received after submitting the form. This has a few values and is very useful:

  - _blank shows the response in a new window or tab.

  - _self, by default, is used and displays response in the current frame.

  - _parent, the response is displayed in the parent frame.

  - _top, the response is displayed in the full body of the window.

  - *Framename* will display the output in a named frame "*framename*".

- **Method** defines the http method to use for sending form data.

- **Get** sends the form data as URL variables by appending the form data to the URL as name/value pairs. This is the default which you get if you don't explicitly define a method:

  - URL is limited to about 3000 characters which varies depending on the browser you are using. It is often 2048 characters. Any parts that don't fit are just truncated without any warning, so you can get unexpected results.

  - You should never send sensitive data with GET since it can be seen on the URL.

  - URL can be bookmarked.

- **Post** appends the form data inside the body of the HTTP request:

  - Data is not shown in the URL so it is more secure.

  - There are no size limitations. If you need many parameters and length is an issue, then use this.

  - Can't bookmark the URL, since not all the information is there.

In order to change our previous code to use a POST method, we would just add method="post" to the form tag as shown in Listing 3-15.

Listing 3-15. Form that uses a POST method, rather than a GET (which is default)

```
data menu ;
  input ;
  line=_infile_;
  datalines ;
<html>
<form action="http://d351tq92/SASStoredProcess/do?" method="post">
<input name="_program" value="/User Folders/phil/My Folder/test12"
type="hidden">
<input name="age" value="14">
<input type="submit">
</form>
</html>
```

Persistence – How to Pass Data Between Stored Processes

Stored Processes can be used in a large number of flexible ways. In some applications of Stored Process technology, you may want to keep data in between runs. For instance, rather than asking for a name every time, you can keep the name and default to the last one used by that user. We might want to keep some count or record of activity which can then be reported back to the user. We might even just want to take some result(s) from one Stored Process and pass to another Stored Process to be used. This is what I call persistence of data. By that I mean that certain data can persist after a Stored Process has run. Usually data entered by a user is transient, meaning that it is used by the Stored Process and then lost.

Storage

One major consideration for persistence is whether you want to store the data locally on a client that is being used or remotely on the server being used. If saved locally, then moving to another client means you don't have access to your data. There are a range of solutions available for this:

- localStorage is an HTML5 technology that provides a way to store, retrieve, and remove items that are stored for use by the web browser on the client. It involves calling some JavaScript functions to do this, but they are very simple to use.

- indexedDB is another web API that can be used but is far more complex.

- Sessions are provided by SAS as a way of providing persistence for a limited amount of time.

Cookies

Cookies are a web technology that lets us store small items of text locally on the client as a cookie. Other kinds of objects can often be converted to text and stored and then converted back when retrieved. Cookies can be set using the stpsrv_header function in SAS which can call the "Set-Cookie" method. You have to specify a name and value for each cookie that is set. You can optionally specify a path and expiry date too.

The following example shows some code which can be used in a Stored Process via the web application. We set a value for the cookie and then write some JavaScript code out which gets the value of the cookies (Listing 3-16) and displays it in an alert box.

Listing 3-16. Setting a cookie with SAS function and then displaying it with JavaScript

```
* set cookie ;
data _null_ ;
  old=stpsrv_header("Set-Cookie","CUSTOMER=Phil Mason") ;
run ;
* use some javascript to display the cookie that was set ;
data _null_ ;
  file _webout ;
  put "<script>alert(document.cookie);</script>" ;
run ;
```

Figure 3-22 shows the alert box displayed.

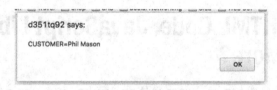

Figure 3-22. *Alert box in web browser showing cookie that was set from SAS*

You can access cookies via the _HTCOOK automatic macro variable. The following code in Listing 3-17 shows how to access the value.

Listing 3-17. Examining cookies from a web page using SAS code

```
proc sql ;
select * from dictionary.macros
where name="_HTCOOK" ;
run ;
```

Figure 3-23 shows what is displayed.

Macro Scope	Macro Variable Name	Offset into Macro Variable	Macro Variable Value
GLOBAL	_HTCOOK	0	@abda10387356840f07c01590095d6bd7_Cluster=0C5D4525A66E09F6F7CD65182CF3EE3C.abda10387356840f07c01590095d6bd7_SASServer1_1 CUSTOMER=Phil Mason®

Figure 3-23. *Cookies from the web browser visible in the SAS macro variable*

Files or Tables

Files or tables can be used quite easily to store the data you want to make available again and then for another Stored Process to read that data in. You will need to manage multiple users who might try to write to a shared table at the same time. This can be done by locking the table before writing to it. You might decide to have a separate table for each user and then the locking issue virtually is eliminated.

URL

Passing parameters on URL is probably the easiest way and achieves persistence by passing data from one process to the next. So, when one Stored Process wants to pass data to the next one, it is simply passed as name/value pair parameters on the URL.

Where to Put HTML Code, JavaScript Libraries, Images, and More?

When you are using the SAS Stored Process Web Application, you need to understand a few things about the environment you are working in. It runs within a web application server, which is often known as a servlet container. If you are running on SAS 9.4, you may be using the SAS-provided web application server, which is highly recommended. For a start, it can be automatically installed with SAS 9.4 and is well integrated. If you use an alternate web application server (e.g., WebSphere), then there is likely to be a bit of extra customization required during setup. When running in the web app server, there will be certain directories on that server which are easily accessible to your Stored Process to use. Some other locations on that server may need permissions changed or to be referred to with a specific path in order to access them or may be inaccessible.

If your Stored Process specifies a relative pathname, then the key thing to remember is that the root is not the root of the machine you are running on, but is the root of the web application server, as defined in its configuration. So, on my SAS 9.4 system with a default configuration, the root for the web app server is C:\SAS\Config\Lev1\Web\WebServer\htdocs on the SAS server. Note that this will be different to the C: drive on the client machine.

So, if I code up a statement like this

```
filename x 'my_file.txt' ;
```

then this will actually be pointing at the server HOME directory, which is C:\SAS\Config\Lev1\Web\WebServer\htdocs\my_file.txt on my server. If I want to use sub-directories, then I would define a `fileref` like this:

```
Filename x 'orders\2018\my_file.txt' ;
```

Then this would actually be point at C:\SAS\Config\Lev1\Web\WebServer\htdocs\orders\2018\my_file.txt.

And in case you are wondering, a `fileref` like this

```
Filename x '/orders.txt' ;
```

would point to something like c:/orders.txt, since this is not a relative path but instead is an absolute path. You can always run the preceding code and then use the following code to see exactly where this `fileref` is located:

```
Filename x list ;
```

If you are wanting to write a file temporarily to a location that you are allowed to write to, then you can always find a temporary location that you have permission to in a number of different ways. You could get the location of the work library by using the pathname function, which returns the physical path to a SAS library which is already allocated. This code will get the location and write it to the log:

```
%put %sysfunc(pathname(work)) ;
```

If you are using a UNIX system, then you might want to find out where your HOME directory is by getting the value of the HOME environment variable. You can use the sysget function to get the value of an environment variable, so this code will print the value to the log:

```
%put %sysget(HOME) ;
```

Remember that UNIX is case sensitive, so you need to look for HOME, not home or Home.

Another way to find your home directory is to run some code like this, which allocates a `fileref` to the home directory and then shows its location:

```
Filename test '.' ;
Filename test list ;
```

Summary

In this chapter, we have learned about HTML and specifically some ways to use it with SAS and stored processes:

- Using forms in HTML which is a major way to prompt the user for information and get it to your SAS code in the form of SAS macro variables

- Generating HTML code in several different ways:

  - ODS (Output Delivery System) to generate HTML

  - HTML produced by data steps in SAS code, resolving macro references if required

  - Proc Stream to produce HTML code while resolving macro variables and macro programs

  - Using the %stpbegin and %stpend macro programs provided by SAS to produce ODS

- Making a stored process that generates a form with prompts that then calls itself to produce the results and display them

- Using form attributes to make stored process calls

- Passing data between stored processes using browser storage, cookies, files, or URLs

CHAPTER 4

JavaScript

JavaScript is a language usually used with HTML to add functionality especially involving interactivity. It was invented by Brendan Eich in 1995 and is not the same thing as Java, which was released four years earlier. The official name of the JavaScript language is actually ECMAScript, and it became a standard in 1997. It is now supported by most modern web browsers, and it is a powerful tool that you can use as you build web-based applications.

JavaScript is an easy-to-learn language that lets us do many things that are very useful, including

- Validate input on the client machine, rather than having to send a request to the server first. This reduces network traffic and load on your servers.

- Provide instant feedback to users, rather than waiting for a page refresh.

- Ability to make interactive interfaces since it can detect when the mouse is hovering over something, when keys are pressed, single and double clicks, and so on. Once something is detected, it can carry out various actions that modify the screen.

- Ability to use items such as drag-and-drop components, sliders, interactive tables, and so on.

JavaScript does limit you in doing some things you might like to do, mostly due to the fact that it runs in your browser on your client machine and does not run on the server you connect to. Some of JavaScript's limitations are

- No reading or writing files on the client. This is a security measure. You wouldn't want a JavaScript program to read some information from your machine and send somewhere else.

© Philip Mason 2020
P. Mason, *SAS Stored Processes*, https://doi.org/10.1007/978-1-4842-5925-2_4

- No access to web pages from another domain with JavaScript.

- No support for multi-threading or use of multi-processors on the client. So, we are not supposed to do compute heavy operations on the client.

- No access to databases on a server without some kind of server-side script. Fortunately, SAS Stored Processes can fulfill this function.

- No access to most of your local devices with JavaScript.

- JavaScript can be disabled in a browser, which means that many web applications will no longer work.

There are many places to learn JavaScript: the Internet, books, web training, live classroom training, and so on. I want to recommend a few things that I find very helpful. Firstly, the print series *In Easy Steps* has books about HTML5, JavaScript, jQuery, and CSS3.[1] This series is very easy to dip into and get basic useful information quickly. The other major resource that I love to use for learning is the W3Schools online tutorial website (w3schools.com). It has a wealth of excellent information about JavaScript,[2] HTML,[3] CSS,[4] jQuery, and more.

Basic Example of a JavaScript Program

Here is a simple JavaScript example:

```
<HTML>
<body>
<p id="hello"></p>
<script>
document.getElementById("hello").innerHTML = "Hello World!";
</script>
</body>
</HTML>
```

---

[1] http://ineasysteps.com/books-by-category/programming-2/
[2] JavaScript info – www.w3schools.com/js/default.asp
[3] HTML info – www.w3schools.com/HTML/default.asp
[4] CSS info – www.w3schools.com/css/default.asp

In this example, we use an HTML paragraph tag `<p>` and give it an id called "hello". We put our JavaScript inside the `<script>` and `</script>` HTML tags, which is always where JavaScript code goes.

Looking at the JavaScript statement, on the fifth line of the code

- `Document` refers to the entire HTML document or file.

- `getElementById` looks up the id called "hello" from the document.

- `innerHTML` refers to the HTML code that appears inside that element, which in our case is a paragraph tag.

So, this first part of JavaScript points to the content of the paragraph tag, and using an equals sign then assigns it a new value.

The output produced in the browser is as shown in Figure 4-1.

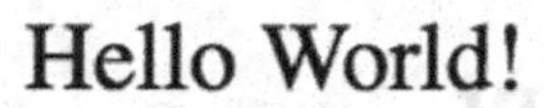

Hello World!

Figure 4-1. *Displayed in web browser when previous JavaScript code is run*

Writing and Testing

All that is required to write JavaScript code is a text editor, preferably one such as Notepad++ which is free. So, you don't need any fancy software, although using software that has been designed for this has some advantages. You can get free software which is very good for this, and I have listed some of these later in this book. A great one I would highly recommend is Notepad++. It has syntax highlighting, powerful search/replace abilities, and many other features. It's a great basic editor for most kinds of text. It also has a Run menu which will take the code you have edited and open it in one of several web browsers for testing. Figure 4-2 shows what the example program from the previous section would look like in Notepad++.

```
1    <html>
2    <body>
3      <p id="hello"></p>
4    <script>
5      document.getElementById("hello").innerHTML = "Hello World!";
6    </script>
7    </body>
8    </html>
```

Figure 4-2. *Program in Notepad++*

There are more powerful editors available of course, such as IDEA, VScode, VSCodium, NetBeans, BBEdit, or Atom (from GitHub). Some of these will let you run and test your code directly from the tool. It's best to think about the most useful features for the way you develop and then to choose the best set of features for that.

Debugging JavaScript

There are various ways to debug JavaScript code. Firstly, you can check the code before it runs. There is a tool called Lint, which exists in a number of different forms such as JavaScript Lint[5] where it can be run online or downloaded to your machine. It will check the JavaScript code for common mistakes such as comments within comments or missing semi-colons at the end of lines. It also looks for less common mistakes such as regular expressions missing a preceding left parenthesis. So, it will basically do a syntax check and will also lay out your code nicely.

The other way to check your JavaScript code is to run it with a debugger. There are debuggers built into most web browsers which enable you to break when errors happen and examine things, see how long it takes for parts of the program to run, check resources used, and so on. You can access developer tools in the following ways:

- **Chrome** – Menu item "View/Developer".

- **Firefox** – Menu item "Tools/Web Developer".

- **Internet Explorer** – Press F12.

- **Safari** – Menu item "Develop".

---

[5]JavaScript Lint – `www.JavaScriptlint.com/index.htm`

There are lots of developer tools available in these browsers, some having far more than others. For example, some browsers have a responsive design mode as well, which will let you change your screen size to match that of another device such as an iPad so you can see what your application looks like on that. Another good one is some browsers have a switch to let you emulate different browsers, so you can see what your code looks like in other browsers while only using one. It's best to install them all and try out the different tools before you settle on one that you like best.

Using JavaScript with HTML

To use JavaScript in your HTML documents, there are two main ways to do so. Firstly, you can use <script> tags and put your code between it. For example, if you wanted an alert box to pop up on the screen saying "Hello World!", then you could use this code:

```
<script>
alert("Hello World!") ;
</script>
```

Secondly, you can use JavaScript in some parameters of some of the HTML attributes of tags. For example, if you wanted a pushbutton on your page which would call a JavaScript function called my_function when it was pressed, then you could use this code:

```
<button onclick="my_function()">Click here</button>
```

There are lot of these attributes that let us do different things in JavaScript based on some kind of event that happens – these are often referred to as event handlers. The main event handlers are shown in Table 4-1.

Table 4-1. *JavaScript event handlers*

Event Handler	Description
Onabort, Onerror	Responds when user aborts download of page or an error occurs
Onblur, Onfocus	Responds when user moves focus onto or off an element
Onchange, Onselect	Responds when user changes or selects an element
Onclick, Ondblclick, Onmousedown, Onmouseup	Responds when user clicks or double-clicks the mouse button
Onload	Responds when the page has finished loading
Onmousemove, Onmouseover, Onmouseout	Responds when user moves mouse over an element
Onsubmit	Responds when user submits a form to server
Ondragstart, Ondragover, Ondragend, Ondragenter, Ondragleave, Ondrag, Ondrop	Responds when user drags or drops an element

Basic DOM

When an HTML document is loaded into a web browser, a Document Object is created which is made up of nodes. The Document Object Model (DOM) describes what you will find on a Document Object. There are nodes for elements, attributes, text, and comments. There are methods available to interact with the DOM, so that you can interrogate it and change it. This gives you a massive amount of control over the web page. Interacting with the DOM can be rather slow which has led to the emergence of "virtual DOM" frameworks such as React (made by Facebook). If you are looking for speed, then it may be worth looking into those.

You could use JavaScript to call some DOM methods and change some text on your web page, change the styling of a title, or even add or delete parts of the web page. The DOM is a big and complex thing to understand and is beyond the scope of this book. I suggest looking online for some good resources to learn about it.[6]

---

[6]W3Schools has some good info about the DOM here: www.w3schools.com/js/js_HTMLdom.asp

Using Stored Processes to Generate Pure JavaScript

In the same way that Stored Processes can generate HTML, it can also generate JavaScript. JavaScript can handle a lot of the logic required for a web application; in fact, it is almost essential for any reasonable functionality.

With SAS, you can use ODS to produce output in a range of forms, including HTML. HTML is the form which offers the greatest potential for creating applications that have multiple screens, are lightweight, are running on multiple platforms, and are secure and interactive. ODS has the ability to add some elements of interactivity but is limited. If you use SAS to generate HTML with JavaScript and CSS code, then you can produce almost anything.

When you run a Stored Process to generate JavaScript code, you will be running SAS code on the server. The JavaScript generated will run in the browser after the SAS code that generated it has run. You can do some clever things like having your Stored Process pause for some time and then deliver some more JavaScript to the browser to run. In fact, there are almost endless possibilities of what you can do. Just imagine all the things you have seen running in a web browser – most of that can be done using JavaScript. And all of your JavaScript can be generated from SAS Stored Processes and delivered to the browser.

Remember that SAS has some limitations around the length of variables in SAS 9, which means if you are dealing with names and values over 32,767 characters long, then there will be truncation. There are techniques to get around this problem and some clever open source software such as SASjs and SASjs-cli on GitHub which makes it easy to do.

You don't need to be an expert in these web technologies to achieve a lot. But you do need to know some basics, which I am trying to cover in this book. I have mentioned how to run JavaScript code by either using script tags or using event-handler attributes. That is the key way that you get some JavaScript to run on your HTML page.

Another key thing to know is how to define JavaScript libraries to HTML. This is also done using a script tag, but you specify a source to get the JavaScript code from. For example, to load the jQuery library so that you can use JavaScript functions defined in it, you would use the following code:

```
<script src="https://ajax.googleapis.com/ajax/libs/jquery/3.2.1/jquery.min.
js"></script>
```

> **Note**   When loading libraries like this that are external to your network, you should ideally use an integrity hash to avoid possible URL interception.[7]

You could just as easily save a lot of your own JavaScript code into different files and load them in using this technique. This is the most important thing for a SAS programmer to know, as it gets you access to a wealth of great JavaScript code that is out there in the free and open source community.

The most important thing to know is how to use the event-handler attributes, which I have already described. Knowing this allows the SAS programmer to do many things like detecting clicks and button presses and then taking actions like running Stored Processes and passing various values to them.

How Data Is Stored and Used

In JavaScript, you can load data from various data structures using a range of methods. This might be loading data in from plain text, JSON files, XML, HTML, CSV, databases, and more. The data can be loaded into various structures in memory for use with JavaScript, such as arrays or objects.

You can hard-code data into your JavaScript programs, and this is often a good way to get started when writing some new code since you can enter some sample data easily.

Most of the time, you will load data from somewhere into JavaScript to then be used. If you are using a JavaScript framework like D3, then you might use a provided function to load a CSV file into a data structure that is compatible with other parts of that framework.

How SAS Stored Processes Can Feed Data to Objects

When building a normal web application using HTML and JavaScript, the programmer would usually point to data that is being provided from some data source such as a CSV file or which is being loaded from a database. It is easy to use a Stored Process to provide

---

[7]https://developer.mozilla.org/en-US/docs/Web/Security/Subresource_Integrity
https://sasjs.io/security/#integrity-checking-for-javascript-files

data when it is needed in the appropriate format. This means that you can use any kind of SAS programming on the server to assemble the data you need to be delivered to the code in the web browser that needs it.

A simple example of this comes from the world of D3, which is a powerful JavaScript visualization library. It has a function used for loading data from a CSV file into a JavaScript object where it is able to be used with many other functions. The code used to do this would be something like this:

```
D3.csv
// Get the data
d3.csv("data.csv", function(error, data) { } ) ;
```

If you wanted to use a Stored Process to provide the CSV data rather than the data. csv file, then you could substitute in a call to a Stored Process as the data source for the CSV function:

```
// Get the data
d3.csv("http://my.server.com/SASStoredProcess/do?_program=tools/
csv&table=sashelp.class", function(error, data) { } ) ;
```

The basic principle in using a Stored Process to feed data to an object is to use the appropriate syntax to point to the Stored Process via the Stored Process Web Application. As long as the function you are using is capable of pointing to a URL, then it should work. If you have to simply specify a hard-coded JavaScript array or object in order to use the function/object that you wish to use, then you won't be able to point to a Stored Process to do this. However, you can use techniques discussed in the Proc Stream section of this book. You can basically generate values as a result of a macro program or macro variable, and proc stream will resolve those so that they appear in the appropriate place in the HTML/JavaScript code.

More About Where to Put Files on Your Web Server

Usually when creating JavaScript code, you would put that in a place that is accessible to your web server, so that it can be referred to with a URL, or by using relative or absolute paths in a program. Most web servers have a home directory which is the top level used when URLs are used. It is often called HTDOCS, and all HTML, JavaScript, CSS, and other files needed for web pages would be put in directories or under that.

Directories

For example, when entering a URL into a web browser such as `www.sas.com/en_gb/`
`home.html`, firstly the IP address for that website would be found by looking up sas.com
in a DNS.[8] With this IP address, the computer containing the website can be accessed.
The browser then looks for the file home.HTML in the directory en_gb for the web
server, which often will be something like this: **C:\SAS\Config\Lev1\Web\WebServer\
htdocs**\en_gb\home.html. The part in bold is likely to be similar on another windows
installation.

The HTDOCS directory being the root directory for the web server means that
anything you put there is easily referred to with reference to it. So, if we had another file
such as C:\SAS\Config\Lev1\Web\WebServer\htdocs\reports\report1.HTML, then this
could be found using a URL like this: `www.sas.com/reports/report1.HTML`. Notice that
the slashes for a path in windows are "\", whereas when used in a URL, they are the UNIX
style slashes which are "/". And we have put a directory "reports" after the website, which
takes us down to that directory on the web server before looking for the file "report1.
HTML".

Usually it's best practice to have a directory on your web server for the web
application with sub-folders for JavaScript libraries, another for CSS files, another for
images, and so on. Although there is no reason, you can't put them anywhere under
the root directory. Generally, there is no way to refer to files above a root directory or
elsewhere on a system which is not under that web server root directory. Of course, if
you have shared resources, they should be combined into an area accessible to the apps
that will be using them, rather than having multiple copies of them.

Relative Paths

You can use relative paths to point to things on a root directory though. Suppose you
have an HTML file that is located in the reports directory. Then if you specify an image
as "logo.png" without a path specified, then it will look for that in the reports directory
too, since that is where the HTML file containing that reference is. Suppose the HTML
file was in the /reports directory, but the image was in the /images directory, then you
could use a path like <img src="**..**/images/logo.png" /> where the "**..**" means go up one

---

[8]DNS (Domain Name Server).

level, and then it goes down to the images directory to find the logo. Or you could specify "/images/logo.png" which means go to the root directory and then down to the images directory to find the logo.

Specifying Libraries

If you want to make use of libraries such as the jQuery JavaScript library or the w3.css CSS3 library, you can refer to them from your HTML code like this, which would look for the libraries in your web server's root directory:

```
<script src="jquery-3.2.1.min.js"></script>
<link rel="stylesheet" href="w3.css">
```

You could refer to these libraries in sub-directories under your web server root directory like this. If you start the path with a "/", it means that it starts at the web server root. So the path in the following example might be "C:\SAS\Config\Lev1\Web\WebServer\htdocs**JavaScript\jquery-3.2.1.min.js**":

```
<script src="/JavaScript/jquery-3.2.1.min.js"></script>
<link rel="stylesheet" href="/css/w3.css">
```

Or if you don't have the libraries on your web server, then you can refer to them on another web server like this:

```
<script src="https://code.jquery.com/jquery-3.2.1.min.js"></script>
<link rel="stylesheet" href="https://www.w3schools.com/w3css/4/w3.css">
```

You need to be aware of your organization's security policies, since many companies don't like you to point to external libraries like this. If that is the case you may need to obtain a copy of the library, pass it through some security procedure (such as virus checking) and then to load it onto your internal network where it could then be referred to.

When you specify libraries in your HTML code in this manner, the contents of those files will be loaded in and processed, so you are then ready to make use of the functions and classes that they define in the rest of your code.

Building Interactivity with JavaScript

JavaScript can add interactivity to your web pages. It enables you to do everything from displaying a message when something happens to displaying a complex table enabling you to sort the columns in it – and much more. I will outline a few things that you can easily do without much expertise.

Pop-Up Windows

There are three different kinds of functions in JavaScript which will pop up a window.

Alert displays a box with some text, which you can then close, useful for messages to the user.

Confirm will display a box with some text and an OK and Cancel button. This allows the user to confirm that something is OK or not.

Prompt will display a window with some text and an input box in which the user can type some text. It is good for asking the user for a text response to a question.

Examples of these three pop-up windows follow here:

```
<script>
window.alert('Hello!') ;
window.confirm("Press a button!") ;
window.prompt("What's your name?","Phil") ;
</script>
```

These JavaScript calls display the following series of pop-up windows shown in Figures 4-3, 4-4, and 4-5.

Figure 4-3. *Result of window.alert*

Figure 4-4. *Result of window.confirm*

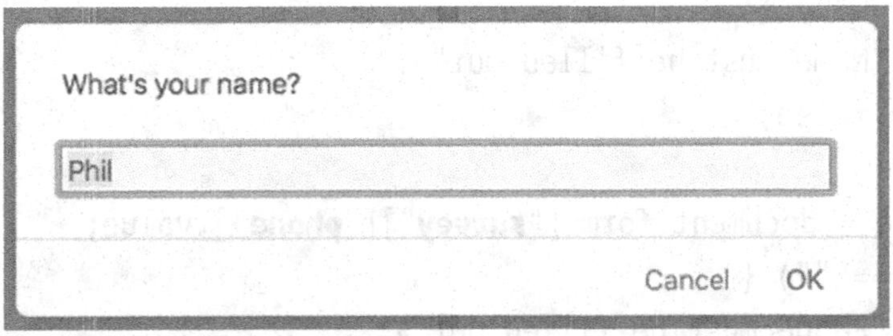

Figure 4-5. *Result of window.prompt*

The JavaScript functions can return values and be used to capture those values to do something with them. For instance, the following variable definition will prompt for the name and assign it to the variable person when the user clicks OK, or if they click Cancel, then it will return a null value:

```
var person = prompt("What's your name?", "Phil");
```

Notice that you can also write the methods without the window prefix.

Validating Form Fields

You can either do client-side or server-side validation or both! Client-side validation happens on the client computer in the web browser. Server-side validation happens back on the server once the form content has been sent there. To do client-side validation, you can use JavaScript. You are able to get the value of a field that has been typed into or even detect each character as it is typed.

The following HTML and JavaScript example in Listing 4-1 shows a simple way to get you started doing client-side validation. The numbers (①,②,③, and ④) just show lines that have a relationship of some kind.

Listing 4-1. HTML and JavaScript example

```
<HTML>
<head>
<script>
①function validateForm() {
②  ③ var name = document.forms["survey"]["name"].value;
    if (name == "") {
        alert("Name must be filled out");
        return false;
    }
③ ④  var phone = document.forms["survey"]["phone"].value;
    if (phone == "") {
        alert("Phone must be filled out");
        return false;
    }
}
</script>
</head>
<body>
③ ①<form name="survey" onsubmit="return validateForm()" method="post"
action="run.php">
② Name: <input type="text" name="name"><br>
④ Phone: <input name="phone" type="text" onkeypress='return event.charCode
>= 48 && event.charCode <= 57'></input>
<input type="submit" value="Submit">
</form>
</body>
</HTML>
```

We have a function which gets the value of name and checks if it is empty, in which case a message is shown and the function returns a false, meaning that the action is not done. If the name had some content, then it gets the value from the phone field and does the same test.

Also, on the phone field, we have specified onkeypress, which carries out the JavaScript in quotes each time a key is pressed. That will return the value of the text typed if it is between the ASCII codes of 48 and 57, which are the digits 0–9. This ensures that we can only type numbers into the phone field, and any other characters will be ignored.

The HTML produced is shown in Figure 4-6.

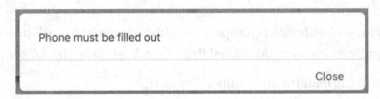

Name:
Phone: [Submit]

Figure 4-6. *HTML results in this displayed in browser*

If we don't enter a name, then the text in Figure 4-7 is displayed.

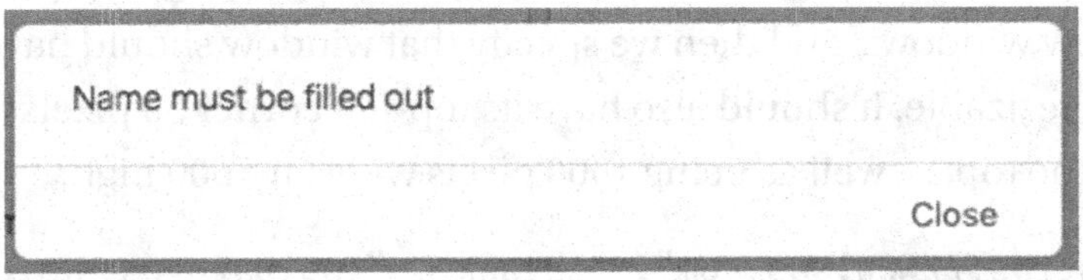

Name must be filled out

Close

Figure 4-7. *Message when Submit is pressed without specifying a Name*

If we don't enter a phone number, then the text in Figure 4-8 is displayed.

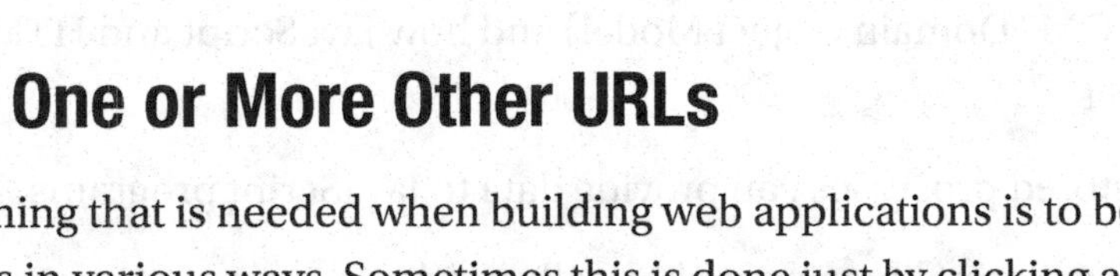

Phone must be filled out

Close

Figure 4-8. *Message when Submit is pressed with specifying a Phone number*

Linking to One or More Other URLs

One common thing that is needed when building web applications is to be able to call other web pages in various ways. Sometimes this is done just by clicking a link, which is simply done using an anchor tag. These show up as blue underlined links usually, although we can change how they look with CSS. Here is some HTML code for a link:

```
<a href="https://www.sas.com">SAS Web Site</a>
```

Clicking a link like this will open a web page replacing the one you are currently on. If you specify a target attribute on the anchor tag, then you can choose where to open the web page. _blank will open the link on a new window/tab, _self will open it on the same frame as it was clicked, _parent opens it in the parent frame, _top opens it in the full body of the current window/tab, or you can specify the name of a frame to open it in that. Using links like this will always require the user to click the link to make the action happen. However, you can use JavaScript to open other URLs automatically. The following JavaScript code will open the SAS home page when it is executed:

```
window.open("https://www.sas.com");
```

You can specify other parameters with **window.open** to control more about how the URL is opened. For instance, the following code specifies the page to open, _blank says to open it in a new windows, and then we specify that window should have a toolbar and scrollbar and be resizable. It should also have its top-left corner 50 pixels in from the left and down from the top, as well as being 1000 pixels wide and 500 high.

```
window.open("https://www.sas.com", "_blank", "toolbar=yes,scrollbars=yes,
resizable=yes,top=50,left=50,width=1000,height=500");
```

Summary

In this chapter, we look at JavaScript especially with a view to what will be useful when creating web applications with SAS Stored Processes. We look at the following things:

- Some of the features and limits of JavaScript

- Debugging JavaScript programs using tools available in web browsers

- The DOM (Domain Object Model) and how JavaScript and HTML interact

- How stored processes can provide data to JavaScript programs

- How JavaScript libraries are basically used

- How to add more interactivity to HTML programs

- Adding validation to HTML forms

CHAPTER 5

JavaScript Libraries

JavaScript libraries are a collection of pre-written JavaScript programs which have a defined Application Programming Interface (API)[1] that can be used by other programs to make use of their functionality. For instance, a library might provide a collection of useful objects such as tables and graphs of different kinds. Those objects would have parameters defined so that you could provide data to them and define things about the layout of the objects.

If you have used SAS/AF in the past, you will see similarities between JavaScript libraries and SAS/AF. Both allow you to interact with a client by building a user interface, detecting responses, and taking various actions. I have built applications in the past using SAS/AF, and now JavaScript together with HTML lets me build quite similar applications.

Benefits of a Library

JavaScript libraries have some useful benefits over writing your own code to achieve the same results. The primary benefit is that the code has already been written and used by many people and is now shared for others. Other benefits of libraries include

- **Browser support** – Often a library will have code that supports multiple browsers. If you don't have code that does this, then you can sometimes find inconsistencies in the behavior of your code.

- **Cross-platform support** – Libraries will often support differences in how multiple platforms operate. For instance, using a library can allow your applications to run properly on computers, tablets, and mobile phones.

---

[1]Application Programming Interface, or API, is a definition of how a program can make use of another program. It defines the input, outputs, parameters, and so on.

© Philip Mason 2020
P. Mason, *SAS Stored Processes*, https://doi.org/10.1007/978-1-4842-5925-2_5

- **Functionality** – Code and widgets from libraries can provide objects with lots of functionality that can be used with very little coding. The library of functionality means you can use them rather than developing a lot of code to do similar things. This is similar to the collection of widgets provided with SAS/AF which provided lots of pre-built functionality.

- **Extensible** – With libraries, you get the source code and then have the ability to extend and enhance any code provided. This is only really applicable to expert JavaScript programmers though and is far beyond the scope of this book.

- **Learning** – Often a JavaScript library has a community of users providing support and sample code. This can provide a great resource to learn from or base your own code on with some modification of examples you like.

- **Quality** – Since the code is used by many people and has been well tested, you get high-quality code to build upon.

- **Speed of development** – Using a library means you have a huge amount of code available which you don't need to write yourself, thus saving a lot of development time.

Choosing a JavaScript Library to Use As a Framework

There are quite a lot of libraries around today and even more are being developed all the time. Some of them have been around for a long time, and many form a foundation for other ones which tends to ensure their longevity. So, I can be confident in recommending the libraries in the next section. When picking a library, I suggest evaluating them on the following criteria:

- **Popularity** – This tends to ensure ongoing development and bug fixing. More popular libraries will have more examples floating around the Web and more problems solved on forums.

- **Functionality** – The key thing you're after. Look at what the library gives you in the way of functions, objects, widgets, and so on. It's easy to look through a library's example to see a showcase of what it can do. You might want to get one library because it gives you the best grid that you are looking for, but it might not do graphs. So, you might choose another library that does graphs really well. If you mix and match, you need to make sure that the libraries operate together well.

- **Ease of use** – Varies between libraries, especially if you are not a proper JavaScript programmer and just dabble.

- **Available via CDN** – Means that you will be able to point to the libraries on a publicly available Code Delivery Network. If the library you want is not available on one of these, then you need to install the file on your server and point to it there.

- **W3Schools** – See if your library is covered on the W3Schools website which provides free reference and training resources on a number of web technologies. If a library is covered here, then you can be sure it is a good choice.

- **Cost** – Most libraries can be downloaded and used for free at least for a while. Even the ones that cost will allow free use for personal development/non-commercial uses. However, some of the really good ones charge by number of developers, websites, servers, or some combination. So, you need to be aware of the potential cost before investing a lot of expense in development.

Recommended Libraries

There are a huge number of libraries around, but to get you started, I would suggest looking at the following ones:

- **jQuery** – Perhaps the best known of all libraries. Its strapline is "write less, do more". And it's free. You can learn more about jQuery in the next section of this chapter.

- **jqGrid** – A great jQuery grid plug-in with some variations for pivot tables, tree view, and so on.

- **Highcharts** – One of the best for graphs and other visualizations.

- **D3** – Lets you do amazing visualizations and has several other libraries built on top of it such as C3, Dimple, and DC.

- **Crossfilter** – Lets you have linked objects in which selecting something in one will apply filters to the others. Simple and powerful.

- **Handsontable** – A grid library that is almost like having Excel in a web browser.

- **Highmaps** – Not free but does a great job at maps.

- **Highstocks** – Also not free, but has some great graph types commonly used with stocks but not exclusively.

- **Sencha Ext JS** – Great, but not cheap. It has a very useful designer which is a point and click interface to build applications using its library.

You will usually want a mix of libraries, since you will want jQuery for doing many basic things; however, it doesn't come with a grid or graphs. So, you might then add in a grid like Handsontable and graphs like Highcharts. If money is no object, you might just get Ext JS which will give you everything you need. If you don't want to spend anything, then a combination like jQuery with dataTables, DC.js, and dyGraphs is something that I have used with great success.

Content Delivery Networks (CDNs)

A great place to get libraries like jQuery is from a Content Delivery Network or CDN. They are a collection of distributed servers which deliver content to users efficiently based on factors such as geographical location. In practice, they are extremely useful for loading JavaScript libraries. I have found that often it is difficult to get permission to host a JavaScript library on a server of a client I am working for; however, I can point to a CDN and just load that library when it is needed. Additionally, if people load the library a lot, then it is held in cache and becomes very efficient to load.

A Google search of "CDN jQuery" will come up with a range of CDNs that have jQuery libraries available. You will see that there are many versions of jQuery, and with major new versions generally new functionality and support for older browsers is dropped and newer browsers added. So generally, if you are using the latest browser, then choose the latest version.

You will also notice that there are usually several versions of each library on a CDN. There is a normal version, a version with comments through it (which is bigger), and a minimized version which has all the white space, carriage returns, comments, and so on taken out so it is as small as possible while still working properly. We usually use the minimized version since it is smallest and so is quicker to load. However, if you are developing and using a debugger, you might want the bigger version with comments.

If using a CDN, you need to be aware of potential security issues. Using a CDN, you are going to an external website and including JavaScript code which will then run on your machines. That should be OK, but there might potentially be some malicious code that someone hacks into a CDN so that it is used by many people. It is best to find copies of libraries that you trust and run through virus and malicious code checkers. Then keep a copy of the scanned libraries on your own web server and use that version rather than a CDN version. Although, sometimes people don't have the permission to update their web servers like this and will reply on a CDN, or perhaps use a CDN for ease of use. You can mitigate the risks by using an integrity hash.[2]

jQuery

jQuery is a JavaScript library which greatly simplifies JavaScript programming. You can usually achieve quite a lot with far less statements than it would take with standard JavaScript. You can do things like manipulate the HTML on a web page, such as changing things displayed and loading items into a list of items; modify the CSS on a web page, such as changing the font/size/color of text and laying out items on a screen; attach event handlers to things on a web page such as pressing a button, pressing the "Y" key, or hovering over some text that can carry out an action; and create dynamic effects and animations like having text slowly appear and grow in size as a web page opens.

One of the most useful things you can do with jQuery is to make use of AJAX, which stands for Asynchronous JavaScript and XML. It lets you fire off requests from one web page to do other things. So you might use AJAX to load three selection lists on a page with values. The great thing about AJAX is that the rest of the web page will load and display while AJAX requests are off running, and when they return, you are able to update the web page with things they return. It's a key feature that makes it possible to build great web applications.

---

[2]https://sasjs.io/security/#integrity-checking-for-javascript-files

Getting Started

A great place to learn about jQuery, HTML, CSS, and more is at W3Schools website. The jQuery section (www.w3schools.com/jquery) has lots of examples, tutorials, references, and more. W3Schools uses a page for all examples which displays the code on the left and the results on the right. You are able to modify the code and then see results on the right updated, which makes it a great place to try things out and learn about jQuery.

To use jQuery, we need to include the jQuery library by using a script tag and then have some JavaScript that makes use of some jQuery. A simple "hello world" example is as follows in Listing 5-1.

Listing 5-1. Hello World example

```
<HTML>
<head>
<script src='/Users/philipmason/Downloads/jquery.min.js'></script>
<script>
  $(document).ready(function() {
    alert("Hello World!") ;
}) ;
</script>
</head>
<body>
<h1>jQuery test</h1>
</body>
</HTML>
```

This HTML produces a page like the one shown in Figure 5-1.

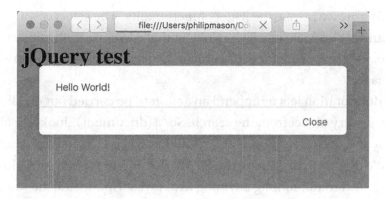

Figure 5-1. *Alert is shown when web page loads*

If you are using code like jQuery from outside your business, there are security implications. You need to make sure you get a safe copy of it checked and loaded onto your own infrastructure to reduce any possible risk. If you just connect to a CDN, then you will always be grabbing the code from an external source every time you use your web app. You can mitigate the risk by using integrity hashes.[3] And having said that, these libraries are used by millions of websites around the world and are very safe.

One important thing to note is that when you load the jQuery library to make use of all the jQuery functionality, this statement should be used:

```
<script src='/Users/philipmason/Downloads/jquery.min.js'></script>
```

Here I have loaded the library from my Mac; however, you can load it from your own web server or load it from somewhere online. A great place to load things like jQuery is from a CDN which is described in the next section.

The other important thing in this example code is the piece of jQuery code:

```
$(document).ready(function() {
  alert("Hello World!") ;
}) ;
```

You use jQuery by using the following syntax:

```
$(selector).action() ;
```

---

[3]https://sasjs.io/security/#integrity-checking-for-javascript-files

The $ sign is how we invoke the jQuery functionality. The selector will look through the HTML document and return a jQuery object that contains all the objects that match. In our example, we are looking for a "document" object, which is how we refer to the whole HTML page.[4]

JavaScript dot notation lets us append an action to be carried out on all the objects returned in the jQuery object from the search. So "$(document)" looks for objects that are a document and then ".ready" sets an action that will be carried out when the ready event occurs. We do this to make sure the HTML document is completely loaded and ready before we start manipulating anything with JavaScript. Inside the round brackets, we have the code that will run when the document is ready. Here we define a function to run, which contains the statement we want to run. "function()" indicates that this is a function object, and the statements to run occur within the curly brackets. Within the curly brackets, we simply have a standard JavaScript alert function which pops up a box with some text in it.

Using this kind of code is a standard way you can use when you want to do something once a web page is loaded. All you need is the following jQuery, as we have seen in our example, and replace the code with whatever jQuery or JavaScript that you want to run:

```
$(document).ready(function () {
//    your code goes here
}) ;
```

Selecting Elements in jQuery

There are a number of ways to select elements in an HTML document with jQuery. They are quite flexible, and we are able to select things by referring to the name of the tag, the id used on a particular tag, the class defined, attributes used, and much more. Here are some of the major ones that you are likely to need.

---

[4]If you're a bit worried at this stage that things are getting a bit deep and that you will need to learn all about the Domain Object Model, which is how HTML documents are represented in a web browser, then don't worry as we will be learning just enough to get things done and not delving deep into web technologies as that is far beyond the scope of this book. We only need a bit of knowledge about all this and some examples to work from in order for us to do a lot.

Selecting by Tag Name

You can specify the name of an HTML tag to select elements. In the following code, I select the list item tag ("li") and then use the jQuery text method to set the text for each tag.

Listing 5-2. List item tag and jQuery text method example

```
<HTML>
<head>
<script src='/Users/philipmason/Downloads/jquery.min.js'></script>
<script>
$(document).ready(function () {
    $('li').text('new value')
}) ;
</script>
</head>
<body>
<ol>
<li>1</li>
<li>2</li>
<li>3</li>
</ol>
</body>
</HTML>
```

This results in the output shown in Figure 5-2.

1. new value
2. new value
3. new value

Figure 5-2. Result of JavaScript selecting all li tags and changing them

Selecting by ID

If you have specified an id with any of your tags, then you can select them by using that id. If you put a hash symbol (#) in front of what you are selecting, then that indicates it is an ID rather than a tag name. So in the code in Listing 5-3, we select the elements (see ①) with an ID of "one" (see ②).

Listing 5-3. Select by ID example

```
<HTML>
<head>
<script src='/Users/philipmason/Downloads/jquery.min.js'></script>
<script>
$(document).ready(function () {
$('#one').text('new value')        ①
}) ;
</script>
</head>
<body>
<ol>
<li id='one'>1</li>                ②
<li id='two'>2</li>
<li id='three'>3</li>
</ol>
</body>
</HTML>
```

This results in the output shown in Figure 5-3.

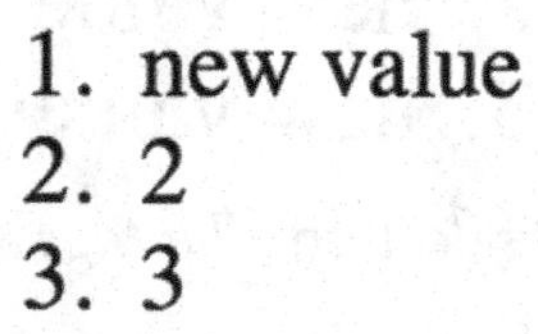

1. new value
2. 2
3. 3

Figure 5-3. *Result of JavaScript selecting one specific id and changing it*

Selecting by Class

If you have specified a class with any of your tags, then you can select them by using that class. If you put a dot (.) in front of what you are selecting, then that indicates that it is a class. So, in the code in Listing 5-4, we select the elements (see ①) with a class of "odd" which results in selecting two lines (see ② and ③).

Listing 5-4. Selecting by class example

```
<HTML>
<head>
<script src='/Users/philipmason/Downloads/jquery.min.js'></script>
<script>
$(document).ready(function () {
$('.odd').text('new value')          ①
}) ;
</script>
</head>
<body>
<ol>
①  <li class='odd'>1</li>              ②
<li class='even'>2</li>
①  <li class='odd'>3</li>              ③
</ol>
</body>
</HTML>
```

This results in the output shown in Figure 5-4.

1. new value
2. 2
3. new value

Figure 5-4. *CSS class was used to select number 1 & 3, resulting in "new value" being used*

It is best practice to specify the tag name, followed by the class ①, so in the previous example that would be done like this:

```
$(document).ready(function () {
    $('li.odd').text('new value')        ①
}) ;
```

Other Ways to Select Things

I won't go into all this much more, but just to let you know of some of the possibilities in case you ever want a bit more control over what you select. Table 5-1 shows some other examples of ways to select things.

Table 5-1. *Some ways to select things in jQuery*

HTML Code	jQuery Code	What It Does
<li lang='en'>	$('[lang="en"]')	Select elements which have an attribute called lang equal to "en"
<li>1</li> <li>2</li>	$('li:even')	Select "li" elements which with even row numbers. Can also select :first, :last, :odd, :lt, :gt, :eq
<ul> <li>1</li> <li>1</li> <li>3</li> </ul>	$('ul span')	Select the element with a span tag which is within a ul tag
<h1>heading 1</h1> <h2 id='2'>heading 2</h2> <h3>heading 3</h3>	$('h1,#2')	Select the element with a span tag which is within a ul tag

You can find many more examples on the W3Schools website (www.w3schools.com/jquery/jquery_ref_selectors.asp).

Fundamental jQuery Techniques

jQuery gives us a lot of tools to detect things happening on our HTML page and then modify the page in various ways. That is the basis for building a web application. We want to display some information and allow a user to interact with the page by moving the mouse around, clicking, and typing. Based on those interactions, we might load some more content, go to another page, hide or reveal something, and so on. The extent of your imagination is the limit. We could even throw in some speech recognition or virtual reality.

Listing 5-5 shows some examples of simple jQuery to show a few of the things we can do with it and how little code is needed to achieve this:

- The code on the left will load a text file into a section of a web page when a button is clicked.

- The code at the top right will hide all paragraphs on a web page when a button is pressed.

- And code on the bottom right does some animation of some sections of HTML when a button is pressed.

Listing 5-5. jQuery example code

```
<script>

$(document).ready(function(){
    $("p").click(function(){
        $(this).hide();
    });
});

</script>

$(document).ready(function(){
    $("button").click(function() {
        $("#div1").load("demo_test.txt");
    })
});

</script>
```

```
$(document).ready(function(){
   $("button").click(function() {
      $("#div1").fadeIn();
      $("#div2").fadeIn("slow");
      $("#div3").fadeIn(3000);
   })
});
```

Now let's look at some of the fundamental jQuery techniques you can build on.

Actions

We can use jQuery to easily attach actions to elements of a web page. We just need to select an element on the web page and then attach a method to it which will handle an event. We are able to detect things such as in Table 5-2.

Table 5-2. *Methods that can be used in jQuery to detect events*

Jquery Method	Explanation
click()	Single click of mouse button
dblclick()	Double click of mouse button
mousedown()	Mouse button is pressed down
mouseup()	Mouse button is released
mouseover()	Mouse has moved over an element
mouseout()	Mouse has moved off an element
mousemove()	Mouse has moved on the screen; we can get the x and y coordinates of where the mouse is
keypress()	A key has been pressed; we can get the ASCII code for that key (e.g., 65 is "A", 97 is "a")
keydown()	A key was held down. It is useful to recognize things like arrow keys (ASCII codes 37–40)
keyup()	A key was released

There are also some other actions that can be taken when the screen is resized (resize()), when something is scrolled (scroll()) and more.

The following example in Listing 5-6 shows how we can define a function for single (②) and double (③) clicks. Additionally, you can see a way to identify if it was the left, middle, or right mouse button that was pressed. The parameter "e" that I passed to the click method returns an object which we can find the button from by using the button method ①. A value of 0 indicates the left button, 1 is the middle button, and 2 is the right button.

Listing 5-6. Define a function for single and double clicks

```
<HTML>
<head>
<script src='/Users/philipmason/Downloads/jquery.min.js'></script>
<script>
$(document).ready(function () {
②    $('#box').click(function (e) {
①        $(this).text('clicked button: ' + e.button)
         .css('background','yellow');
    })
③    $('#box').dblclick(function () {
        $(this).text('double clicked').css('background','red');
    })
}) ;
</script>
<style>
#box {width:200px;height:100px;border:3px solid black}
</style>
</head>
<body>
<div id='box'>click</div>
</body>
</HTML>
```

Here is what the screen looks like at first (Figure 5-5), after a single click (Figure 5-6), and then a double click (Figure 5-7).

Figure 5-5. *Browser shows this when page is first shown*

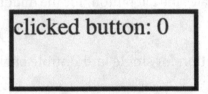

Figure 5-6. *Browser shows this after one click with left mouse button*

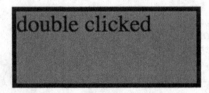

Figure 5-7. *Browser shows this after a double click with left mouse button*

Many other JavaScript libraries work well with jQuery. In fact, out of the many libraries I have seen, I have never found any that conflict with jQuery. jQuery uses a $ sign to make calls to it, but this can even be substituted with "jquery" and the $ deactivated in case it conflicts with other web usage.

Summary

In this chapter, we look at JavaScript libraries which can provide lots of pre-built functionality to save you having to do a lot more programming:

- There are many benefits of using a library of JavaScript code.
- Some libraries provide a framework that you can.

- The best and most popular libraries change from time to time, but currently some of the best are

  - jQuery

  - Highcharts

  - D3

  - Crossfilter

  - Data tables

- Content Delivery Networks provide a source of libraries you can reliably use from your web applications.

- We went into some more detail with jQuery about how to select things on screen and detect when the user clicks with a mouse or hits a key.

Data

Among many of the tools that SAS has in its arsenal, SAS can generate data for multiple uses. This chapter allows the reader to determine how they plan to use the data. Are you looking to interact with data managed by SAS using a spreadsheet? Are you looking to bring SAS data into another application page, static HTML page, or in an Excel spreadsheet (i.e., Office Analytics)? This section will help you see who SAS can be used for all of these and more.

This section will talk about using data from SAS with other things such as some kind of application that needs to consume data. For instance, it might be that you want to import some data into Microsoft Excel. Or you might want to display a graph in a web browser which uses the data from SAS. The possibilities are endless.

Dynamic Data

Dynamic data is data produced by a SAS program at the point that it is needed. This means it can always be completely up to date. So, we might have a SAS Stored Process that can be called and will produce JSON data when it is needed based on a live system in order to give up to the minute information to the calling application.

Dynamic data is easily produced with Stored Processes but could also potentially be produced by running a standard SAS program in batch and then picking up the output produced from it.

© Philip Mason 2020
P. Mason, *SAS Stored Processes*, https://doi.org/10.1007/978-1-4842-5925-2_6

Using Stored Processes to Create Dynamic Data

SAS allows Stored Processes to produce data which can be consumed by JavaScript objects and libraries. As the newest web data transport format, JSON will be the most common format; some processes may use CSV or XML. The key points in achieving this are as follows:

- Exclude stpbegin and stpend macros from your Stored Process. These are usually used by default if making a Stored Process with Enterprise Guide.

- Produce the data using any method you like such as a data step, PROC EXPORT, PROC JSON, and so on.

- Set the Stored Process to return streaming output.

- Write the output to the `fileref _WEBOUT`, since that will stream the data directly to whatever has called the Stored Process.

The data called in the Stored Process will stream directly back to what has called it. If you place the URL directly in a browser address bar, then the data will be shown in the format designated in the stored process directly in the browser. Similarly, if you place the URL inside a JavaScript function, the data will be available for consumption by the JavaScript function or library. Stored Process production of web data allows us to build flexible applications which use web-based data for generating grids, graphs, lists, and many other objects on your web pages and applications.

The following code is a simple example of a Stored Process that uses a parameter for the name of the table and writes CSV data to _webout so that it is streamed back to the web application. We also have to specify `replace` for it to work; otherwise, the Stored Process can't write to _webout. In the metadata for the Stored Process, you just need to define the table parameter so that the Stored Process can be called and specify those values for use:

```
proc export data=&table outfile=_webout dbms=csv replace ;
run ;

proc export  data=sashelp.class outfile=_webout dbms=csv replace ;
run ;
```

Here is another simple example showing a Stored Process which returns JSON data. It uses a parameter for libname and memname ① to specify the data required. In the metadata for the Stored Process, you just need to define the libname and memname parameters so that the Stored Process can be called and specify those values for use:

```
proc json out=_webout ;
    export &libname..&memname ; ①
run ;

proc json out=_webout ;
    export sashelp.orsales ;
run ;
WARNING: PROC JSON in SAS 9 can truncate what it produces if it is over
32,767 in length.
```

How SAS Stored Processes Can Feed Data to Objects

Many JavaScript objects use data provided via a URL. This could be a static file on a web server, a PHP script, a file on a WebDAV server, or even a Stored Process. The JavaScript object will typically be able to use some code to point to a data source. You will often find example code or documentation that shows exactly how to associate data with a file, since that is the simplest thing to do. For example, the following code uses jQuery to point to a JSON file which will be used as input to a grid:

```
$('#table1').DataTable( {
    "ajax": "http://d351tq92/sales.json"
} );
```

So, we could generate a file from SAS to be used as input to an object like this, although we can also just associate an object directly to a Stored Process. That Stored Process will return a stream of content in the same way as reading from a file would return a stream of content. For example, to change the previous example to use a Stored Process, I could use some code like this:

```
$('#table1').DataTable( {
    "ajax": "http://d351tq92/SASStoredProcess/do?_program=%2FUser+Folders%2
    Fphil%2FMy+Folder%2Fgrid_json"
} );
```

The preceding Stored Process can further be enhanced by adding some parameters to it. This adds a whole new level of benefit for us. If we point at a file, then we simply get the content of that file. If we point at a Stored Process, we get the content of it. If we add parameters to the Stored Process enabling us to specify the SAS table we want, then we can have the Stored Process return us the data we select. This makes the Stored Process into a general purpose one that could now drive a JavaScript grid which would be able to show us any table. For example, the following code adds a libname and memname parameter. To be clear, this only works if you are using a Stored Process with something like Proc Stream so that the values of &libname and &memname are resolved when the following code is written out. You can see this method shown in Listing 6-1.

```
$('#table1').DataTable( {
    "ajax": "http://d351tq92/SASStoredProcess/do?_program=%2FUser+Folders%2
    Fphil%2FMy+Folder%2Fgrid_json%nrstr(&libname)=&libname%nrstr(&memname)=
    &memname"
} );
```

Here is the Stored Process code for the entire example that would make a grid object and point to another Stored Process that would provide its data.

Listing 6-1. Stored process code example

```
* generate a list of variable names to use as table headers and footers ;
proc sql noprint ;
    select '<th>'||strip(name)||'</th>' into :th
        separated by ''
        from dictionary.columns
        where libname="%upcase(&libname)" and memname="%upcase(&memname)" ;
quit ;
%put &=th ;

* write content out ;
data _null_ ;
    file _webout ;
    input ;
    line=resolve(_infile_) ;
    put line ;
cards4 ;
```

```
<HTML>
<head>
<script src="http://code.jquery.com/jquery-1.12.4.js"></script>
<script src="https://cdn.datatables.net/1.10.15/js/jquery.dataTables.min.
js"></script>
<script>
$(document).ready(function() {
    $('#table1').DataTable( {
        "ajax": "http://d351tq92/SASStoredProcess/do?_program=%2FUser+
        Folders%2Fphil%2FMy+Folder%2Fgrid_json%nrstr(&libname)=&libname%
        nrstr(&memname)=&memname"
    } );
} );
</script>
<link rel="stylesheet" href="https://cdn.datatables.net/1.10.15/css/jquery.
dataTables.min.css">
</head>
<body>
<table id="table1" class="display" cellspacing="0" width="100%">
<thead>
<tr>
&th
</tr>
</thead>
<tfoot>
<tr>
&th
</tr>
</tfoot>
</table>
</body>
</HTML>
;;;;
run ;
```

The Stored Process that provides the data is shown here. The code is very straightforward as it produces some JSON data written out. The pretty parameter lays the JSON out in a nice way that is easier to see the structure. We also need some write statements to produce the exact form of JSON required for the object we are using. Often, I find that PROC JSON doesn't automatically provide the right JSON needed as the format will vary depending on the JavaScript object you use. But the write statements let you customize it quite a lot to make any kind of JSON you might need. We also use nosastags to turn off some SAS JSON written out which is not required:

```
proc json out=_webout pretty ;
    write open object ;
    write value "data" ;
    write open array ;
    export &libname..&memname / nokeys nosastags ;
    write close ;
    write close ;
run ;
```

Static Data

Static data is data that is produced by a SAS program at some point in the past and then is used as is by an application. So, we might produce an XML file and place it on a server. Various applications could then come along and pick up that file to use in different ways. For it to be useful, we might need to update that file each week, so that applications will always have the latest available data for the previous week. So there will be various things to think about regarding

- How recent must the data be?

- Where is the best location for it, to be secure but available?

- Should it be password protected or encrypted?

- What volume of usage will it get? Should it be on fast storage? Does it matter?

This data could be stored in a file somewhere or could even be delivered in the form of a Stored Process report which is a cached version of a Stored Process. When you download some static data, then that data will be fixed until you download some more data to update it. So any changes to the data elsewhere will not be reflected in the data you downloaded.

In this book, I am trying to show you how to use dynamic data rather than static data. Dynamic data will be up to date and always go back to the source bringing you fresh data when it is needed.

CSV

CSV stands for comma-separated values. It's a way of representing data which is usually structured as a table. The usual way that people come to know about CSV is through using a spreadsheet program such as Microsoft EXCEL or Apple Numbers from which data can be saved to or loaded from CSV files. Having looked at JSON in the previous chapter, you may realize that this is a bit more limited in its functionality since it can only represent tabular data, whereas JSON can handle far more types of data.

Each line of a CSV file is a list of values separated by a delimiter which is traditionally a comma, although can also be another character, often a semi-colon. The values would tend to have quotes around those that are text and not around numerics to make the distinction clear. If a value contained commas within it, then that would be OK as it would be surrounded by quotes. If a value contained quotes within it, then it would often have double quotes to indicate that. This can vary with applications that use CSV data though.

Typically, a CSV would use the first row to have the names for the columns. These names might indicate variable names or just be descriptions for what is each column. Most of the time, these headings are desirable and there is little reason to drop them, as they are easily ignored if not required. However, data in CSV format does not insist on column headings.

One last important thing to mention is that if values are missing, then we might have CSV data that just has consecutive commas that indicate a value is missing by having whitespace or nothing between them. Consecutive commas can be handled differently in different programs, so if you might have them, you need to know the behavior of the application using your data. They might be ignored by treating multiple consecutive commas the same as one comma or as a number of missing values.

Making a CSV with a Data Step

In Chapter 4, we talked about the role of CSV files and the availability of CSV data available over the Web. Some JavaScript libraries require a CSV input. Here we will show you a couple of ways to generate CSV with SAS.

It is easy to make a CSV file from a data step. It just requires pointing to a file and writing out values separated by commas. See Listing 6-2.

Listing 6-2. CSV file from a data step

```
filename temp temp;

data _null_;
    file temp;
    set sashelp.class;
    put name ',' age;
run;

data _null_;
    infile temp;
    input;
    put _infile_;
run;
```

The log from this having run in SAS Studio shows the CSV data produced (in **bold**) (Listing 6-3).

Listing 6-3. CSV data example

```
56          filename temp temp;
57
58          data _null_;
59          file temp;
60          set sashelp.class;
61          put name ',' age;
62          run;
```

NOTE: The file TEMP is:
      Filename=/tmp/SAS_work4BDB00005068_localhost.localdomain/#LN00031,
      Owner Name=sasdemo,Group Name=sas,
      Access Permission=-rw-rw-r--,
      Last Modified=21 April 2017 12:05:33 o'clock

NOTE: 19 records were written to the file TEMP.
      The minimum record length was 8.
      The maximum record length was 11.
NOTE: There were 19 observations read from the data set SASHELP.CLASS.
NOTE: DATA statement used (Total process time):
      real time   0.01 seconds
      cpu time   0.01 seconds

```
63
64         data _null_;
65         infile temp;
66         input;
67         put _infile_;
68         run;
```

NOTE: The infile TEMP is:
      Filename=/tmp/SAS_work4BDB00005068_localhost.localdomain/#LN00031,
      Owner Name=sasdemo,Group Name=sas,
      Access Permission=-rw-rw-r--,
      Last Modified=21 April 2017 12:05:33 o'clock,
      File Size (bytes)=198

Alfred ,14
Alice ,13
Barbara ,13
Carol ,14
Henry ,14
James ,12
Jane ,12
Janet ,15
Jeffrey ,13

```
John  ,12
Joyce ,11
Judy  ,14
Louise ,12
Mary  ,15
Philip ,16
Robert ,12
Ronald ,15
Thomas ,11
William ,15
NOTE: 19 records were read from the infile TEMP.
      The minimum record length was 8.
      The maximum record length was 11.
NOTE: DATA statement used (Total process time):
      real time           0.01 seconds
      cpu time            0.01 seconds
```

There are some even easier ways to do this in SAS. The following code uses the DLM= parameter to specify a delimiter to use when writing values out. That means there is no need to write the delimiter in our PUT statement:

```
filename temp temp;

data _null_;
    file temp dlm=',';
    set sashelp.class;
    put name age;
run;
```

If I modify the code to include a variable that does not exist, then I will have missing values written out to my file:

```
filename temp temp;

data _null_;
    file temp dlm=',';
    set sashelp.class;
    put name x age;
run;
```

This results in some CSV data like this. Notice the missing value indicated by a . between the commas:

```
Alfred,.,14
Alice,.,13
Barbara,.,13
```

However, if I use the DSD parameter, then that means that I won't write out missing values, but just leave the commas following on from each other with nothing in between them. So the modified code is this:

```
filename temp temp ;
data _null_ ;
file temp dlm=',' dsd ;
set sashelp.class ;
put name x age ;
run ;
```

And you can see that now we don't have missing values written out:

```
Alfred,,14
Alice,,13
Barbara,,13
```

If I wanted to just simply write all the variables out in CSV format, then the most efficient code is something like this. The part with "name--weight" is how we specify a list of variables including all variables between name and weight inclusive:

```
data _null_;
  file temp dlm=',' ;
  set sashelp.class;
  put name--weight ;
run;
```

This produces output that looks like Listing 6-4.

Listing 6-4. Output

```
Alfred,M,14,69,112.5
Alice,F,13,56.5,84
Barbara,F,13,65.3,98
Carol,F,14,62.8,102.5
Henry,M,14,63.5,102.5
James,M,12,57.3,83
Jane,F,12,59.8,84.5
Janet,F,15,62.5,112.5
Jeffrey,M,13,62.5,84
John,M,12,59,99.5
Joyce,F,11,51.3,50.5
Judy,F,14,64.3,90
Louise,F,12,56.3,77
Mary,F,15,66.5,112
Philip,M,16,72,150
Robert,M,12,64.8,128
Ronald,M,15,67,133
Thomas,M,11,57.5,85
William,M,15,66.5,112
```

Using PROC EXPORT to Make CSV

Another nice easy way to generate CSV data from SAS is by using PROC EXPORT. We will cover this elsewhere in more detail, but basically the code is as follows:

```
filename temp temp ;
proc export data=sashelp.class
            outfile=temp
            dbms=csv ;
run ;
```

By default, PROC EXPORT will give us column headings for our data. If we didn't want the column headings, we could specify PUTNAMES=no to suppress them.

SASHELP.SAS in CSV

Using the PROC EXPORT code, we can generate the following CSV output. I have included this so it can be easily compared to other types of output for sashelp.class. See Listing 6-5.

Listing 6-5. PROC EXPORT generated CSV output

```
Name,Sex,Age,Height,Weight
Alfred,M,14,69,112.5
Alice,F,13,56.5,84
Barbara,F,13,65.3,98
Carol,F,14,62.8,102.5
Henry,M,14,63.5,102.5
James,M,12,57.3,83
Jane,F,12,59.8,84.5
Janet,F,15,62.5,112.5
Jeffrey,M,13,62.5,84
John,M,12,59,99.5
Joyce,F,11,51.3,50.5
Judy,F,14,64.3,90
Louise,F,12,56.3,77
Mary,F,15,66.5,112
Philip,M,16,72,150
Robert,M,12,64.8,128
Ronald,M,15,67,133
Thomas,M,11,57.5,85
William,M,15,66.5,112
```

XML

XML stands for eXtensible Markup Language, which was created to store and transport data. It is designed to be readable by machines and humans, though it is not as easy to read as JSON (in my opinion). It has been around a lot longer than JSON though, so is a bit more embedded into things on the Internet.

XML is stored as a text file, like JSON and CSV. It is quite easy in SAS to deal with simple XML files which have a table like structure, as the next examples will show. We can also deal with far more complex types of XML; however, to do this requires the use of XMLMaps which are beyond the scope of this book. Just be aware that there is a great program available with SAS called the XML Mapper[1] that helps you create XML maps, or you can create them manually. You then specify a map that you are using in order to map more complex XML structures into the simpler SAS table layout.

Reading XML Data into SAS

The following SAS program in Listing 6-6 writes some XML data to a temporary file. I then get the filename that was created (using pathname function). Using that I can use the XML engine on the libname statement to point to the file. Because the XML is stored in this way, I can easily read it into SAS and use it.

Listing 6-6. XML data to temporary file

```
filename temp '/tmp/class.xml';

data _null_;
    file temp;
    input;
    put _infile_;
    cards;
<?xml version="1.0" encoding="windows-1252" ?>
<TABLE>
 <PEOPLE>
 <FirstName> Phil </FirstName>
 <Age> 52 </Age>
 </PEOPLE>
 <PEOPLE>
 <FirstName> Esther </FirstName>
 <Age> 48 </Age>
 </PEOPLE>
```

---

[1]http://support.sas.com/documentation/cdl/en/engxml/64990/HTML/default/viewer.htm#n
 0mxvt7afwoqron1pioilwOvzxq1.htm

```
<PEOPLE>
<FirstName> Jake </FirstName>
<Age> 20 </Age>
</PEOPLE>
</TABLE>
;;
run ;

libname temp xml;

data PEOPLE;
    set temp.PEOPLE;
run;

proc print data=PEOPLE;
run;
```

The output produced is shown in Figure 6-1.

The SAS System

Obs	AGE	FIRSTNAME
1	52	Phil
2	48	Esther
3	20	Jake

Figure 6-1. *Result of Proc Print from XML data*

Using the XML Engine to Create SASHELP.CLASS in XML

Using the following simple code enables us to write some XML to an external file. I use the temp engine on the filename statement to get a temporary file location, since this doesn't work with libname. Then I can use pathname to find where it is pointing to and then use that with my libname statement which uses the XML engine to create an XML file. Once that is done, it is simple to just create a table in that XML file, in the usual way.

```
filename temp temp;
libname temp xml;

data temp.class;
    set sashelp.class;
run;
```

The file contents are as follows in Listing 6-7. Compare it back to the SASHELP. CLASS output for CSV and JSON data formats. CSV is much more compressed down in size, and JSON is a bit more succinct compared to this XML.

Listing 6-7. File contents example

```
<?xml version="1.0" encoding="utf-8" ?>
 <TABLE>
    <CLASS>
        <Name> Alfred </Name>
        <Sex> M </Sex>
        <Age> 14 </Age>
        <Height> 69 </Height>
        <Weight> 112.5 </Weight>
    </CLASS>
    <CLASS>
        <Name> Alice </Name>
        <Sex> F </Sex>
        <Age> 13 </Age>
        <Height> 56.5 </Height>
        <Weight> 84 </Weight>
    </CLASS>
    <CLASS>
        <Name> Barbara </Name>
        <Sex> F </Sex>
        <Age> 13 </Age>
        <Height> 65.3 </Height>
        <Weight> 98 </Weight>
    </CLASS>
```

```
<CLASS>
    <Name> Mary </Name>
    <Sex> F </Sex>
    <Age> 15 </Age>
    <Height> 66.5 </Height>
    <Weight> 112 </Weight>
</CLASS>
</TABLE>
```

JSON

JSON stands for JavaScript Object Notation. It is a way of encoding data for use by computer programs. It is similar to XML but is simpler. One of its main advantages is that it is quite easily readable by humans, as well as computers. It can represent tabular and hierarchical data structures which makes it very flexible. JSON is widely used on the Web as a data source for JavaScript objects.

One of the best places on the Internet to find out about JSON is the section on the W3Schools website.[2]

There are some useful things to know though:

- Data is always in name/value pairs which separate the name and value with a colon, for example, "name":"Phil".

- Data is always separated by commas, when there is more than one data item obviously, for example, "name":"phil","lastname":"mason".

- Objects are defined within curly brackets.

- Arrays are defined within square brackets.

Putting all these things together lets you define all kinds of data. You can have arrays of objects, objects made up of arrays, and so on.

---

[2]www.w3schools.com/js/js_json_intro.asp

Example of JSON

For this example in Listing 6-8, you will notice some things about it:

- The curly brackets indicate that this structure is an object.

- The first item is just a text string, since we have the name for the object followed by its value.

- The next item is an object, because we have a name for the item followed by something enclosed in curly brackets indicating another object.

  - This object has four items in it: town, phone, current home, and ages.

  - The first item has a text value (quotes around the text value).

  - The next item has a numeric value (notice there are no quotes since this is a number).

  - The next item has a Boolean value (true/false).

  - The last item is an array, indicated by the square brackets.

  - Within the array, we have five items which are all numeric separated by commas.

Listing 6-8. JSON example

```
{
    "name": "Phil Mason",
    "home": {
        "town": "Wallingford",
        "phone": 1491824891,
        "current home": true,
        "ages": [
            51,
            46,
            18,
            16,
            13
        ]
    }
}
```

Read in JSON

From SAS 9.4 Maintenance Release 4 onward, we can use the JSON libname engine to read JSON data in very easily. A JSON map is used to read the JSON data in, which describes how the data is structured. The following code shows how we can create a map to use for the JSON reading by specifying a libref where the map will be stored and by specifying automap=create which will automatically create a JSON map:

```
* generate a map to see what is in the JSON, and what datasets are
automatically made ;
filename ex 'C:\Users\phil\Documents\My SAS Files\9.4\example json.sas' ;
filename jmap temp ;
libname in json fileref=ex map=jmap automap=create ;
```

We could then take a look at the map that was created using a data step like this:

```
* look at the map that was generated ;
data _null_ ;
   infile jmap ;
   input ;
   put _infile_ ;
run ;
```

Looking either at the fileref directly or in the log, we can see the map as shown in Listing 6-9.

Listing 6-9. JSON map that was automatically created by the libname statement using the JSON engine

```
{
  "DATASETS": [
    {
      "DSNAME": "root",  ①
      "TABLEPATH": "/root",
      "VARIABLES": [
        {
          "NAME": "ordinal_root",
          "TYPE": "ORDINAL",
```

```
      "PATH": "/root"
   },
   {
      "NAME": "name",
      "TYPE": "CHARACTER",
      "PATH": "/root/name",
      "CURRENT_LENGTH": 10
   }
   ]
},
{
   "DSNAME": "home",  ②
   "TABLEPATH": "/root/home",
   "VARIABLES": [
      {
         "NAME": "ordinal_root",
         "TYPE": "ORDINAL",
         "PATH": "/root"
      },
      {
         "NAME": "ordinal_home",
         "TYPE": "ORDINAL",
         "PATH": "/root/home"
      },
      {
         "NAME": "town",
         "TYPE": "CHARACTER",
         "PATH": "/root/home/town",
         "CURRENT_LENGTH": 11
      },
      {
         "NAME": "phone",
         "TYPE": "NUMERIC",
         "PATH": "/root/home/phone"
      },
```

```
      {
        "NAME": "current_home",
        "TYPE": "NUMERIC",
        "PATH": "/root/home/current home"
      }
    ]
  },
  {
    "DSNAME": "home_ages",   ③
    "TABLEPATH": "/root/home/ages",
    "VARIABLES": [
      {
        "NAME": "ordinal_home",
        "TYPE": "ORDINAL",
        "PATH": "/root/home"
      },
      {
        "NAME": "ordinal_ages",
        "TYPE": "ORDINAL",
        "PATH": "/root/home/ages"
      },
      {
        "NAME": "ages1",
        "TYPE": "NUMERIC",
        "PATH": "/root/home/ages/ages1"
      },
      {
        "NAME": "ages2",
        "TYPE": "NUMERIC",
        "PATH": "/root/home/ages/ages2"
      },
      {
        "NAME": "ages3",
        "TYPE": "NUMERIC",
        "PATH": "/root/home/ages/ages3"
      },
```

```
      {
        "NAME": "ages4",
        "TYPE": "NUMERIC",
        "PATH": "/root/home/ages/ages4"
      },
      {
        "NAME": "ages5",
        "TYPE": "NUMERIC",
        "PATH": "/root/home/ages/ages5"
      }
    ]
  }
 ]
}
```

Reading through the map, we can see that three datasets have automatically been mapped (shown as ①, ②, and ③). We can look at them by using some PROC PRINT statements (Figure 6-2).

Obs	ordinal_root	name
1	1	Phil Mason

Obs	ordinal_root	ordinal_home	town	phone	current_home
1	1	1	Wallingford	1491824891	1

Obs	ordinal_home	ordinal_ages	ages1	ages2	ages3	ages4	ages5
1	1	1	51	46	18	16	13

Figure 6-2. *Proc Print output of one record from each JSON mapped table*

So you can see how easy it is to read simple JSON data in with the new JSON engine. It's great.

Using JSON Lint

Lint refers to a collection of tools which analyze a computer program and flags any errors in it. They are usually free tools and often can be run by just using a web browser. It will often also lay out the code in a standard way to make it easier to understand. There are Lint tools available for various languages including JSON. Searching for JSON Lint will find these tools, which can then be used to check your JSON and lay it out clearly. This is especially useful if you are building some custom JSON yourself. Users should be aware that web-based Lint tools will upload the code to be analyzed to a web server to be analyzed. This is a potential security risk since your code could be seen by others. You could buy Lint tools that could be run locally on a computer in which case the code would not have to be uploaded for analysis.

Many text editors (such as Notepad++) allow the language for a file to be set and then do context-sensitive highlighting. This can indicate where there are errors in syntax especially things like non-matching brackets and quotes. If you are looking at JSON, you can set the language to JavaScript since JSON is a form of JavaScript and it will show if your JSON is valid or not.

For example, here is some badly formatted JSON:

```
{"name":"PhilMason","home":{"town":"Wallingford","phone":1491824891,
"current home":true,"ages":[51,46,18,16,13]}}
```

And here is that same JSON when it has been run through JSONLINT.COM:

```
{
    "name": "PhilMason",
    "home": {
        "town": "Wallingford",
        "phone": 1491824891,
        "current home": true,
        "ages": [51, 46, 18, 16, 13]
    }
}
```

Using a Data Step to Make JSON

You can make JSON data from a data step (Listing 6-10).

Listing 6-10. JSON data from a data step

```
data _null_ ;
    set sashelp.class end=_end ;
    if _n_=1 then put '[' ;
    put '{' ;
    put '"Name":"'    name   +(-1) '",' ;
    put '"Sex":"'     sex    +(-1) '",' ;
    put '"Age":"'     age    +(-1) '",' ;
    put '"Height":"' height +(-1) '",' ;
    put '"Weight":"' weight +(-1) '"' ;
    put '}' ;
    if not _end then put ',' ;
    else put ']' ;
run ;
```

Using Proc JSON

Listing 6-11 shows an easy way to take SAS data and produce JSON data.

Listing 6-11. SAS data to produce JSON data

```
filename temp temp;

proc json out=temp;
    export sashelp.class / tablename="class";
run;

data _null_;
    infile temp;
    input;
    put _infile_;
run;
```

SASHELP.SAS in JSON

Using PROC JSON, we can transform SAS tables into JSON, as we have done here in Listing 6-12 with SASHELP.CLASS. This gives you a good idea of how the table is an object which has the rows represented as an array of objects – you can tell that by the square bracket indicating the start of an array (I **bolded** them). In other words, each row is a separate object in an array which holds all the rows in the table. You can see that each row is contained within curly brackets, making it an object. Each row object consists of a collection of name/value pairs, each of which represents a variable and its value. I think this is a great example of how JSON is not only machine-readable but also human-readable.

Listing 6-12. Transform SAS tables into JSON

{"SASJSONExport":"1.0","SASTableData+class":**[**{"Name":"Alfred","Sex":"M", "Age":14,"Height":69,"Weight":112.5},{"Name":"Alice","Sex":"F","Age":13, "Height":56.5,"Weight":84},{"Name":"Barbara","Sex":"F","Age":13,"Height":65.3, "Weight":98},{"Name":"Carol","Sex":"F","Age":14,"Height":62.8,"Weight":102.5}, {"Name":"Henry","Sex":"M","Age":14,"Height":63.5,"Weight":102.5},{"Name": "James","Sex":"M","Age":12,"Height":57.3,"Weight":83},{"Name":"Jane", "Sex":"F","Age":12,"Height":59.8,"Weight":84.5},{"Name":"Janet","Sex":"F", "Age":15,"Height":62.5,"Weight":112.5},{"Name":"Jeffrey","Sex":"M","Age":13, "Height":62.5,"Weight":84},{"Name":"John","Sex":"M","Age":12,"Height":59, "Weight":99.5},{"Name":"Joyce","Sex":"F","Age":11,"Height":51.3,"Weight": 50.5},{"Name":"Judy","Sex":"F","Age":14,"Height":64.3,"Weight":90},{"Name": "Louise","Sex":"F","Age":12,"Height":56.3,"Weight":77},{"Name":"Mary", "Sex":"F","Age":15,"Height":66.5,"Weight":112},{"Name":"Philip","Sex":"M", "Age":16,"Height":72,"Weight":150},{"Name":"Robert","Sex":"M","Age":12, "Height":64.8,"Weight":128},{"Name":"Ronald","Sex":"M","Age":15,"Height":67, "Weight":133},{"Name":"Thomas","Sex":"M","Age":11,"Height":57.5,"Weight": 85},{"Name":"William","Sex":"M","Age":15,"Height":66.5,"Weight":112}**]**}

Summary

In this chapter, we look at aspects of using data with Stored Processes especially when using them with web applications. We looked at some of these things:

- How stored processes can produce dynamic data and deliver it in various formats such as CSV and JSON

- How to produce CSV data with Proc Export and data steps in flexible ways

- How to produce XML using the XML libname engine

- How to produce JSON using a data step or PROC JSON

- Reading in JSON data with the JSON libname engine

CHAPTER 7

Stored Processes

In this chapter, we will focus on SAS Stored Processes and look at the details around them so we can get a good understanding of how to create them along with all the details around that. Let's start by looking at how we move from a SAS program that every SAS programmer understands to a Stored Process.

Converting a SAS Program into a Stored Process

It is very easy to take a normal SAS program and make it into a Stored Process. Here is a normal SAS program which extracts some data, summarizes it, and prints it:

```
* take a random sample ;
data sample ;
    set sashelp.class ;
if ranuni(1)<0.5 ;
run ;
* work out average height and weight by sex ;
proc summary data=sample ;
  class sex ;
  var height weight ;
  output out=class_sum
        mean= ;
run ;
proc print data=class_sum ;
run ;
```

And here is the same program code, once it has been converted to a Stored Process. All that is needed for the SAS code is to add in the %stpbegin macro at the start and %stpend macro at the end. No special program is needed to do this, just a simple text

© Philip Mason 2020
P. Mason, *SAS Stored Processes*, https://doi.org/10.1007/978-1-4842-5925-2_7

editor like Notepad++. Note that the stpbegin and stpend macros are called from SAS autocall libraries that are provided and will be pointed to by default. If you modify the sasautos option, then it might be that you no longer point to where these are stored and may get errors.

```
%stpbegin
* take a random sample ;
data sample ;
    set sashelp.class ;
if ranuni(1)<0.5 ;
run ;
* work out average height and weight by sex ;
proc summary data=sample ;
  class sex ;
  var height weight ;
  output out=class_sum
         mean= ;
run ;
proc print data=class_sum ;
run ;
%stpend
```

If you were to have the program in Enterprise Guide and choose to make it into a Stored Process using the wizard, then Enterprise Guide would produce the following code:

```
*  Begin EG generated code (do not edit this line); ①
*
*  Stored Process registered by
*  Enterprise Guide Stored Process Manager V7.1 ②
*
*  ====================================================================
*  Stored Process name: test9 ③
*  ====================================================================
*;

*ProcessBody; ④
```

```
%STPBEGIN; ⑤

*  End EG generated code (do not edit this line); ⑥
⑦
* take a random sample ;
data sample ;
   set sashelp.class ;
if ranuni(1)<0.5 ;
run ;
* work out average height and weight by sex ;
proc summary data=sample ;
   class sex ;
   var height weight ;
   output out=class_sum
          mean= ;
run ;
proc print data=class_sum ;
run ;

*  Begin EG generated code (do not edit this line); ⑧
;*';*";*/;quit; ⑨
%STPEND; ⑨

*  End EG generated code (do not edit this line); ⑧
```

Notice that Enterprise Guide adds some code to the code that you enter. The following things are added:

- ①First you get a comment indicating that the EG generated code starts here and that you shouldn't edit this line. This is so that when the code is read in to Enterprise Guide, it knows what part it generated and what part you entered.

- ②You get a block of comments at the top which identifies that the code was generated by Enterprise Guide and the version used.

- ③Then you get some more comments that have the name of the Stored Process, along with a description if that was entered in the Stored Process.

- ④Next you get a special comment which is always this –
  *ProcessBody; – and it is used in SAS 9.2 and earlier Stored Processes
  to indicate that the parameters should be read in and set as macro
  variables at this point.

- ⑤The macro invocation is added next – %STPBEGIN – which is a
  special macro supplied by SAS which does many things related to
  setting the ODS output correctly.

- ⑥Now you get another specially formatted comment that you
  should not edit. This indicates to Enterprise Guide that the code it
  generated ends here.

- ⑦Your code appears after this, as it was entered in the Enterprise
  Guide editor.

- ⑧Now there is some more code generated by Enterprise Guide, so
  you have a comment line at the start and end of it which is specially
  formatted and should never be edited.

- ⑨Preventing SAS programs from prematurely ending: inside the
  generated block of code, there is a special comment line which is
  designed to assist with stopping errors that may stop SAS working
  properly. By itself, the line does nothing; however, it has been
  carefully crafted so that it will end unmatched quotes, finish
  unfinished statements, finish unfinished comments, and quit
  procedures that haven't been finished properly. Here is the line – a
  handy one to use at the end of non-Enterprise Guide SAS programs
  too.

  ```
  ;*';*";*/;quit;
  ```

- ⑩Inside the generated block of code, there is an invocation to
  %stpend, which is a SAS-supplied macro which basically finishes off
  the ODS output properly.

A WORD ABOUT THE PROCESSBODY COMMENT

If you are using SAS 9.2, then the parameters for Stored Processes are not initialized in the same way as later versions. This means that you need to include a comment in your Stored Process code like this:

```
*ProcessBody;
```

When using a Stored Process with a workspace server, none of the parameter values will be available until that comment is processed. If using a Stored Process server, then it is not required though. This means that useful automatic parameters such as _METAUSER as well as any parameters passed in by the user are not available. For SAS 9.3 onward, you don't need to use ProcessBody anymore.

Creating a Stored Process

There are several ways to make a Stored Process:

1. Management Console

2. Enterprise Guide

3. Data Integration Studio

4. Programmatically using SAS metadata calls

We will start with Management Console to make our first Stored Process. I think of it as the purest way of making a Stored Process since it gives you full control over creating the metadata and SAS code which make up the Stored Process. Using Enterprise Guide is a little more restrictive in what can be done. Data Integration Studio is used far less in my experience. The last method is not used much at all but turns out to be incredibly useful, and more recently, some prolific programmers are using it. I will just be covering the first two methods.

Creating a Stored Process with Management Console

We will carefully go through the steps to make a stored process using Management Console. Many users don't have access to this by default, but it is very useful. Permissions can be set by your SAS administrator so you can use this to create stored processes while being prevented from doing any harm by changing settings in the SAS system.

When you open Management Console for the first time, you will need to create a connection profile for the SAS metadata server you want to use. Your SAS administrator can provide the details you need to do this. When I opened Management Console for the first time, I got this message shown in Figure 7-1.

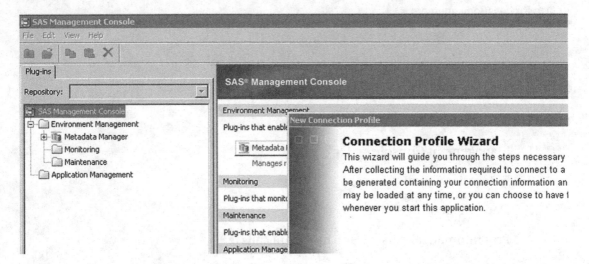

Figure 7-1. *Opening SAS Management Console*

Follow these steps to make your first Stored Process:

1. Start Management Console. In my case, I am using PC SAS, and I have a link to it on my windows desktop. You may also have a link, or you might need to navigate to where it is stored. In my default windows system, the path was "C:\Program Files\SASHome\ SASManagementConsole\9.4\sasmc.exe".

2. Next select the Folders tab as shown in Figure 7-2, which will show you the SAS folders in metadata.

Figure 7-2. *Folders tab in Management Console*

You may not be able to create Stored Processes in all the locations, but there will usually be at least one folder put aside for you. Navigate to a location like the one I have selected (if possible) in Figure 7-3. A restriction of this location (My Folder) is that no other users can execute this Stored Process, so don't use it for anything you want others to use.

Figure 7-3. *Metadata folders in Management Console*

3. Right-click a folder in which you want to create your Stored Process. Click New ➤ Stored Process as shown in Figure 7-4.

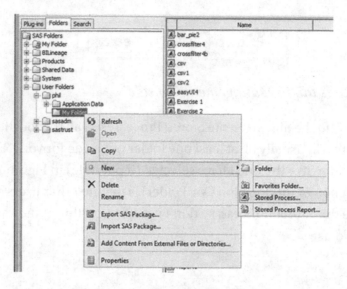

Figure 7-4. *Context menu for a metadata folder*

4. You are presented with the New Stored Process wizard (Figure 7-5)
    which guides you through the process of creating a Stored Process.
    Some parts of the wizard are optional and other parts have
    required fields. The first screen is the General screen for specifying
    the name, description, and keywords for the Stored Process to be
    defined. The only field you have to specify on this screen is the
    Stored Process name. Other fields are not essential, so click Next.

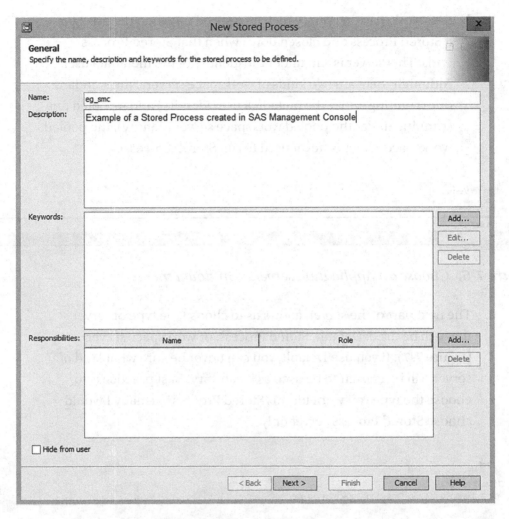

Figure 7-5. *First page of New Stored Process wizard*

5. Next, we must choose where the Stored Process is able to run by
    selecting an application server from the list of available ones as
    shown in Figure 7-6. Sometimes you might only have one choice
    available, so it will be an easy choice. Stored Processes are able to
    run on two kinds of SAS servers:

    a. SAS Stored Process servers, which are started up when required
        and stay up to run Stored Processes for any users that need them
        run. So, this server is run under the general server identity and is
        potentially used by multiple users.

    b. SAS Workspace servers, which are started up when needed by
      a Stored Process and closed down when that Stored Process
      ends. This server is run under the identity of the metadata user.
      Although there are two kinds of workspace servers, the standard
      one (running under the metadata user identity) and a pooled one
      (running under the pooled workspace server identity), the pooled
      workspace server is never used to run Stored Processes.

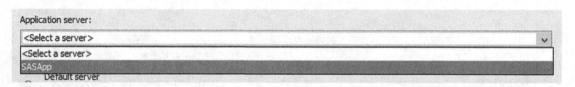

Figure 7-6. *Choose an Application server drop-down menu*

6. The next part of the screen allows us to choose the type of server
   that will be used: Default, Stored Process, or workspace server
   (Figure 7-7). If you use Default, you can never be sure what kind of
   server will be chosen to be used as it can vary. Best practice is to
   choose the type you want for this Stored Process – usually I would
   choose Stored Process server only.

Server type:

  ○ Default server
      Select this option to allow the client application to specify the server.

  ◉ Stored process server only
      Select this option if the stored process uses sessions or if it uses replay (for example, to produce graphics in streaming output).

  ○ Workspace server only
      Select this option if the stored process must be run under the client identity.

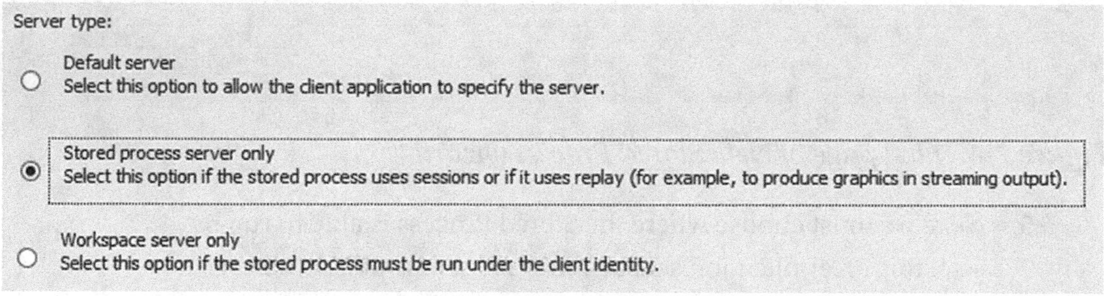

Figure 7-7. *Select type of server*

7. The next part of this screen specifies where the SAS source code
   is located. This could be on a disk somewhere or could be in the
   metadata itself. As shown in Figure 7-8, I usually select the first
   radio button which allows the Stored Process to execute in more
   places and also stores the source code in the metadata.

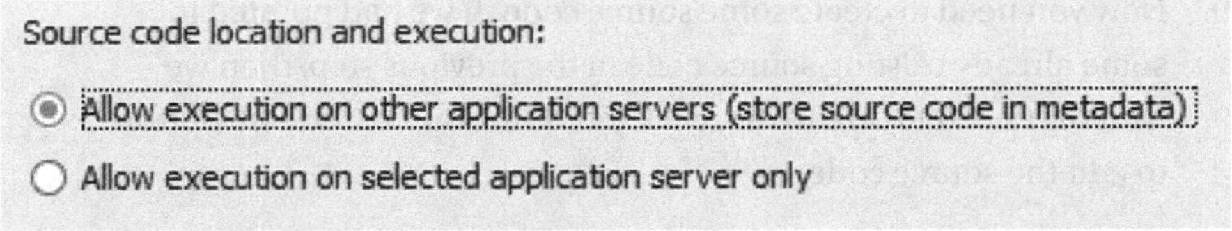

Source code location and execution:

⦿ Allow execution on other application servers (store source code in metadata)

◯ Allow execution on selected application server only

Figure 7-8. *Source code location*

You can also choose to store the code on disk as shown in Figure 7-9.

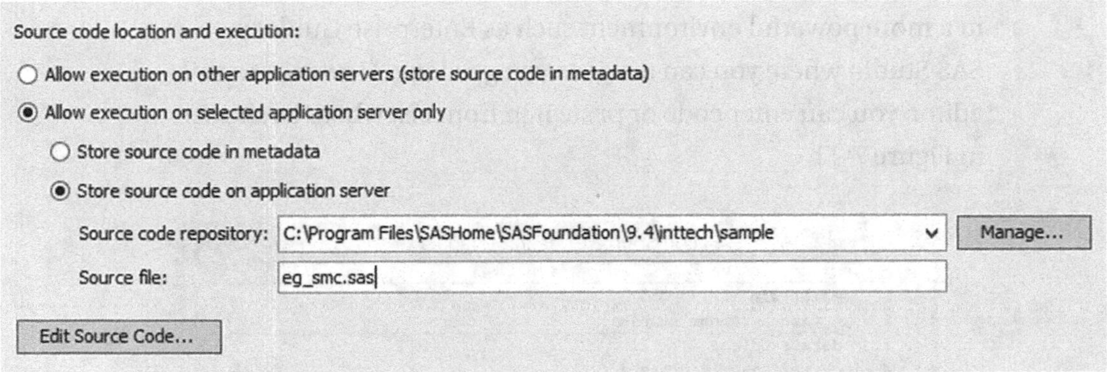

Source code location and execution:

◯ Allow execution on other application servers (store source code in metadata)

⦿ Allow execution on selected application server only

◯ Store source code in metadata

⦿ Store source code on application server

Source code repository: C:\Program Files\SASHome\SASFoundation\9.4\inttech\sample ▾   Manage...

Source file: eg_smc.sas

Edit Source Code...

Figure 7-9. *Storing code on disk requires a path and filename*

8. You can choose from the source code repositories you have defined.
   If you want another location, you can click the Manage button and
   define another Source Code Repository (see Figure 7-10).

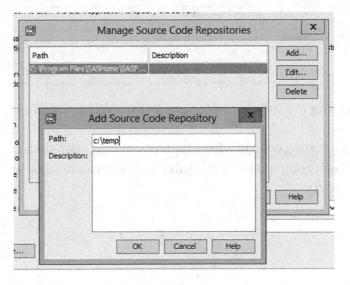

Figure 7-10. *Define a Source Code Repository*

9. Now you need to create some source code. If we had pointed to some already existing source code in the previous step, then we wouldn't need to do this. So, click the "Edit Source Code ..." button to edit the source code.

10. If you are storing your code in metadata or to a file which already exists, then you are put into an editor similar to the enhanced editor in Classic SAS. Syntax is highlighted for you, but functionality is fairly limited. It is best to develop the actual code in a more powerful environment such as Enterprise Guide or SAS Studio where you can test it as you go along. However, in this editor, you can enter code or paste it in from elsewhere as shown in Figure 7-11.

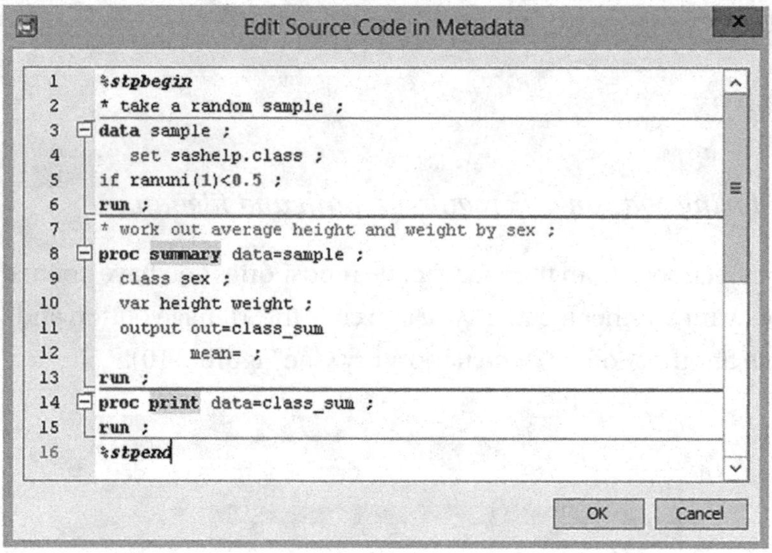

```
1    %stpbegin
2    * take a random sample ;
3    data sample ;
4        set sashelp.class ;
5    if ranuni(1)<0.5 ;
6    run ;
7    * work out average height and weight by sex ;
8    proc summary data=sample ;
9       class sex ;
10      var height weight ;
11      output out=class_sum
12            mean= ;
13   run ;
14   proc print data=class_sum ;
15   run ;
16   %stpend
```

Figure 7-11. *Editing the source code when it is stored in metadata*

11. If you are storing code to a file which doesn't yet exist, then you will be prompted to create it, to which you can answer Yes (Figure 7-12).

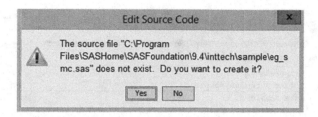

Figure 7-12. *Edit Source Code prompt*

This will then show you an editor window (Figure 7-13).

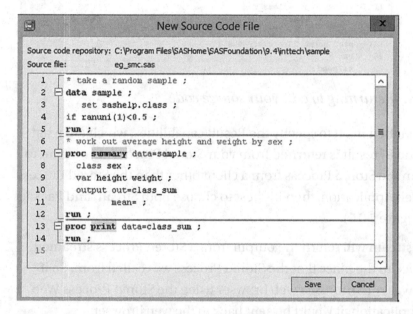

Figure 7-13. *Editing some new source code in a file rather than metadata*

You can then save the code and return to edit it if you like (Figure 7-14).

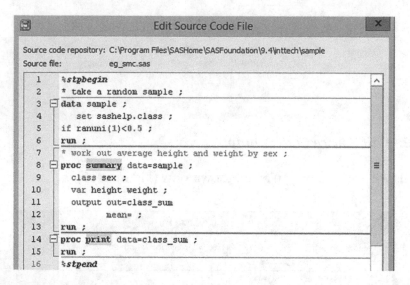

Figure 7-14. Returning to edit your source code

12. You then need to specify the Result capabilities, which are what kind of result is returned from your Stored Process. If you plan to run the Stored Process from a client other than the Stored Process Web Application, then it's best to choose both Stream and Package (Figure 7-15).

A stream will return the output from a Stored Process streamed back to the place that the Stored Process was called from. So if it was run through a web browser using the Stored Process Web Application, it would be sent back to the web browser.

A package is basically a SAS package file, which is pretty much the same as a zip file and can be opened with a program such as WinZip. This is handled by other clients you would run from such as Enterprise Guide and the Microsoft Office Add-In.

Figure 7-15. Result capabilities

13.   At this point, we have entered all the information for the Stored
       Process that is needed, which is why we now have the option of
       pressing the <u>finish</u> button to create the Stored Process. Otherwise,
       we can press next and go on with choosing parameters and other
       things. We will press finish.

14.   You can see your Stored Process in the list of Stored Processes as
       shown in Figure 7-16.

	Name	Description	Type	Last Modified ▽
🖹 eg_smc	Example of a Stored Process created in SAS Management Console	Stored process	29-Apr-2017 16:52:04

Figure 7-16. *Stored Process we created in list*

15.   If you right-click the Stored Process, a number of things you can
       do will be displayed (see Figure 7-17).

   a. Copy the Stored Process and paste it into another metadata folder.

   b. Delete it.

   c. Rename it.

   d. Export it as a SAS Package, which is basically a zip file. You will get the SAS
       code and metadata in the package which means it could then be moved
       somewhere else and imported into another SAS metadata server. For
       example, when developing applications in a controlled environment, this
       enables moving Stored Processes from Development to Test to Production.
       Or should you want to copy from one metadata server to another to make
       changes and test before returning to the original server, then exporting
       enables this to be done easily.

   e. Deploy as a web service, which will let you convert your Stored Process
       into a web service. However, from SAS 9.3 onward, you can run any Stored
       Process as a web service without deploying it as a web service.[1]

---

[1]For more information, look here: http://support.sas.com/documentation/cdl/en/
wbsvcdg/64883/HTML/default/n1arlomsivd9q0n1qalkfhbppln6.htm

f. Make compatible with SAS 9.2, which at the time of writing is still very widely used. Later versions of SAS have some extra features not available on SAS 9.2 Stored Processes so this will make the necessary changes to make them compatible. You could then export a SAS 9.4 Stored Process and import it into SAS 9.2.

g. Properties displays all the information about the Stored Process and allows you to change any of it as long as you have the right permissions.

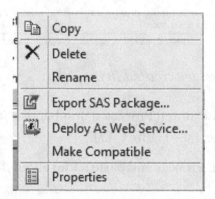

Figure 7-17. *Context menu for a stored process*

That is the end of the process for creating a Stored Process in Management Console. Now let's have a quick look at prompting with a Stored Process administered from Management Console, and then we will see how Enterprise Guide is very similar but has some important differences.

Prompting from Management Console

Should you want to edit the Stored Process, go into Properties which displays the screen shown in Figure 7-18. We can click the various tabs and see the metadata defined for this Stored Process. We can also make any changes to it, so long as we have permission to do so.

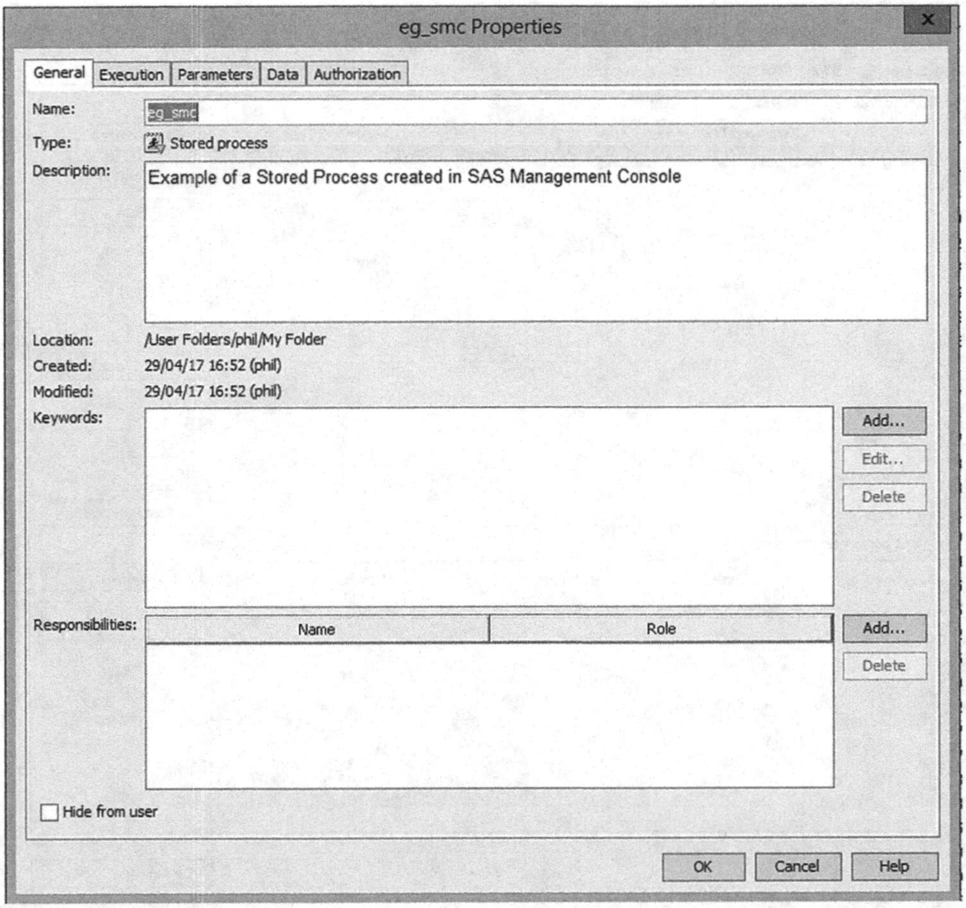

Figure 7-18. General tab of Properties window for a stored process

We can add parameters which will prompt the user for values when the Stored Process is run. So, clicking the Parameters tab takes us to the screen in Figure 7-19. We might want to generalize our code a little by adding a prompt to allow us to summarize our data by different variables. We can do this by clicking New Prompt.

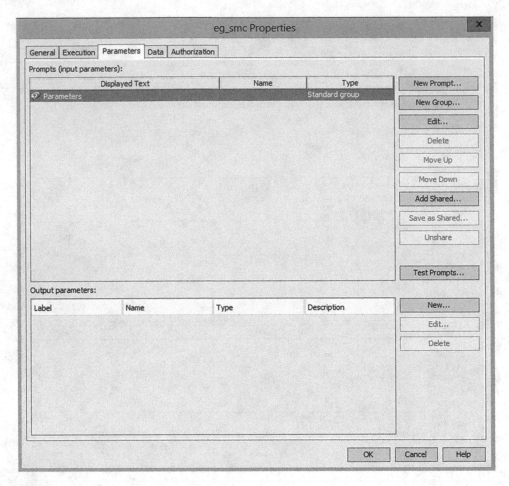

Figure 7-19. *Parameters tab of Properties window for a stored process*

The New Prompt screen allows us to enter a name for the prompt/parameter and text to display when the user is prompted (Figure 7-20).

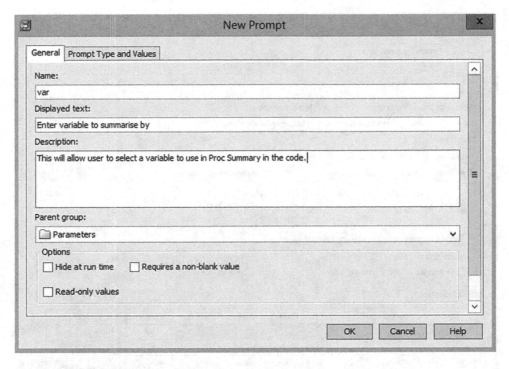

Figure 7-20. *New Prompt window*

Now we can click the Prompt Type and Values tab, which will let us specify what kind of prompt this is – for example, are we asking the user for a number, for some text, for one value or many, to select from a list of values, and so on? In our example, we want to let the user pick one or more variable names from several possibilities, so we will provide a list of values in a static list. My sample list of values is shown in Figure 7-21. I have chosen the following items:

- Prompt type – Text.

- Method for populating prompt – User selects values from a static list.

- Number of values – Multiple ordered values.

- List of values – Sex (which has default checked), name, and age.

- No other tick boxes are checked.

Note   The use of parameters will be explained in more detail later.

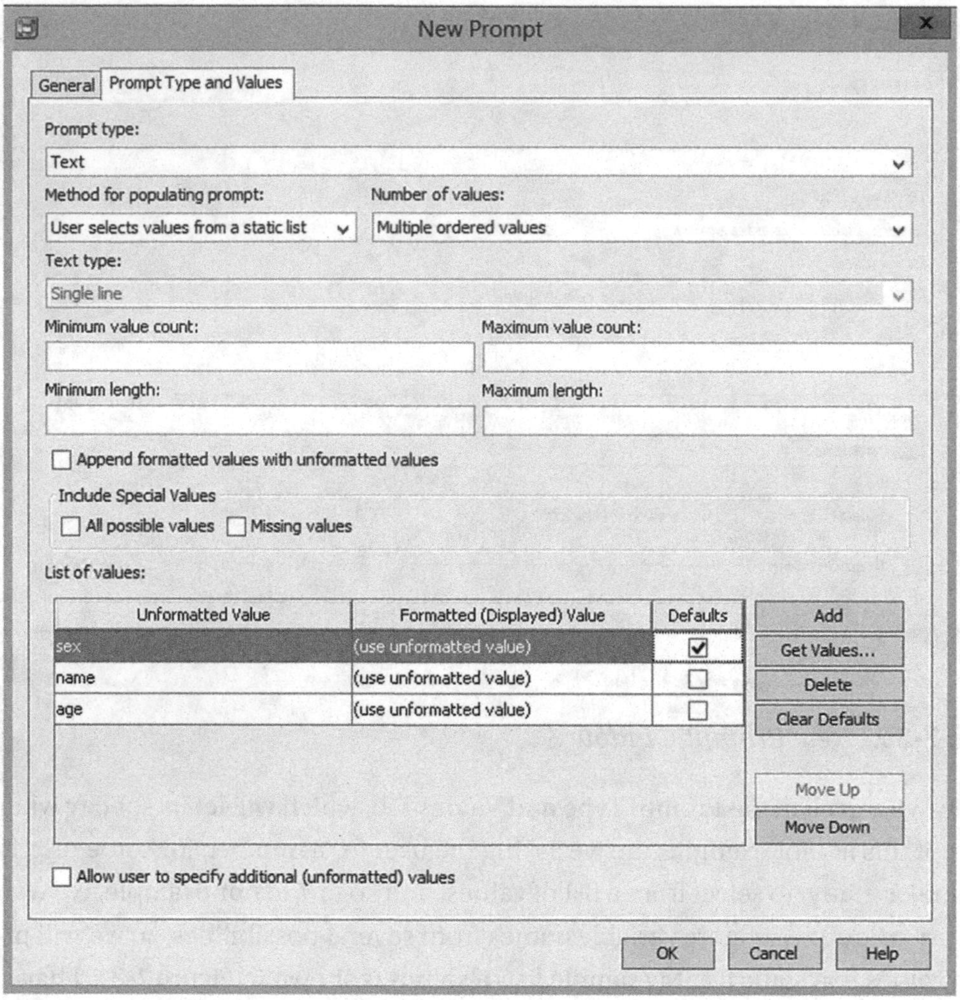

Figure 7-21. *Prompt Type and Values window*

Clicking OK, we will see that our parameter has now been added (Figure 7-22).

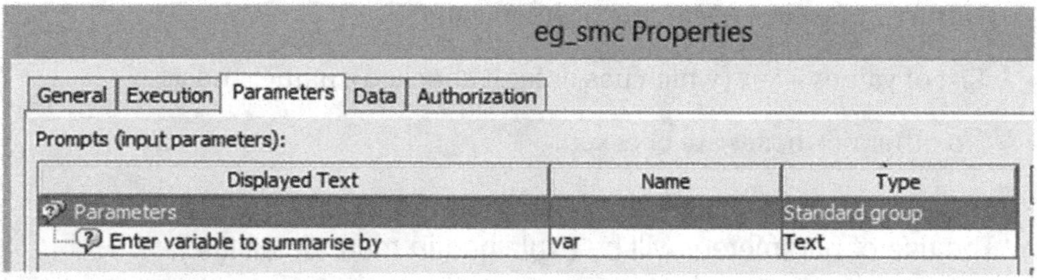

Figure 7-22. *Screen showing parameter we added*

Now we need to modify our SAS code slightly to make use of the parameter. So, we click the Execution tab and select Edit Source Code. In Figure 7-23, I change the variable used in the class statement to use &var, which is a macro variable that is created with the value of the parameter entered by the user.

```
                    Edit Source Code in Metadata                    [×]
 1     %stpbegin
 2     * take a random sample ;
 3   ⊟ data sample ;
 4        set sashelp.class ;
 5     if ranuni(1)<0.5 ;
 6   └ run ;
 7     * work out average height and weight by sex ;
 8   ⊟ proc summary data=sample ;
 9        class &var ;
10        var height weight ;
11        output out=class_sum
12             mean= ;
13   └ run ;
14   ⊟ proc print data=class_sum ;
15   └ run ;
16     %stpend

                                        [  OK  ]  [ Cancel ]
```

Figure 7-23. *Source code in Metadata*

Clicking OK will save the change. Then clicking OK exits the Properties dialog, which saves our changes to the Stored Process metadata.

Now we can test this out by going to Enterprise Guide and running the Stored Process. Find it in the list of Stored Processes in SAS Folders (Figure 7-24). Right-click it and select Open which will add it to your Enterprise Guide project.

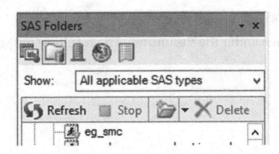

Figure 7-24. *Folder icon that changes view to show metadata folders*

Now you can right-click the Stored Process in the process flow of Enterprise Guide and run it by selecting Run.

The Stored Process runs and prompts you for parameters (Figure 7-25).

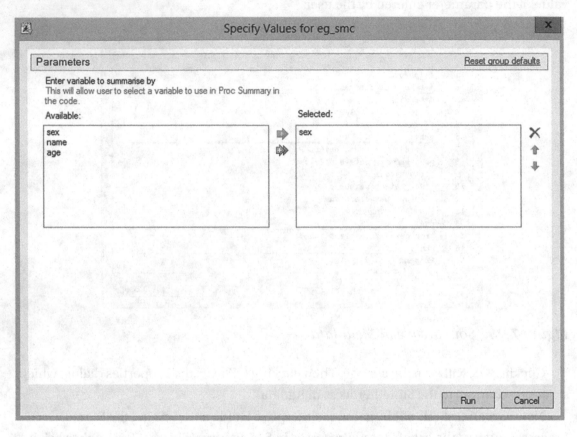

Figure 7-25. *Prompt that appears for parameters when running in Enterprise Guide*

Make any selections you like and click Run.

The results are shown under the Results tab. The results of my Stored Process are shown in Figure 7-26.

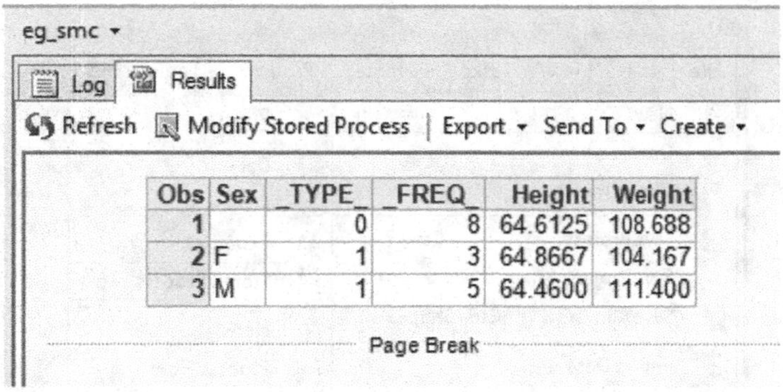
eg_smc
Log
Results
Refresh
Modify Stored Process
Export
Send To
Create
Obs Sex _TYPE_ _FREQ_ Height Weight
1 0 8 64.6125 108.688
2 F 1 3 64.8667 104.167
3 M 1 5 64.4600 111.400
Page Break

Figure 7-26. *Results*

Using Enterprise Guide to Make a Stored Process

SAS Management Console is often just available to administrators, whereas SAS Enterprise Guide tends to be available to most SAS programmers in an enterprise. Enterprise Guide has a great wizard that guides the user through the creation of a stored process, whereas Management Console is a little harder to use:

1. Open up Enterprise Guide, and from the File menu, select New and then Stored Process as shown in Figure 7-27.

Figure 7-27. *Creating a new stored process in Enterprise Guide*

2. **Labelling and saving the Stored Process** – You are shown the first page of a wizard (Figure 7-28) which will gather the information needed to create a Stored Process. Some of the fields are required, but many are optional. For our first Stored Process, we will just fill a minimal number of fields in. On this first page, you must enter a name for the Stored Process. The location is the location of the Stored Process in the metadata. It might default to a suitable place or else you can click browse to find a place to put your Stored Process. The other fields on this page are optional, but I would recommend always filling in the description field so that others finding your work in future will have more chance of understanding what you have done.

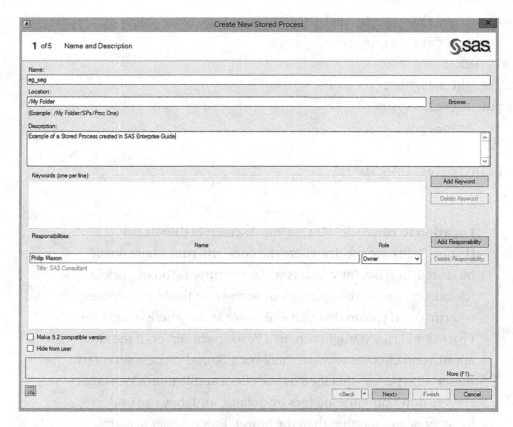

Figure 7-28. *New Stored Process wizard*

3. **SAS code** – The second page of the wizard is for entering the SAS
code. You will have often created the code elsewhere and will
just be pasting in the code at this point. You could type it in if you
wanted to, although you can't run it to test if it works at this point.
The button that is labelled "Include code for" is an important one,
but we will leave that for now. The only thing you must do on this
screen is to enter some code (Listing 7-1).

Listing 7-1. Sample code to enter for stored process

```
* take a random sample ;
data sample ;
   set sashelp.class ;
if ranuni(1)<0.5 ;
run ;
```

```
* work out average height and weight by sex ;
proc summary data=sample ;
  class sex ;
  var height weight ;
  output out=class_sum
         mean= ;
run ;
proc print data=class_sum ;
run ;
```

4. **Location to run code** – On the third screen of the wizard
    (Figure 7-29), we specify where the code will run, where it will
    be stored, and how any results will be returned. You can select
    "default server" as the application server that the Stored Process
    will run on. If you do this, you will never know where your Stored
    Process will run. It might run on a Workspace server (if the client
    application chooses to run it there) or a Stored Process server (if
    no server type was specified by the client application). Workspace
    servers don't produce log files by default, and they run under
    the user account rather than the Stored Process user account.
    So many users consider it risky to let this default and choose the
    server it will run on specifically from the drop-down list.

    I usually specify that I want the code stored in the metadata
    which means that the Stored Process metadata and code are
    kept together. Alternatively, you could put the code in a source
    code repository in a disk somewhere. If you store the code in the
    metadata, then it does mean that when you export or move a
    Stored Process, from one place to another, then the code is still
    with it. However, if you store the code in a source code repository,
    then if you move a stored process, you need to make sure that
    it can access the code or also move the code and define where
    its new location is. If you are following this example through,
    you may not be able to save into the same location shown in my
    screen shot, but that is OK. Just save to metadata if you have any
    problems.

The result capabilities are usually best specified as stream and package. Stream will stream results back to the place the Stored Process was called from. A package is basically a SAS package file, which is pretty much the same as a zip file and can be opened with a program such as WinZip. This is handled by other clients you would run from such as Enterprise Guide and the Microsoft Office Add-In.

It doesn't really matter where you store the code, as it won't affect whether this example would run or not. That goes for most example Stored Processes in this book, so if you don't have access to some location that I store code, then just store it somewhere else or in metadata which you should always be able to do.

At this point in the wizard, you can see that the Finish button has ceased being grayed out. That means that we can finish the wizard now and create the Stored Process. Or else we can continue and potentially enter other optional information.

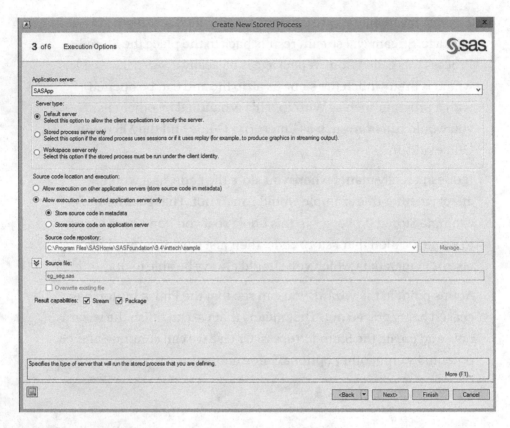

Figure 7-29. *Execution options from the wizard for creating a new stored process*

5. **Process prompts** – The fourth page of the wizard (Figure 7-30)
   allows us to enter prompts (or input parameters) which will
   prompt the user for information when a Stored Process is run.
   That information is then used as the SAS code of the Stored
   Process is executed. Specifying prompts will be covered in the next
   section.

Figure 7-30. *Prompts page in wizard where we can define parameters*

6. **Data sources and targets** – The fifth page (Figure 7-31) is for specifying data sources and targets which are used with web services and the SAS Add-in for Microsoft Office. Note: From SAS 9.3 onward, your Stored Process is available as a web service automatically without any further action required by the user. Access to the web application is described here.

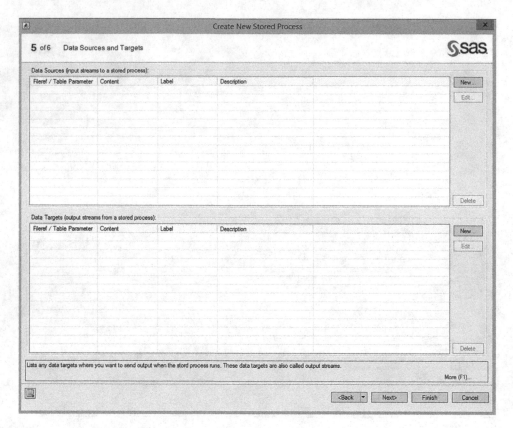

Figure 7-31. *Data sources and targets*

7. The last page of the wizard (Figure 7-32) shows a summary of information that has been entered.

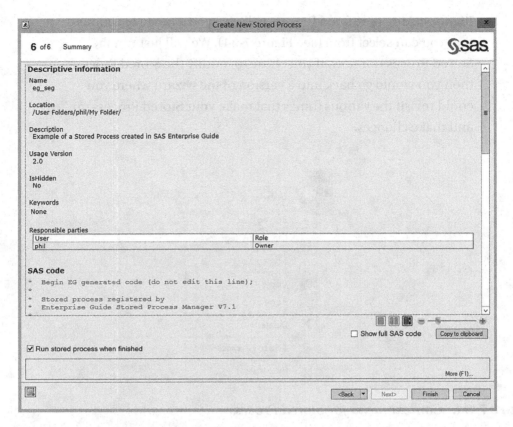

Figure 7-32. *Summary page of wizard*

8. Now that you have finished the wizard, you can see your Stored Process in the Enterprise Guide project process flow as shown in Figure 7-33. If SAS has any problems with the configuration of your stored process, you will get a prompt to tell you. You can always use the Back button to go back and change things before you press Finish to finalize your stored process.

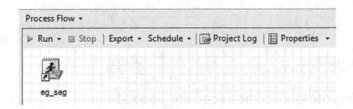

Figure 7-33. *Icon for the Stored Process just created*

9. Right-clicking the Stored Process will give you a range of actions that you can select from (see Figure 7-34). We will just run the Stored Process for now. If you chose to modify the Stored Process, then you would go back into a version of the wizard where you could revisit the various things that make your Stored Process up and make changes.

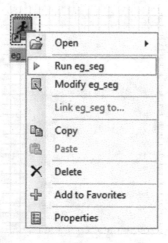

Figure 7-34. *Context menu for Stored Process*

10. After running the Stored Process, you will be shown a Results tab, which has a range of actions along the toolbar. Some of these will only work properly if certain parts of your SAS infrastructure are configured correctly. The results of my Stored Process are shown in Figure 7-35.

Obs	Sex	_TYPE_	_FREQ_	Height	Weight
1		0	8	64.6125	108.688
2	F	1	3	64.8667	104.167
3	M	1	5	64.4600	111.400

Figure 7-35. *Results*

11. Choosing the Log tab shows you the log for the Stored Process (Figure 7-36).

```
eg_seg ▾                                                                                                    ✕
 Log   Results
 Modify Stored Process | Export ▾  Send To ▾ | ⬆ ⬇ | Log Summary | Project Log | Properties
 ⊟ 1                                                      The SAS System                           17:4
 
     NOTE: Copyright (c) 2002-2012 by SAS Institute Inc., Cary, NC, USA.
     NOTE: SAS (r) Proprietary Software 9.4 (TS1M3)
           Licensed to WOOD STREET CONSULTANTS LTD, Site 70195163.
     NOTE: This session is executing on the X64_SRV12  platform.
 
 
     NOTE: Updated analytical products:
 
           SAS/STAT 14.1
           SAS/ETS 14.1
           SAS/OR 14.1
           SAS/IML 14.1
 
     NOTE: Additional host information:
 
      X64_SRV12 WIN 6.2.9200  Server
 
     NOTE: SAS Initialization used (Total process time):
           real time                0.00 seconds
           cpu time                 0.00 seconds
 
     NOTE: The autoexec file, C:\SAS\Config\Lev1\SASApp\WorkspaceServer\autoexec.sas, was executed at server in
 
     >>> SAS Macro Variables:
 
     _APSLIST=_RESULT,_CLIENTVERSION,_CLIENTMACHINE,_ODSDEST,_ODSSTYLESHEET,_ODSOPTIONS,_TIMEZONE,_GOPT_DEVICE,
 ◄  ▐                            III                                                               ►
```

Figure 7-36. *Log from the Stored Process run*

So that is how you create a Stored Process using either Management Console or
Enterprise Guide. You can create your Stored Process in one of those and then modify it
in the other one.

Prompting in Enterprise Guide

Prompting allows the user to be prompted for information which will provide values
to parameters used in SAS code. This enables some code to be written in a more
generalized way to be far more flexible. The user can define that the values provided for
each prompt are macro variables available for use in the project SAS code. For instance,
we might be prompted to choose the parts of a country that we want a report to be
created for.

Enterprise Guide has its own prompting system available, which is not related to
Stored Processes. You can define prompts for a process flow which will prompt you for
information before running that process flow. You can look at and define Enterprise
Guide prompts by going to the Prompt Manager (Figure 7-37).

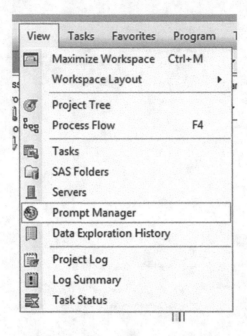

Figure 7-37. *Selecting the prompt manager for Enterprise Guide*

The prompt manager for Enterprise Guide is located in the lower half of the left navigation pane (i.e., where you find the SAS folders and servers). We won't be covering this kind of prompting, but the manager is shown in Figure 7-38.

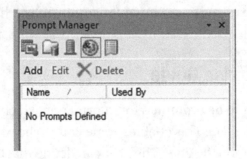

Figure 7-38. *Prompt Manager*

Stored Process prompts can be used with Stored Processes to prompt the user for some input before running the SAS code within the Stored Process. The prompts might be displayed in different ways depending on the client used, but will essentially be the same. There are many kinds of prompts that can be used when making a Stored Process. We will look at a brief example of each kind in the following. You can see a complete list in the SAS documentation online.[2]

Modifying a Stored Process

We can modify the stored process by right-clicking the Stored Process which is in your process flow. When the menu appears, select Modify <name of stored process> (Figure 7-39).

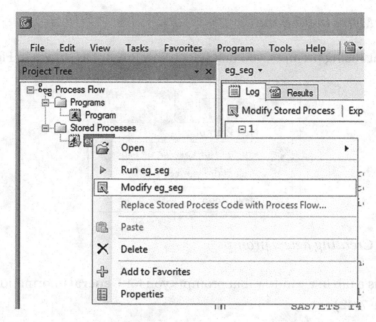

Figure 7-39. *Modify stored process via context menu*

Now you can choose Prompts from the left menu (see Figure 7-40).

---

[2]"Entering Prompt Values" from the SAS Stored Process Documentation - `https://documentation.sas.com/?docsetId=stpug&docsetTarget=n0174t2cve9kekn1tq627pnui5js.htm&docsetVersion=9.4&locale=en` and the quick reference guide on prompts which is here `https://documentation.sas.com/?docsetId=stpug&docsetTarget=n1x5bwm15z6zcmn1jjzrsch14z90.htm&docsetVersion=9.4&locale=en`

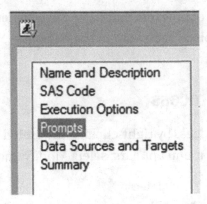

Figure 7-40. *Menu in left pane*

Then to start using prompts, you first select New Prompt as shown in Figure 7-41.

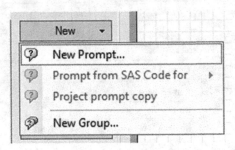

Figure 7-41. *Creating a new prompt*

This reveals a tab in a window that prompts you for **General** information about the prompt (Figure 7-42).

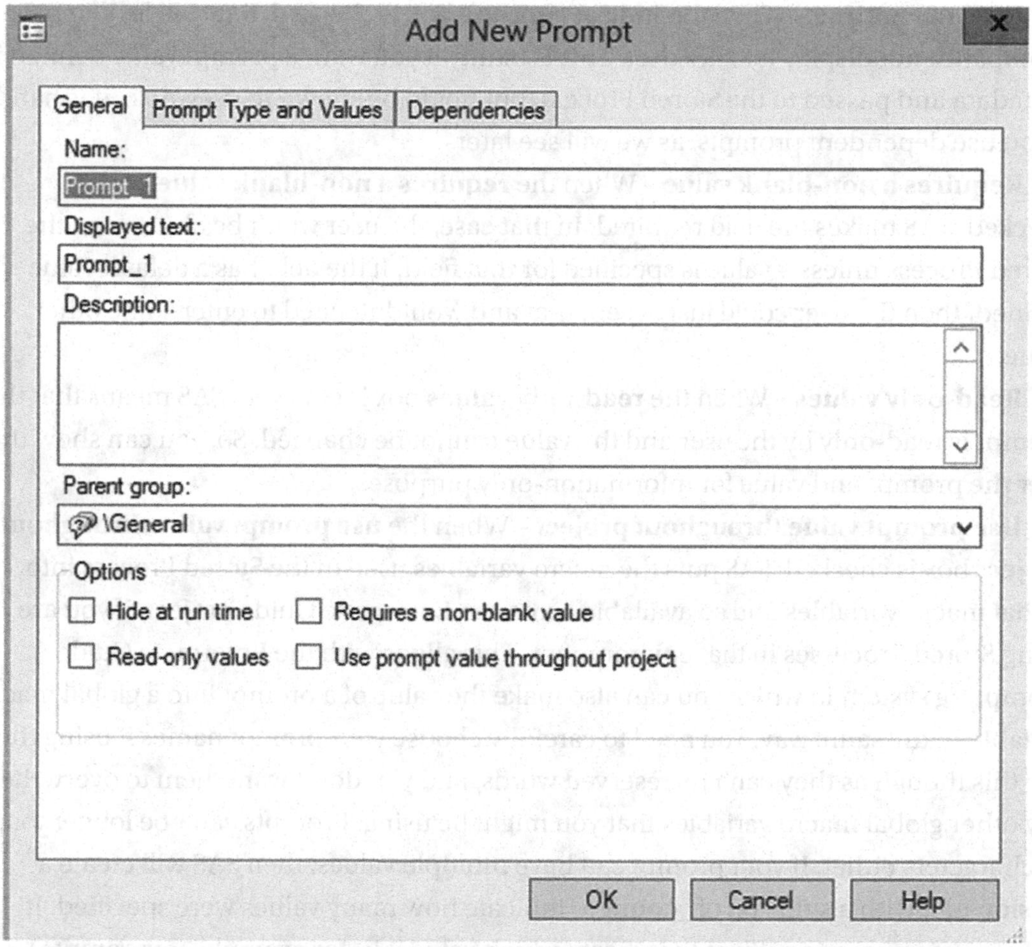

Figure 7-42. General tab of window used to add new prompt

Name – SAS requires a name that is valid under the SAS naming conventions. In this
example, we will use the name Prompt_1. You can give it any name you like, and if it is
not valid (perhaps having spaces in it), then it will be converted to a valid SAS name. The
name you specify and the values the user assigns become a global macro variable. This
allows the prompt and user input to be available to all the SAS code in the Stored Process.

Displayed text – Displayed text is shown next to the prompt, so should describe what
you want the user to enter.

Description – Description will be displayed under the prompt to explain more about
it. You can arrange prompts into nested groups of prompts if you want to. Remember
that the prompt names are required but remaining fields are optional and also that the
fields can be modified later if required by editing the stored process.

Hide at runtime – When the **hide at runtime** box is checked, SAS will let you have a prompt but not display it to the user. This is handy if you want a prompt value defined in metadata and passed to the Stored Process, but not to be shown to user. Also, it is handy if you use dependent prompts, as we will see later.

Requires a non-blank value – When the **requires a non-blank value** box is checked, SAS makes the field required. In that case, the user won't be able to run the Stored Process unless a value is specified for that field. If the field has a default value defined, then the user could just accept that and wouldn't need to enter some other value.

Read-only values – When the **read-only values** box is checked, SAS means that the prompt is read-only by the user and the value cannot be changed. So, you can show the user the prompt and value for information-only purposes.

Use prompt value throughout project – When the **use prompt value throughout project** box is checked, SAS puts the macro variables used in the Stored Process into global macro variables and so available across an Enterprise Guide project, if you are using Stored Processes in that environment. This aligns with the Enterprise Guide prompting system in which you can also make the value of a prompt into a global macro variable in the same way. You need to carefully choose your prompt names if using them like this though as they can't be reserved words, and you don't want them to overwrite any other global macro variables that you might be using. Prompts can't be longer than 32 characters either. If your prompt can have multiple values, then SAS will create a version of it with a suffix on of **_count** to indicate how many values were specified. It will also use numeric suffixes to indicate which value it is, for example, myprompt_1, myprompt_2, and so on. myprompt_0 would be the same as myprompt_count and hold the number of values specified. You need to take this extra variable length requirement into account when naming your parameter.

Once you have specified everything you want to on the first tab, you can move onto the second tab to specify the **Prompt Types and Values** (Figure 7-43).

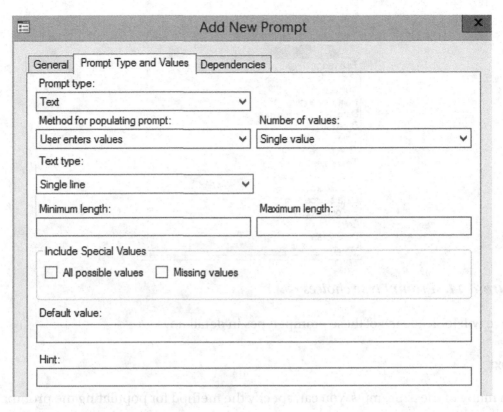

Figure 7-43. *Prompt Type and Values dialog*

Choosing a Prompt Type

Now you have a choice of Prompt type as shown in Figure 7-44.

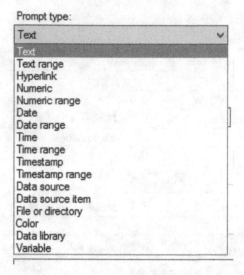

Figure 7-44. *Prompt type choices*

We will look at each of these prompt types in detail now.

1. Text

With many of these prompts, you can specify the method for populating the prompt. For text and many others, this usually can be one of the following options shown in Figure 7-45.

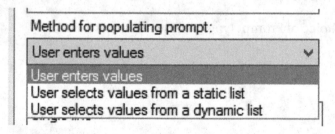

Figure 7-45. *Options for populating values of a prompt*

User enters values – means the user has to type in a value.

User selects values from a static list – where the developer enters a list of values that the user can select from (see Figure 7-46). We can also set one of the values as a default if we want to. Pressing the Add button lets you add a line to the list of values.

☐ Append formatted values with unformatted values

List of values:

Unformatted Value	Formatted (Displayed) Value	Default	
a	Apple	○	Add
b	Banana	○	Get Values...
c	Carrot|	○	Delete
			Clear Default
			Move up
			Move down

☐ Allow user to specify additional (unformatted) values

Figure 7-46. *Entering your own values for a prompt*

You can also click Get Values which will bring up another dialog (Figure 7-47) in which we can specify a data source (either from metadata or a physical location) and column to use to get a list of values to use. For instance, I can navigate using the Browse button and choose SASHELP.CLASS and then pick the column Age. Then if I click Get values, it gets me a list of all the unique values from that table for that column. Then I can copy some or all of them into the selected values list.

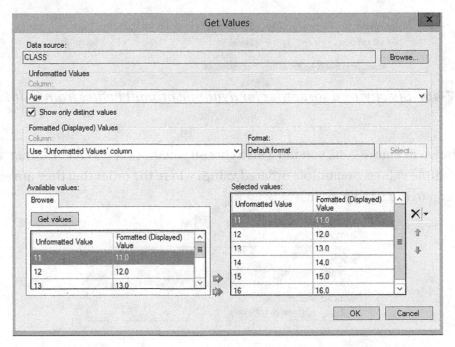

Figure 7-47. *Getting values from a data source and choosing which ones to use*

Next, select values from a dynamic list shown in Figure 7-48. You can navigate to a data source defined in the metadata, choose a column, and get the values to use for selecting from. You can choose either to have all the values or just distinct values. You may choose either the unformatted values to use, the formatted values for variables to use, or to append the formatted values with the unformatted values. You may also specify a sort sequence for displaying the values. And you can choose to allow the user to specify additional (unformatted) values. This is a good option if other values not available from the data are possible, since the user can then enter any values.

Data source:

| ODSSTYLE | Browse... |

Unformatted Values

Column:

| style | ⌄ |

☑ Show only distinct values

Formatted (Displayed) Values

Column: Format:

| Use 'Unformatted Values' colu ⌄ | Default format | Select... |

☐ Append formatted values with unformatted values

Include Special Values

☐ All possible values

Sort order: Default value:

| Default sort order ⌄ | (None) ⌄ | Select... |

☐ Allow user to specify additional (unformatted) values

Figure 7-48. *Specifying a sort order for dynamic prompt values from a data source*

As shown in Figure 7-49, you must also choose whether values can be either a single value, multiple values, or multiple ordered values where the order that they are entered is passed on to the SAS program.

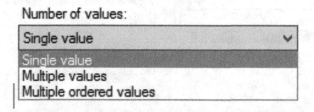

Figure 7-49. *Specifying number of values that can be specified in a prompt*

You also define the formatted value that is shown to the user, as well as the unformatted value which is passed on to the SAS code when it is selected.

When the prompt is displayed, the form it is displayed in will vary depending on the choices you have made.

2. Text Range

Choosing the text range prompt option will let you choose a text range. You can specify some parameters (see Figure 7-50) to restrict the values that can be entered for the range: min/max length of the string, min/max value, and a default value for the range.

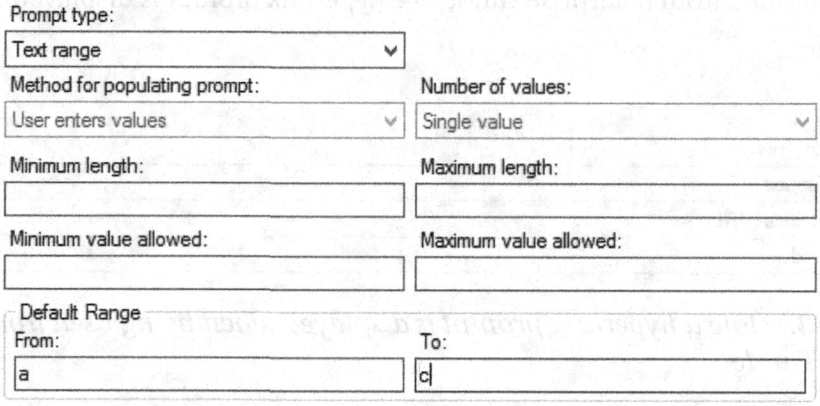

Figure 7-50. *Specifying values for text range prompt*

In Enterprise Guide, the text range prompt is displayed as shown in Figure 7-51.

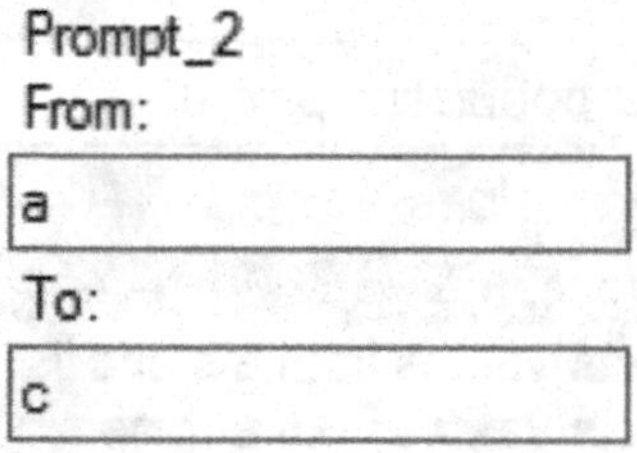

Figure 7-51. *Values for a text range*

3. Hyperlink

This prompt option allows you to enter the text and link for a URL. You can specify defaults if you like as shown in Figure 7-52.

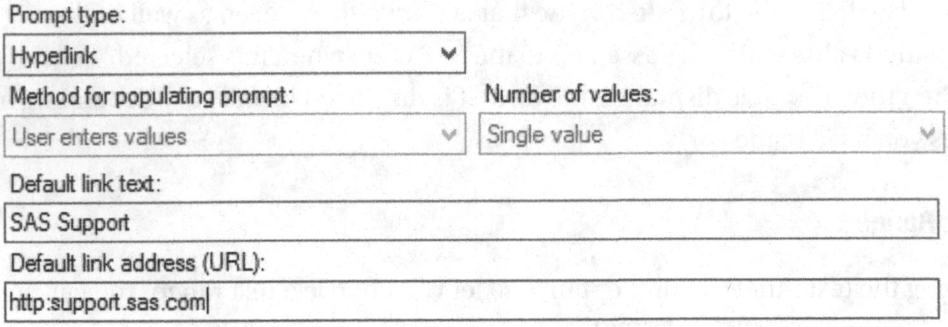

Prompt type:

Hyperlink

Method for populating prompt:

User enters values

Number of values:

Single value

Default link text:

SAS Support

Default link address (URL):

http:support.sas.com

Figure 7-52. *Specifying a hyperlink or URL prompt*

When running from Enterprise Guide, the hyperlink prompt is displayed as shown in Figure 7-53.

Prompt_3
Link text:

SAS Support

Link address (URL):

adasdasd

Figure 7-53. *How a hyperlink prompt is displayed when being used from Enterprise Guide*

4. Numeric

This is similar to the text prompt type. You can populate the prompt with values in a number of ways, as shown in Figure 7-54.

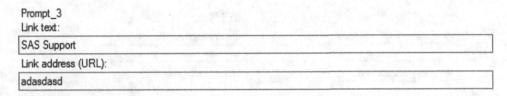

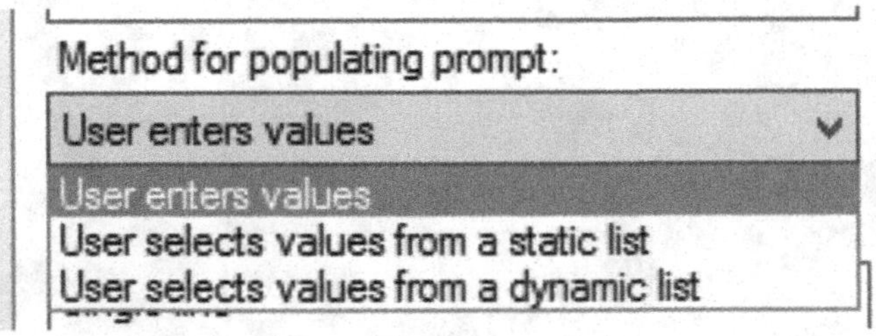

Figure 7-54. *Methods for populating a numeric prompt*

User enters values – means the user has to type in a value User selects values from a static list – where the developer enters a list of values that the user can select from (see Figure 7-55). We can also set one of the values as a default if we want to. Pressing the Add button lets you add a line to the list of values.

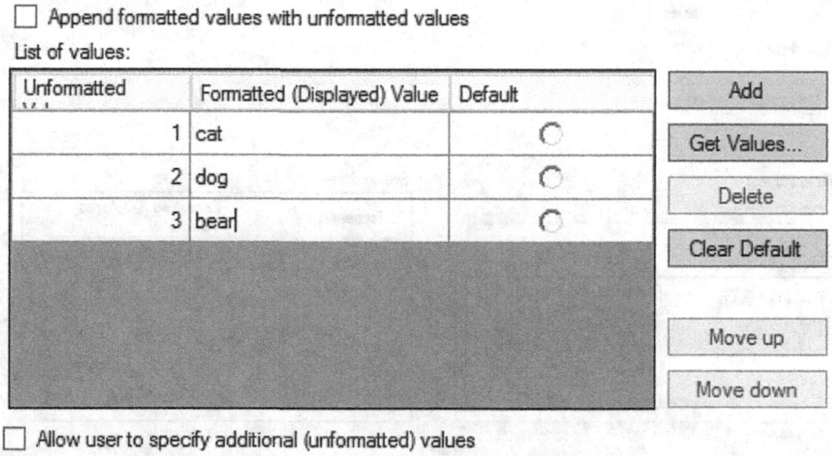

Figure 7-55. *Specifying numeric values and formatted values to display*

User selects values from a dynamic list – where the developer specifies a data source that will provide the values.

For a static list, you can also click **Get** Values which will bring up another dialog (Figure 7-56) in which we can specify a data source (either from metadata or a physical location) and column to use to get a list of values to use. For instance, I can navigate using the Browse button and choose SASHELP.CLASS and then pick the column Age. Then if I click Get values, it gets me a list of all the unique values from that table for that column. Then I can copy some or all of them into the selected values list.

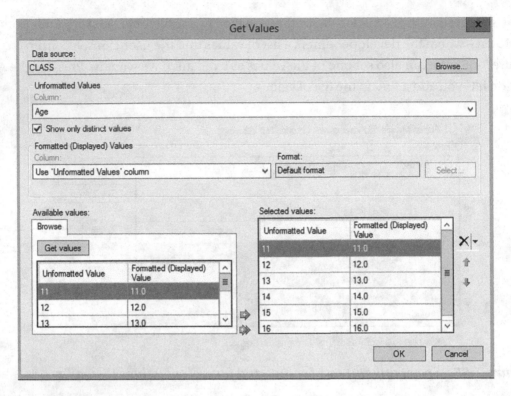

Figure 7-56. Specifying a data source to get values from and which ones to use

For a dynamic list as shown in Figure 7-57, we can navigate to a data source defined in the metadata, choose a column, and get the values to use for selecting from. You can choose either to have all the values or just distinct values. You may choose either the unformatted values to use, the formatted values for variables to use, or to append the formatted values with the unformatted values. You may also specify a sort sequence for displaying the values. And you can choose to allow the user to specify additional (unformatted) values. This is a good option if other values not available from the data are possible, since the user can then enter any values.

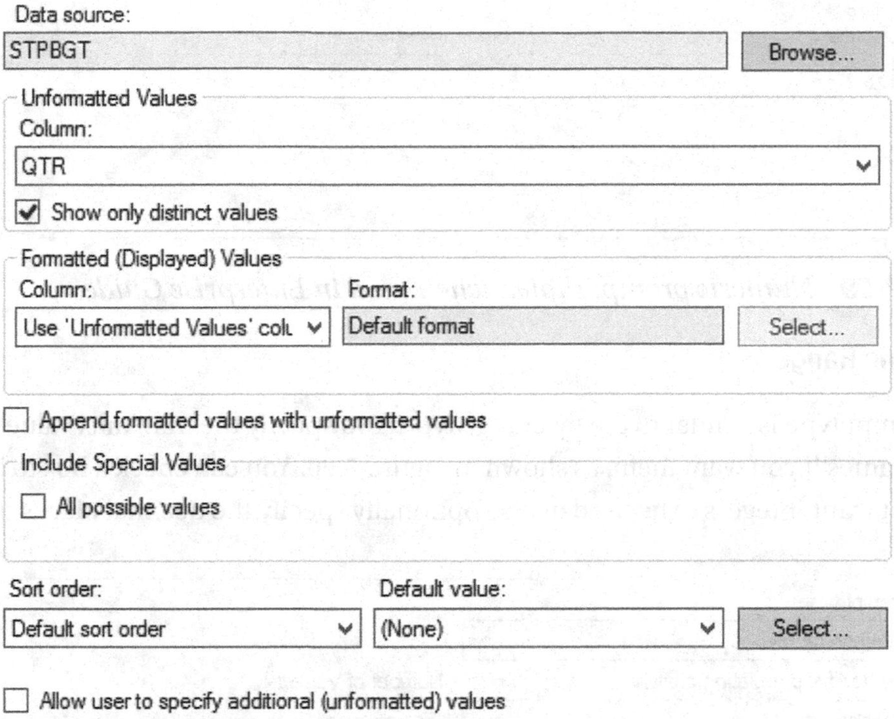

Data source:

STPBGT

Browse...

Unformatted Values

Column:

QTR

☑ Show only distinct values

Formatted (Displayed) Values

Column: Format:

Use 'Unformatted Values' colt ∨   Default format   Select...

☐ Append formatted values with unformatted values

Include Special Values

☐ All possible values

Sort order: Default value:

Default sort order   ∨   (None)   ∨   Select...

☐ Allow user to specify additional (unformatted) values

Figure 7-57. *Specifying a dynamic data source for a numeric prompt*

You must also choose whether values can be either a single value, multiple values, or multiple ordered values where the order that they are entered is passed on to the SAS program (see Figure 7-58).

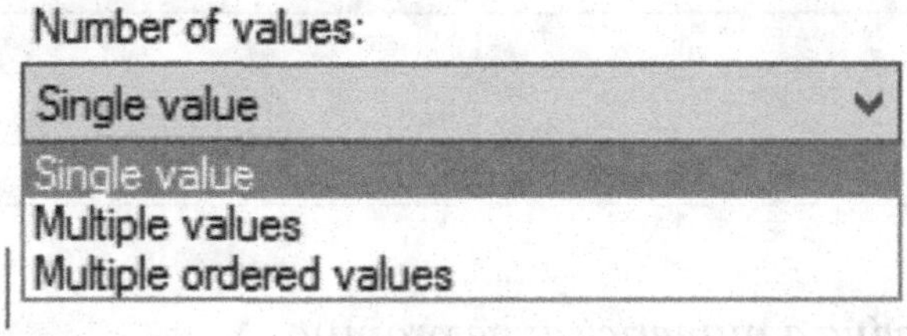

Number of values:

Single value   ∨

Single value
Multiple values
Multiple ordered values

Figure 7-58. *Specifying how many values can be entered for a numeric prompt*

You also define the formatted value that is shown to the user, as well as the unformatted value which is passed on to the SAS code when it is selected.

In Enterprise Guide, this prompt is displayed as shown in Figure 7-59.

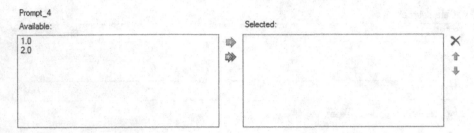

Figure 7-59. *Numeric prompt shown when used in Enterprise Guide*

5. Numeric Range

This prompt type is similar to the text range type. You specify the min/max values and default values if you want them, as shown in Figure 7-60. You can check a box to indicate if you just want integers to be used or else optionally specify the decimal places to use.

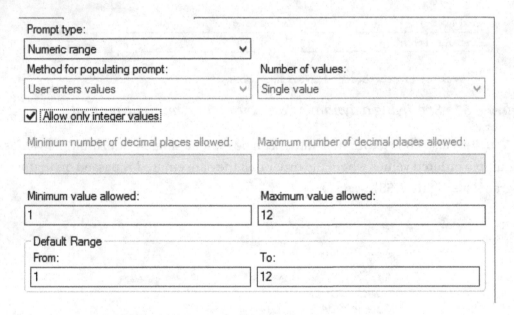

Figure 7-60. *Specifying a numeric range prompt*

When it is running from Enterprise Guide, it is displayed as shown in Figure 7-61.

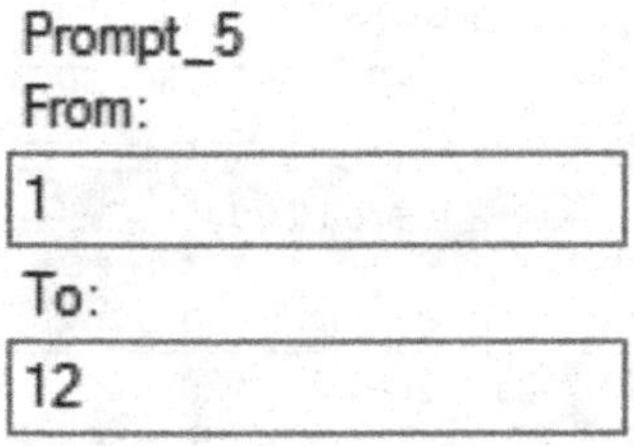

Prompt_5
From:

1

To:

12

Figure 7-61. *Numeric range displayed when used in Enterprise Guide*

6. Date

This prompt type allows you to specify a date for a prompt which can be one of the following types of date shown in Figure 7-62.

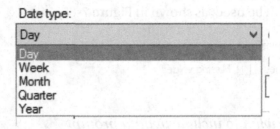

Figure 7-62. *Specify a date type for a data prompt*

You can choose a minimum and/or maximum date to allow by entering it, picking a value from the drop-down list (see Figure 7-63), or choosing a value from the calendar icon ▦ which opens up a calendar to choose from (see Figure 7-64).

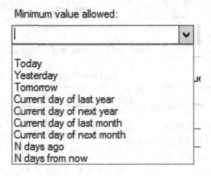

Figure 7-63. *Specify a minimum value for a date prompt with a range of special values*

Figure 7-64. *Choosing calendar icon allows specifying date using a calendar*

You can also choose whether to include all possible values and/or missing values in the list of values that can be used, as shown in Figure 7-65.

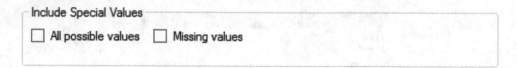

Figure 7-65. *Specify what to include in data prompt*

You can also choose a default value using a drop-down list or calendar picker like those already shown. You can see how to specify a defaul date in Figure 7-66.

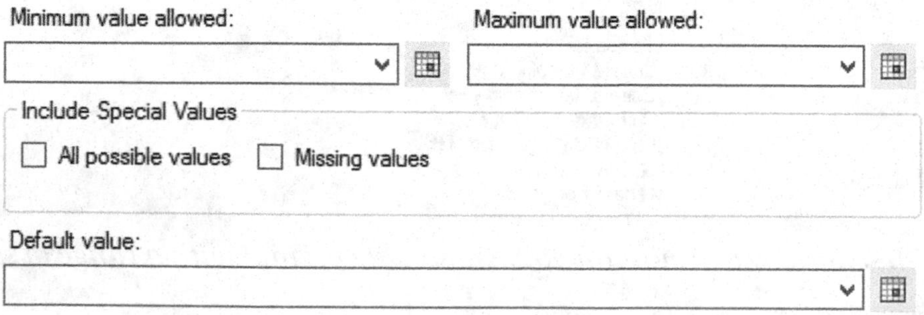

Figure 7-66. *Can specify a default value for date*

If you choose to select values from a static list, then you will have the dialog options we have already seen to make a list of values to choose from (see Figure 7-67).

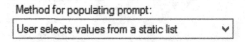

Figure 7-67. *Can specify to get values from a static list*

If you choose to select values from a dynamic list, then you have dialog options to choose a data source and variable to create a list of values from, as shown in Figure 7-68.

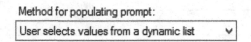

Figure 7-68. *Can specify to get values from a dynamic list*

When it is running from Enterprise Guide, it is displayed like in Figure 7-69.

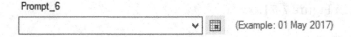

Figure 7-69. *Display of date prompt when running from Enterprise Guide*

7. Date Range

This allows defining a date range to be used as a prompt. You can see how to do this in Figure 7-70.

Prompt type:

Date range ⌄

Method for populating prompt:

User enters values ⌄

Number of values:

Single value ⌄

Date type:

Day ⌄

(Example: 01 May 2017)

Minimum value allowed:

⌄ ▦

Maximum value allowed:

⌄ ▦

Default Range

Range type:

Custom ⌄

From:

⌄ ▦

To:

⌄ ▦

Figure 7-70. *Defining a date range*

Choosing a date type of Day lets min/max range be set up using calendar or drop-down list shown in Figure 7-71.

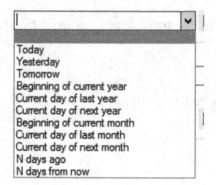

Today
Yesterday
Tomorrow
Beginning of current year
Current day of last year
Current day of next year
Beginning of current month
Current day of last month
Current day of next month
N days ago
N days from now

Figure 7-71. *Special values available for specifying a day*

Choosing week makes the drop-down list appear as in Figure 7-72.

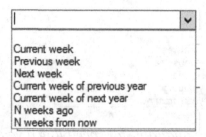

Figure 7-72. *Special values available for specifying a week*

Choosing month makes the drop-down list appear as in Figure 7-73.

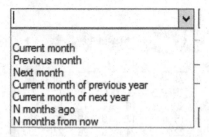

Figure 7-73. *Special values available for specifying a month*

Choosing quarter makes the drop-down list appear as in Figure 7-74.

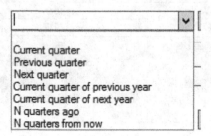

Figure 7-74. *Special values available for specifying a quarter*

Choosing year makes the drop-down list appear as in Figure 7-75.

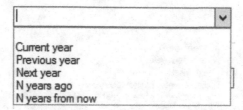

Figure 7-75. *Special values available for specifying a year*

For any date type, you can specify a range which can be specified using the corresponding drop-down menus shown previously or selection dialogs like the ones shown in Figures 7-76, 7-77, 7-78, and 7-79.

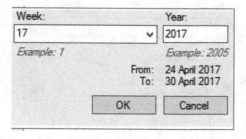

Figure 7-76. *Using calendar widget to specify a date*

Figure 7-77. *Using special week widget to choose a week*

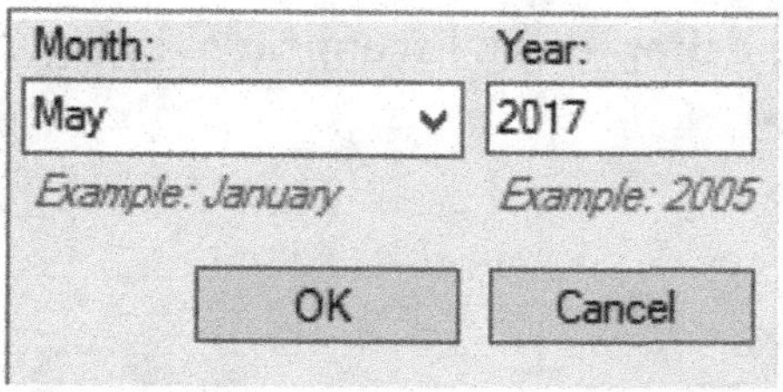

Figure 7-78. *Using special month widget to choose a month*

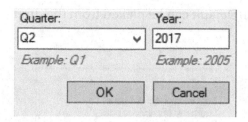

Figure 7-79. *Using special quarter widget to choose a quarter*

When it is running from Enterprise Guide, it is displayed as shown in Figure 7-80.

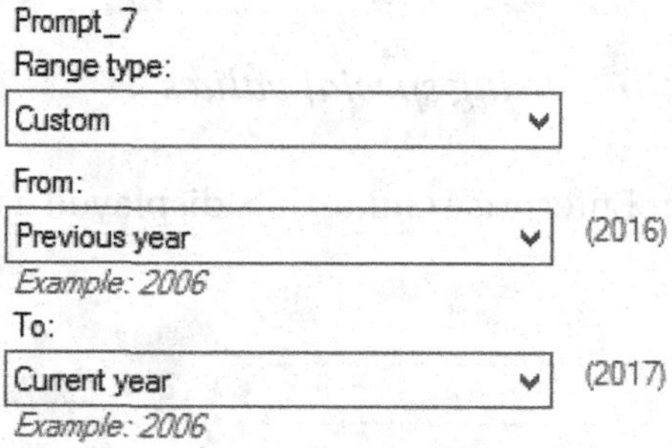

Figure 7-80. *Specifying a date range when run from Enterprise Guide*

8. Time

Choosing time lets us define a time as a prompt as shown in Figure 7-81.

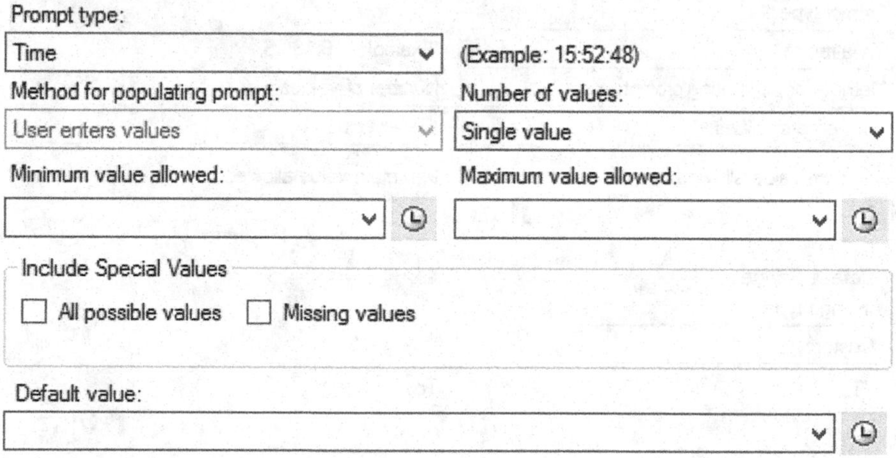

Figure 7-81. *Defining time as a prompt*

Minimum/Maximum/Default can be picked from the drop-down list in Figure 7-82.

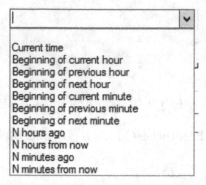

Figure 7-82. *Specifying times using special values*

When it is running from Enterprise Guide, it is displayed as shown in Figure 7-83.

Figure 7-83. *Prompt for specifying a time in Enterprise Guide*

9. Time Range

This prompt type allows specifying a time range (see Figure 7-84).

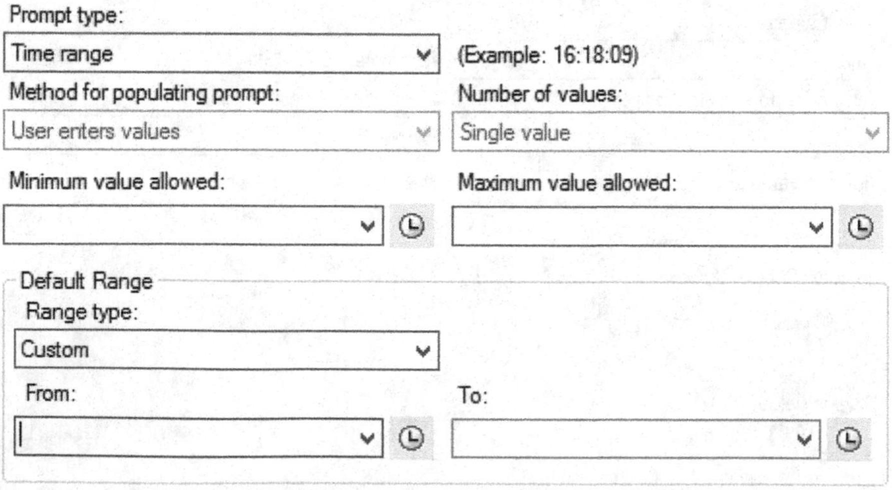

Figure 7-84. *Defining a time range prompt*

Times can be specified using a clock dialog (Figure 7-85) or drop-down list (Figure 7-86).

Figure 7-85. *Specifying a time using clock dialog*

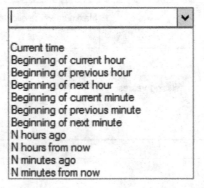

Figure 7-86. *Specifying a time using a special value*

When it is running from Enterprise Guide, it is displayed as shown in Figure 7-87.

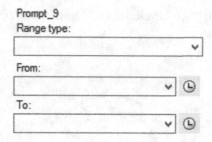

Figure 7-87. *Time range prompt used in Enterprise Guide*

10. Timestamp

You can specify a timestamp as a prompt, which is a combination of a date and time (see Figure 7-88).

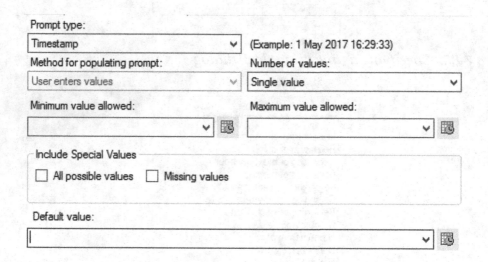

Figure 7-88. *Defining a timestamp as a prompt*

You can choose from the drop-down menu (Figure 7-89) or icon (Figure 7-90) to choose a value for Minimum, Maximum, or Default.

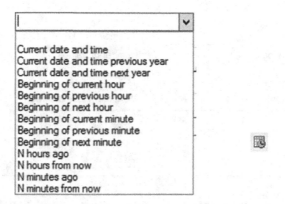

Figure 7-89. *Special values available for a timestamp*

Figure 7-90. *Specifying a datestamp using a combined date and clock dialog*

When it is running from Enterprise Guide, it is displayed as shown in Figure 7-91.

Figure 7-91. *Prompt for a timestamp used in Enterprise Guide*

11. Timestamp Range

The timestamp range prompt type allows you to enter a range or datetime values, as seen in Figure 7-92.

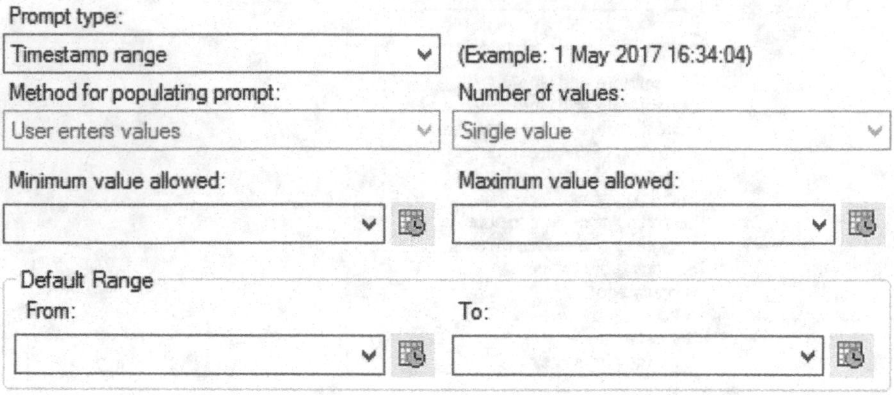

Prompt type:

Timestamp range ⌄   (Example: 1 May 2017 16:34:04)

Method for populating prompt: Number of values:

User enters values ⌄   Single value ⌄

Minimum value allowed: Maximum value allowed:

⌄ 🔲   ⌄ 🔲

Default Range
From: To:

⌄ 🔲   ⌄ 🔲

Figure 7-92. *Defining a timestamp range prompt*

When it is running from Enterprise Guide, it is displayed as shown in Figure 7-93.

Prompt_11
From:

⌄ 🔲

To:

⌄ 🔲

Figure 7-93. *Timestamp range prompt when used in Enterprise Guide*

12. Data Source

The data source prompt allows you to select a data source of one of the types, shown in Figure 7-94.

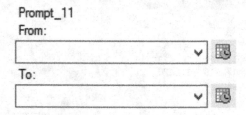

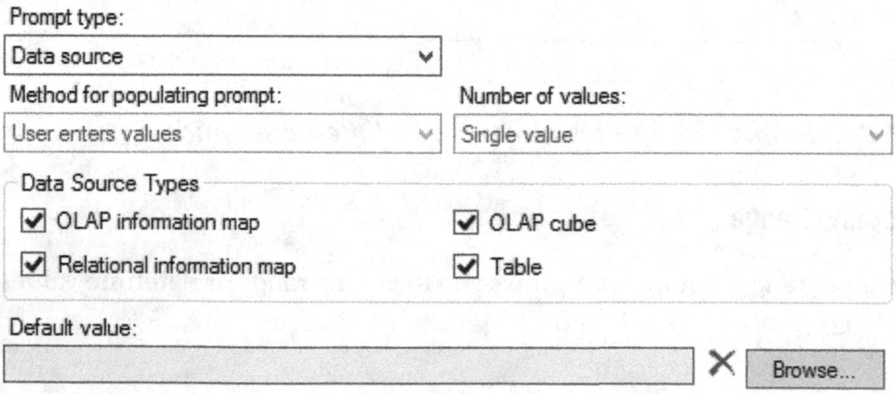

Prompt type:

Data source ⌄

Method for populating prompt: Number of values:

User enters values ⌄   Single value ⌄

Data Source Types
☑ OLAP information map   ☑ OLAP cube
☑ Relational information map   ☑ Table

Default value:

╳ Browse...

Figure 7-94. *Specifying a data source prompt*

When it is running from Enterprise Guide, it is displayed as shown in Figure 7-95.

Figure 7-95. Data source prompt when used in Enterprise Guide

13. Data Source Item

The data source item prompt allows choosing a number of data sources from which you can pick a variable, as shown in Figure 7-96.

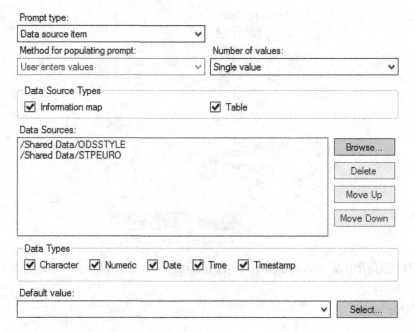

Figure 7-96. Defining a data source prompt

When it is running from Enterprise Guide, it looks like Figure 7-97.

Prompt_13

Figure 7-97. *Using a data source prompt in Enterprise Guide*

When you click the button, you get to choose a variable from the data sources available in the dialog shown in Figure 7-98.

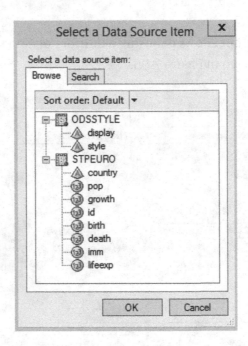

Figure 7-98. *Dialog displayed when browsing for a data source to select*

14. File or Directory

The file or directory prompt lets you choose either a file or a directory (see Figure 7-99). If you choose the file or directory type as input, then that indicates that you will select from things that already exist and so can be used as input. However, if you choose output, then you can create directories or files so that they don't have to already exist.

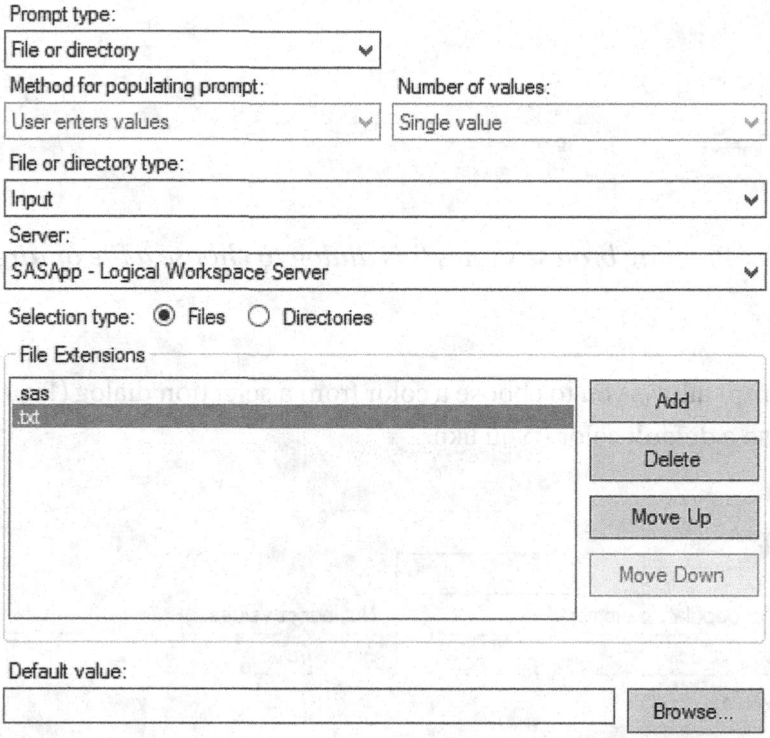

Prompt type:

| File or directory ⌄ |

Method for populating prompt: Number of values:

| User enters values ⌄ | | Single value ⌄ |

File or directory type:

| Input ⌄ |

Server:

| SASApp - Logical Workspace Server ⌄ |

Selection type: ⦿ Files ◯ Directories

File Extensions

.sas		Add
.txt		
		Delete
		Move Up
		Move Down

Default value:

| | | Browse... |

Figure 7-99. *Dialog to specify a file or directory prompt*

If you select to choose a file, you can enter some file extensions, so you will only see files that match those in the list of files as you are browsing. You need to choose a server where the files or directories are located on.

Next, you choose either files or directories, depending on what you want to select. If you choose files, then you can also enter file extensions which will restrict the files that you can use. Lastly, you can enter a default value if you want to.

When it is running from Enterprise Guide, it is displayed as shown in Figure 7-100.

Prompt_14

| | | Browse |

Figure 7-100. *Prompt when used from Enterprise Guide*

Pressing the Browse button brings up a dialog (Figure 7-101) to choose files or directories depending on what you had chosen.

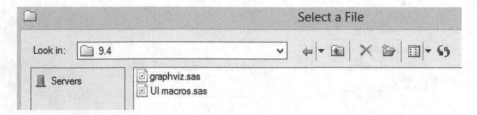

Figure 7-101. *Pressing browse shows this dialog to choose a file or directory*

15. Color

The color prompt allows you to choose a color from a selection dialog (Figure 7-102).
You can choose a default color if you like.

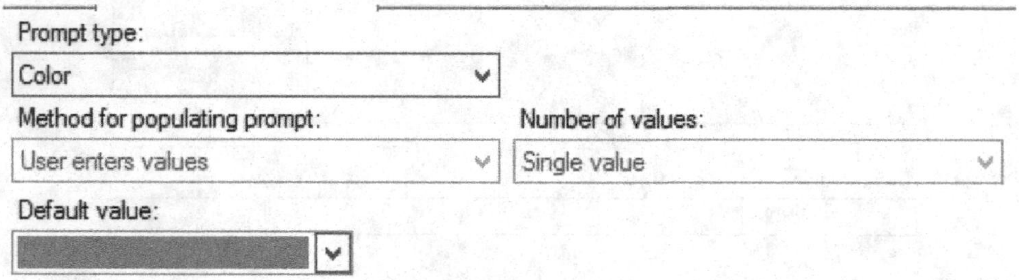

Prompt type:

| Color | ✓ |

Method for populating prompt:

| User enters values | ✓ |

Number of values:

| Single value | ✓ |

Default value:

Figure 7-102. *Defining a color prompt*

When it is running from Enterprise Guide, it is displayed as shown in Figure 7-103.

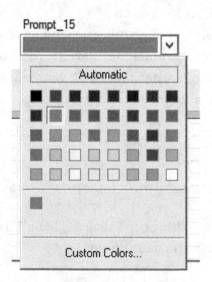

Figure 7-103. *Using a color prompt in Enterprise Guide*

16. Data Library

You can choose a prompt to allow picking a library from the SAS metadata, as shown in Figure 7-104.

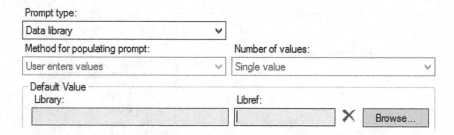

Figure 7-104. *Defining a prompt for a data library*

When it is running from Enterprise Guide, the prompt looks like Figure 7-105.

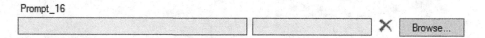

Figure 7-105. *Using a data library prompt from Enterprise Guide*

17. Variable

The variable prompt allows you to choose a variable from a list of variables. You can enter names of variables and set their types manually, as shown in Figure 7-106. Or you can click the Load Values button to select one or more tables and have their variables added to the list.

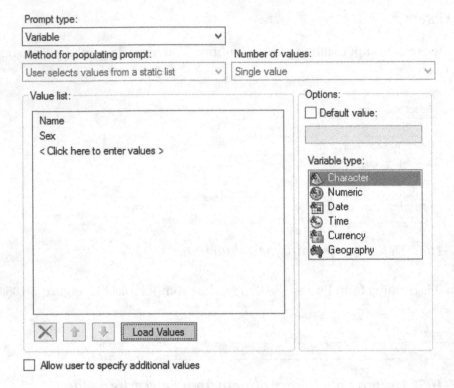

Figure 7-106. Defining a variable prompt

When it is running from Enterprise Guide, it is displayed as shown in Figure 7-107.

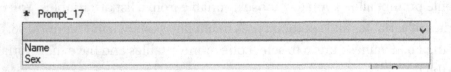

Figure 7-107. Using a variable prompt from Enterprise Guide

Adding Dependencies

The third tab when defining prompts is used when you are using dependencies. Dependencies are great for making your prompts work together. To illustrate, I will make a Stored Process which will print out some of the table sashelp.class. This table has variables: name, age, sex, height, and weight. I would like to prompt the user for sex and then display a list of the names that match that sex. So if the user chooses "F" for female, then they will get a list of female names.

Figure 7-108 shows the SAS code I will use, which will make use of two macro variables in a where clause that are provided by the prompts.

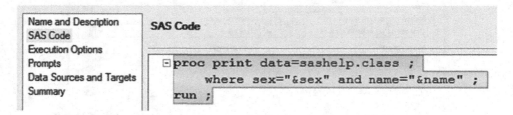

Figure 7-108. *SAS code used for stored process*

Next, I will define my prompts. Firstly, I want a prompt for Sex which must have a value specified as I am using it in the where clause. So, I check the "Requires non-blank value" check box in Figure 7-109.

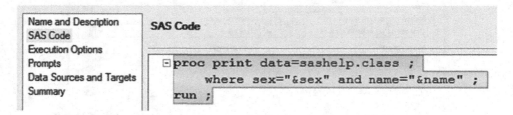

Figure 7-109. *Defining a prompt for sex*

This will have two possible values: M or F, which are added as shown in Figure 7-110.

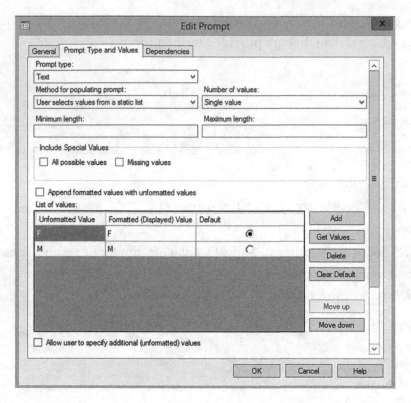

Figure 7-110. *Defining possible values for sex*

Now I want to make a new prompt for name, which I also don't want to have any blank values since it is being used in a where clause in my code (Figure 7-111).

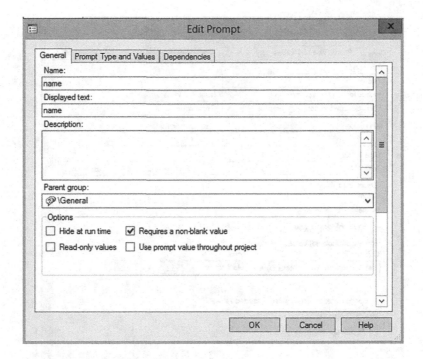

Figure 7-111. *Defining a prompt for name*

This prompt will get its values from a table that is defined in the metadata. Defining a table in the metadata is easily done using Management Console using the Data Library Manager plug-in. First, you define the library, if it isn't already defined, and then you register the table. That enables the table to be used in prompts like this, among other things. For my examples, I added a library for sashelp and then registered all the tables to it. That enables me to pick them out using metadata.

The key thing in defining this prompt is to choose "User selects values from a dynamic list" as the "Method for populating prompt". Then, you click the Browse button to find the table you want to use. Next, you choose the column name to use as an unformatted value and whether to just display distinct values rather than any repeated values. Usually, you will just want distinct values for this kind of thing. You can see the dialog used to do this in Figure 7-112.

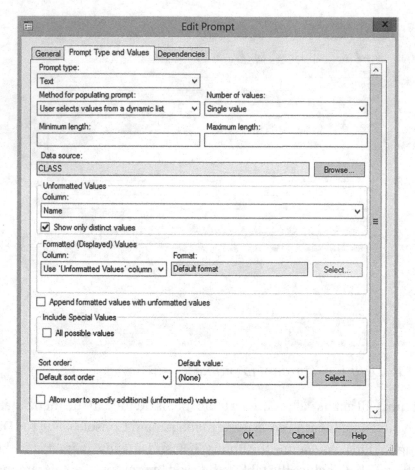

Figure 7-112. *Defining that values will be provided from a variable in a table*

The final thing to define is how the values defined in this prompt will be dependent on values from another prompt. In this example, if the user chose Sex='F', then I just want to display names for females. To define the dependency, I just do a few things shown in Figure 7-113.

Click the Add button to add a new dependency.

Choose the prompt I want to use as a dependency.

Define what the dependency actually is by creating a condition that will be used. In this case, Sex = "*whatever the value of the sex prompt is*".

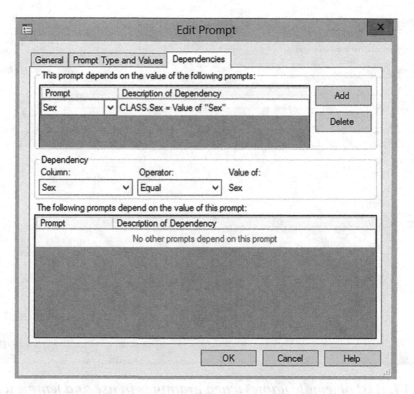

Figure 7-113. *Defining a dependency so we only get names matching the sex chosen*

Now when we run the Stored Process and go to select a name, we will see only names that have a sex of whatever the value of the sex prompt is, as shown in Figure 7-114.

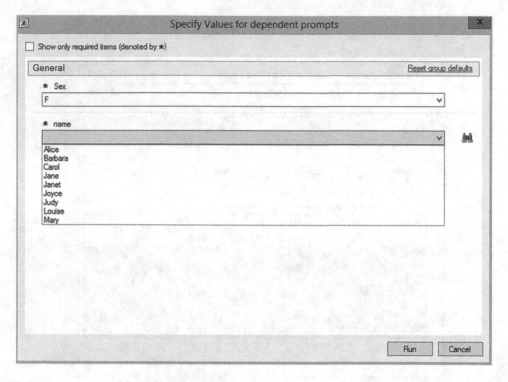

Figure 7-114. *List of female names when prompt is in use and female was chosen for sex*

Running the Stored Process after selecting a sex and name will produce the report in Figure 7-115 using those values.

Obs	Name	Sex	Age	Height	Weight
3	Barbara	F	13	65.3	98

Figure 7-115. *Result of stored process when it is executed using the prompt values specified*

Using Input Streams and Output Prompts

Input streams are defined when you set up a Stored Process and can be used to read data in as it is run. The data comes from a location that is defined as an input stream, such as part of an EXCEL spreadsheet.

Output prompts are also defined when you set up a Stored Process and can be used to output parameter values when it is run. For example, if you wanted to store the number of records that match the criteria of the query, you could perform a sql record count and store the output in an output prompt for use elsewhere. Parameter values are equivalent to macro variable values as the end of the stored process. So this will let you write macro values out to a defined destination, such as a cell in an EXCEL spreadsheet.

Input streams and output prompts work really well when used with the Office Add-in using Microsoft EXCEL. I will describe how to use both by making an example Stored Process.

As we go through the Stored Process wizard in Enterprise Guide, we can enter our stored process code which will be used to read in some data from EXCEL, write results back to it, and also write macro values to EXCEL.

The following code has some key features for use with input streams, which are highlighted in bold. The libname statement uses an XML engine to read data in from EXCEL, since the input stream will be defined to produce XML data. The _webin_ sasname automatic macro variable is created by SAS and populated with the table name that should be used with the XML input stream in order to read the data in properly. If there are multiple input streams, then SAS will create a series of automatic macro variables to use.

We create a macro variable that will be used with an output prompt, which is highlighted in bold italics. An output prompt will be populated with the value from this macro variable. We will also create two other output prompts which will be populated with the values of automatic macro variables.

The Proc Print in Listing 7-2 will produce ODS output which will be written back to EXCEL.

Listing 7-2. Producing ODS output to Excel

```
libname instr xml ;
data input_from_excel(drop=i) ;
    set instr.&_webin_sasname ;
    array numbers(*) _numeric_ ;
    do i=1 to dim(numbers) ;
        calculated_total+numbers(i) ;
    end ;
run;
```

```
* ODS output ;
title "Data read in from EXCEL, numbers totalled and written back to EXCEL"
;
title2 "Ran at %sysfunc(datetime(),datetime.)" ;
proc print ;
run;

%* Get the number of observations in the table, and assign to output
parameter ;
%let dsid=%sysfunc(open(input_from_excel)) ;
%let out_value=%sysfunc(attrn(&dsid,nobs)) ;
%let dsid=%sysfunc(close(&dsid)) ;
```

As we go through the Stored Process wizard, we get to the page where we can define output parameters, and we can define three parameters shown in Figure 7-116. The first takes the value of &out_value, next is &_clientuserid, and last is &_clientusername. The displayed text will be shown to the user as explanation of what the parameter is. The user can then specify where the value will be placed.

Output Parameters:

Name	Type	Displayed Text
out_value	String	Number of observations
_CLIENTUSERID	String	Client Userid
_CLIENTUSERNAME	String	Client User Name

Figure 7-116. *Defining output parameters*

We can specify a new data source for an input stream (see Figure 7-117). Since we are using EXCEL, we should choose XML-based data, which then sets the expected content type to text/xml. We could set this to anything we want to read in to match what is being streamed to the stored process.

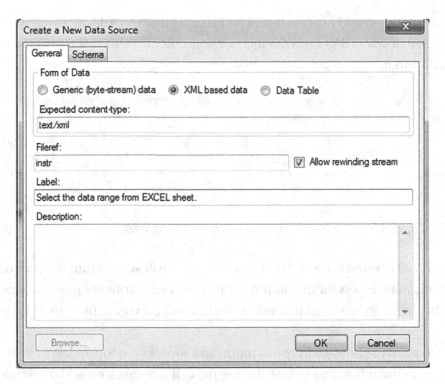

Figure 7-117. *Creating a new data source*

The filheref specified can be any valid filheref but needs to match the one used in the stored process code.

For EXCEL, we should check the box to allow rewinding stream.

The label will be displayed to the user as a prompt at the point that they can specify where the data is located which will be streamed in.

After specifying all this, we see it in the list of data sources and targets, shown in the spreadsheet in Figure 7-118.

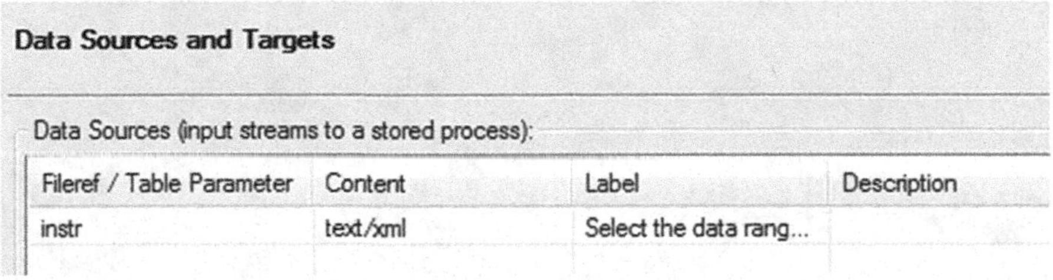

Data Sources and Targets

Data Sources (input streams to a stored process):

Fileref / Table Parameter	Content	Label	Description
instr	text/xml	Select the data rang...	

Figure 7-118. *List of data sources and targets*

We can run the stored process from EXCEL using the SAS Add-in, as shown in Figure 7-119. Just select SAS from the menu, choose Reports, navigate to the stored process, and run it.

Figure 7-119. *SAS tab when EXCEL has the SAS add-in*

Figure 7-120 is some sample data I made, which I will stream into the stored process. I also created some labels for the output parameters I will write out from the stored process. On running the stored process, a window will pop up to prompt us for values needed.

First, we need to choose where our input data sources are located. We can do this by either typing in the references or just clicking the cell selector icon and then choosing the range.

Next, we choose where we want the results from the stored process to go. This could be a new sheet, a new workbook (which will be a new EXCEL file), or just a location in an existing sheet which can also be chosen by using the cell selector icon.

Finally, we tick which of the output parameters we want to use and then choose where the values go to.

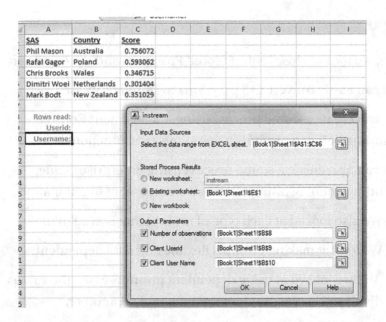

Figure 7-120. *Specifying where output parameters from a stored process go*

After making the selections shown in the previous screenshot and pressing OK, the stored process will run and populate sheet as shown in Figure 7-121. The ODS results have been put into columns E–I. The output parameters have been put into the cells in column B on the last three rows of the figure.

E3				fx	Ran at 28NOV17:08:35:38			
A	B	C	D	E	F	G	H	I
				Data read in from EXCEL, numbers totalled and written back to EXCEL				
SAS	**Country**	**Score**						
Phil Mason	Australia	0.499987						
Rafal Gagor	Poland	0.32871			Ran at 28NOV17:08:35:38			
Chris Brooks	Wales	0.80207						
Dimitri Woei	Netherlands	0.104055		Obs	SCORE	COUNTRY	SAS	calculated_total
Mark Bodt	New Zealand	0.352505		1	0.7560719	Australia	Phil Mason	0.756071872
				2	0.5930616	Poland	Rafal Gagor	1.349133507
Rows read:	5			3	0.346715	Wales	Chris Brooks	1.695848529
Userid:	8726117			4	0.3014035	Netherlands	Dimitri Woei	1.997252046
Username:	Mason, Philip (Contractor - Simp E)			5	0.3510294	New Zealand	Mark Bodt	2.348281405

Figure 7-121. *Results of running the stored process with cells populated in EXCEL*

Summary

In this chapter, we took at close look at Stored Processes and the details around them:

- You can easily convert SAS programs to stored processes.

- You can create a stored process using Management Console, including defining prompts using some great functionality.

- You can also create a stored process using Enterprise Guide, including defining prompts using a similar set of functionality:

  - We also looked at each type of prompt that is available.

  - We look at making prompts flexible and data dependent.

  - And we looked at using dependent prompts when the values displayed in one prompt might depend on another.

- We looked at how to use input streams and output streams for reading and writing to Microsoft EXCEL.

CHAPTER 8

SAS Stored Process Web Application

The SAS Stored Process Web Application is a Java web application that can execute stored processes and return results to a web browser. There are several parts to the Stored Process Web Application which will let you carry out different tasks. Let's explore some of these features before moving on to discussing macro parameters.

Index Page

There is an index page which is a very useful place to find your Stored Processes and Stored Process reports. You get to it by using a URL in your web browser like this:

```
http://your-server/SASStoredProcess/do?_action=index
```

Just put your server machine name or IP address in place of "your-server". You will need to authenticate by entering your user id and password, but then you will get the index page, shown in Figure 8-1.

© Philip Mason 2020
P. Mason, *SAS Stored Processes*, https://doi.org/10.1007/978-1-4842-5925-2_8

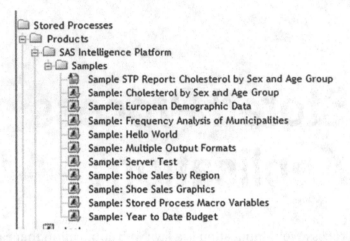

Figure 8-1. Index page

The index page is a helpful visual tool for seeing the following :

- **List of Stored Processes –** If you want to see what Stored Processes and/or Stored Process reports are available to you with the credentials you are currently using, then the Stored Process web app will give you a list of them.

- **Metadata folder structure –** As you look at the list of Stored Processes, they are displayed within the folder structure in the metadata. If this folder structure is set up well, then it can be used to provide a nice logical arrangement for your Stored Processes (see Figure 8-2).

- **Run Stored Processes –** You can run any of these Stored Processes, and the results will appear to the right of the folder list on the same page. This is quite useful to find Stored Processes, try them out, see if they use any prompts, and so on.

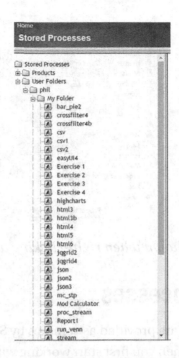

Figure 8-2. *List of stored processes in Enterprise Guide*

The index page also provides an easy way to get a link for a Stored Process. You can right-click any of these Stored Processes displayed and copy the link (see Figure 8-3). You can then take that link and use the URL in a web browser or elsewhere to run that Stored Process. Or perhaps an easier way is to right-click the Stored Process and choose "Open in new tab" or "Open in new window". That will open it and show the URL at the top of the window. Once you have a URL, you can add things to the end of it such as "&_debug=log,trace" which will run the Stored Process producing a trace and show the log, which is great for troubleshooting.

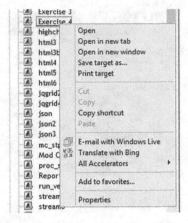

Figure 8-3. *Context menu shown when right-clicking a stored process*

Sample Stored Processes

Some simple Stored Processes are provided as samples by SAS (see Figure 8-4). It is useful to look through these when you first start working with Stored Processes to make sure you understand the examples. You can then go off and look at the code and metadata used for each of these to see exactly what techniques have been used.

SAS Stored Process Web Application   Log Off Philip Mason
                                                                                              §sas

Welcome to the Version 9 SAS Stored Process Web Application. This application allows you to execute SAS Stored Processes from a Web browser.

- Stored Process Samples

The following samples display some of the capabilities of stored processes. Many of the samples allow you to view the SAS log and see the SAS program used to generate the HTML or graphic output. Click on one of the following program names to execute the stored process.

Stored Processes	Description
Sample: Cholesterol by Sex and Age Group	Creates box plots using ODS.
Sample: European Demographic Data	Dynamically generated map with drilldown capabilities using ODS.
Sample: Frequency Analysis of Municipalities	Uses ODS to generate output.
Sample: Hello World	DATA Step-generated output using PUT statements.
Sample: Multiple Output Formats	Uses ODS to generate PDF, PostScript, RTF and other output.
Sample: Server Test	Simple ODS-generated output used to test server response.
Sample: Shoe Sales by Region	Creates a drillable bar chart using ODS.
Sample: Shoe Sales Graphics	ODS-generated output with table of contents and pie charts.
Sample: Stored Process Macro Variables	Illustrates how macro variables are created and used.
Sample: Year to Date Budget	ODS-generated output with table of contents, charts and tables.

- List Available Stored Processes and Reports
- Search for Stored Processes and Reports
- SAS Stored Processes: Developer's Guide - requires Internet access

Figure 8-4. *Sample Stored Processes*

Sample stored processes are also a good way to test if your software is working. If you are making a new install of SAS or have applied some major maintenance, then you can run these sample Stored Processes as a test to make sure that your Stored Process Web Application and all the associated SAS configuration work correctly.

Reserved Macro Parameters

There are many reserved macro parameters that we can use for the Stored Process Web Application. Some are used to pass information in, and some are just automatically set by the Stored Process Web Application and provide useful information for you to use. All of these start with an underscore, so it is generally best to avoid using underscores when you write your application in case you clash with a SAS one. If you do use macro variables starting with underscores, then you need to ensure that they don't clash with any existing SAS ones. Some of these variables are available all the time, but others are only used in conjunction with a specific client such as the Stored Process Web Application.

Some of these parameters are extremely useful. For instance, if you are debugging your stored process, you can set "_action=debug" and you will get the SAS log displayed at the end of your stored process execution. Using "_action=index" will display a list of all the stored processes that you can select and run them from. And using "_result=streamfragment" will generate just the HTML code directly produced by your SAS procedures such as Proc Print, without all the extra front and bottom matter usually generated by SAS.

Macro Variables Used with %stpbegin

Some of the following macro variables will be populated by the web application and you can look at the value to use it in your Stored Process (e.g., _metauser). Other values can be set by you prior to %stpbegin being called, and then the stpbegin macro will make use of the values you set.

Some of the most useful parameters are described here.

_ACTION

This tells the web application to carry out an action of some kind. It can be one of two values: Background or Data.

Background runs the Stored Process in the background like a batch job. So you can fire off your Stored Process, and control is immediately returned to the caller. When you do this, you just get a message back indicating that it has been submitted (Figure 8-5).

Stored Process /*User Folders/phil/My Folder/venn* submitted for background processing.

Figure 8-5. *This is displayed when a stored process is run in the background*

Data displays a summary of the general Stored Process data, not covering parameters you might submit with a Stored Process. So, you get the kind of data you have defined when creating your Stored Process as shown in Figure 8-6.

Stored Process venn	
Metadata path	/User Folders/phil/My Folder/venn
Source code location	Metadata
Source file	
SAS server type	Stored Process Server
Result type	Stream/Package
Created	02 May 2016 19:07:06 BST
Last modified	02 May 2016 20:39:51 BST
Keywords	
Description	

Run

Figure 8-6. *Information displayed with _action=data*

EXECUTE runs the Stored Process. It's the default action anyway. You can use _ACTION=EXECUTE in combination with other _ACTION= values.

PROPERTIES displays the property page, which enables you to set input parameters and execution options and to execute the Stored Process. This is really useful and flexible when you want to run an unfamiliar Stored Process since it is built automatically based on the registered prompt metadata.

BACKGROUND executes the Stored Process in the background. It is useful if your Stored Process runs for a long time, especially since browsers will usually time out after about 30 minutes, and if your Stored Process runs longer, then you can lose track of it. The Stored Process Web Application timeout is set to 30 minutes by default, although this timeout can be increased.

INDEX displays a page which lists Stored Processes on the left in a tree structure. This is very useful if you just want to browse all the Stored Processes that are defined and then select which one you want to run.

FORM displays a custom input form which is a JSP with the same name as the Stored Process, if one exists. Additionally, if you specify _form=<path to a JSP custom input form>, then it will look for a custom input form using the path and name that you specify. This allows you to have custom input forms for your Stored Process, which is quite a useful technique. If you don't specify _form=, then it will look for custom forms in the input folder under the SASStoredProcess directory.

Combining Values on _ACTION

_ACTION=FORM,EXECUTE

This displays a custom input form if one exists, otherwise executes the Stored Process. If EXECUTE was not listed and no form was found, then an error would be generated.

_ACTION=FORM,PROPERTIES,EXECUTE

This displays a custom input form if one exists, and if none is found, then the client app will look for metadata-defined prompts, and if there are no metadata-defined prompts, then just execute the Stored Process. If EXECUTE was not listed and no form was found plus no parameter prompts were defined, a web page with a "Run" button would be displayed to the client. So using EXECUTE is useful in those situations.

JSPs Used with _ACTION=FORM

Form will look for a "form" to display which corresponds to the Stored Process being called. So if our stored process is called "x", then it will look for a form called "x.jsp". Forms are pieces of JavaServer Page (JSP) code. A JSP basically lets you run Java code on the server, and the resulting output is displayed inside your web browser. That means that the Java code is executed at runtime when your web page is displayed. So our stored process called "x" would run "x.jsp" if it found that file. That file could generate some HTML and display it perhaps to prompt us for some choices. In its simplest form, you can just take an HTML file and change its suffix to JSP, and you have a JSP file that will run as one. If you then add bits of Java code to it inside the right tags, then they will be resolved at runtime. Writing JSP code is beyond the scope of this book, but I wanted to let you know that it is a useful way to create pages to prompt the user for information and allows you to execute code that could get data from the server to help create the page that is displayed.

The JSPs for the sample Stored Processes are, by default, deployed with the SAS Stored Process Web Application under the associated directory for each sample:

`<SASBIConfigDir>\Config\Lev1\Web\WebAppServer\SASServer1_1\sas_webapps\sas.storedprocess.war\input\Samples`

For example, the JSP file for the "Hello World" sample is found here:

`<SASBIConfigDir>\Config\Lev1\Web\WebAppServer\SASServer1_1\sas_webapps\sas.storedprocess.war\input\Samples\stphello`

You can read more about this in "Usage Note 38621: Tips for creating a Custom Input Form for a SAS Stored Process"[1] and also in "Specifying Custom Input Forms".[2]

_DEBUG

Debugging flags[3] have a range of possible values:

- **Fields** – Shows the input parameters for the Stored Process.

- **Dump** – Shows output in hexadecimal format.

- **Log** – Shows the SAS log after the Stored Process runs.

- **Trace** – Traces the execution of the Stored Process, which is helpful to understand the stages in the Stored Process execution process. It will also show you the HTTP headers that the server returns.

- **List** – This doesn't run the Stored Process, but instead displays a list of known Stored Processes.

- **Env** – Displays the environment parameters for the Stored Process Web Application.

- **Time** – Shows the real time taken by the Stored Process at the end.

---

[1]Usage Note 38621: Tips for creating a Custom Input Form for a SAS Stored Process – `http://support.sas.com/kb/38/621.HTML`

[2]Specifying Web Application Input – `http://support.sas.com/documentation/cdl/en/stpug/68399/HTML/default/viewer.htm#webinput.htm`

[3]Debugging in the SAS Stored Process Web Application – `http://support.sas.com/documentation/cdl/en/stpug/68399/HTML/default/dbgsrvlt.htm`

You can combine several _debug flags with commas like this: "_debug=log,time". A particularly useful combination is _debug=trace,time,log.

You can also use SAS/Intrnet style numbers to specify these flags[4]. My favorite is using "_debug=2179". This is a decimal converted from a binary, in which I set bits for various _debug options I want. I arrive at 2179 by taking Trace (2048) + Log (128) + Time (2) + Fields (1). Or another way to look at this is that the binary number equivalent to 2179 is 100010000011. Each bit turns on one of these debug options. The leftmost "1" bit is Trace, the next "1" bit is Log, and the last two "1" bits are Time and Fields.

_GOPT_DEVICE

This sets the goption device parameter. I usually use sasemf for this, although other popular choices are Java, activex, and png. One nice thing about using sasemf on UNIX is that true type fonts are more easily used from it.

_GOPT_HSIZE

This parameter sets the goption hsize parameter. It is useful if you want to specify the horizontal graph size precisely.

_GOPT_VSIZE

This parameter sets the goption vsize parameter. It is useful for specifying the vertical graph size.

_GOPT_XPIXELS

This parameter sets the goption xpixels parameter. I usually query my browser to work out the width,[5] allow for any other things taking up space on the screen, and then set the width appropriately. I need to adjust this when I change destinations though, since producing a graph for an RTF document is best done by customizing its size for the page.

---

[4]Application Dispatcher Debugging – http://support.sas.com/documentation/cdl/en/ dispatch/64895/HTML/default/viewer.htm#debuging.htm

[5]Use document.documentElement.clientWidth in JavaScript to get the width of window. Alternatively, use the jQuery $(window).width().

_GOPT_YPIXELS

This sets the goption ypixels parameter. In addition to the comments for _GOPT_
XPIXELS, I use this parameter when I have lots of items I want to put on my y axis. I can
make the graph very long and then display them all clearly as the user scrolls the HTML
page down.[6]

_GOPTIONS

This sets any valid SAS/Graph options, and you can use multiple options if you separate
them with a space - for example, &_goptions=htext=2 hsize=3.

_ODSDEST

This specifies the ODS destination (default is HTML). It can also be one of CSV, CSVALL,
TAGSETS.CSVBYLINE, HTML, HTML5, LATEX, NONE (which produces no ODS
output), PDF, PS, RTF, SASREPORT, WML, XML, or any other tagset destination.

_ODSOPTIONS

This specifies options that are added to the end of the ODS statement. One key use of
this is if you want titles and/or footnotes to be included in graphs, since NOGTITLE and
NOGFOOTNOTE are default options. You can override them by specifying GTITLE and/
or GFOOTNOTE in _ODSOPTIONS.

_ODSSTYLE

This sets ODS STYLE= option.

_ODSSTYLESHEET

This sets the ODS STYLESHEET= option.

---

[6]To get the height of the window, use the JavaScript document.documentElement.clientHeight or
 the rather simpler jquery $(window).height().

_RESULT

This specifies what kind of final result is produced by the Stored Process. It can be one of the following:

- **STATUS** – Produces no output to client, since the ODS LISTING destination is closed.

- **STREAM** – Output is streamed to client through the `_WEBOUT` fileref.

- **STREAMFRAGMENT**[7] – Just like stream but kind of a cut-down version. This is not documented, but I find it really useful for producing HTML when I want to have more control over my HTML. What it actually does is set the ODS no_top_matter and no_bottom_matter options, which means that only the HTML body is returned.

- **PACKAGE_TO_ARCHIVE** – Package is published to an archive file.

- **PACKAGE_TO_REQUESTER** – Package is returned to the client. The package can also be published to an archive file in this case.

- **PACKAGE_TO_WEBDAV** – Package is published to a WebDAV server.

- **PACKAGE_TO_EMAIL** – Package published to one or more email addresses.

- **PACKAGE_TO_QUEUE** – Package published to a message queue.

- **PACKAGE_TO_SUBSCRIBERS** – Package published to a subscriber channel.

Automatic Macro Variables in Stored Processes Run via SAS Stored Process Web Application

When you run a Stored Process using the Stored Process Web Application, you will find that there are a number of macro variables automatically created and populated with some useful values. Some of these values are set by some clients but not others, so it will

---

[7]StreamFragment has been undocumented in SAS up to the time of publishing this book. As with any undocumented feature, it may disappear or be renamed in a future release of SAS.

depend on the client you are using as to what macro variables are available. If you want to use values like this, it is sometimes necessary to check if they exist or what the client is rather than assuming they will exist.

_METAPERSON

This will show the name from the metadata which is associated with the user who is running the Stored Process. If there is no name defined, then this will be empty. It can be quite useful to use this when personalizing your web app so that you can use the user's name when asking them questions or for personalizing reports.

_METAUSER

This contains the userid which was used to access the SAS metadata.

_PROGRAM

This is the name of the Stored Process. This can be really useful for building web apps. You might want to build up a link from the current Stored Process to itself, for instance, which can be useful if you want to call itself again with some different parameters.

_SRVNAME

This is the host name of the server. This is very useful when you want to write Stored Processes that can build URLs for links.

_SRVPORT

This is the port number on which this request was received. It is also useful in building up a URL for links. Usually, you can leave this off URLs since it will default to port 80; however, if your web application server uses a different port, then you may need to specify that (e.g., 8080).

_STPERROR

The global error variable is 0 if everything worked properly, otherwise, non-zero. So this is useful in picking up some kinds of errors.

_URL

This specifies the URL of the web server middle tier used to access the Stored Process. This is also useful in building up a URL to use with links.

_USERNAME

This is the username obtained from web client authentication.

How to Use Macro Variables

Your Stored Process could produce a report with a little bit of HTML that gives you some other options, such as choosing a different product type for your report. The HTML could show some options along with different links, which have been generated by your code. These links would be the same as your current Stored Process call, which has shown this page, except you would want to change the value of the product type. Therefore, you would want to get the current URL being used and then add or change the product type parameter for it. You can construct the URL currently being used as follows:

```
http://&_srvname:&_srvport&_url?_program=&_program
```

If you need to dissect it and replace the value for a parameter, then that is quite easily done. If you just need to add a parameter onto the end of it, then that is even easier to do.

You could use some of the other macro variables from the previous section in ways like this:

```
title1 "Good morning &_metaperson, userid: &_metauser" ;
title2 "Username: &_username" ;
proc print data=sashelp.class ;
run ;

%macro check_for_errors ;
   %if &_stperror>0 %then %put ERROR: Stored Process Error: &=_stperror ;
%mend check_for_errors ;
%check_for_errors
```

Step-by-Step Guide to Building a Web Application Using Stored Processes

If you haven't built a web application with SAS Stored Processes before, then this chapter is a good place to get a quick start. It will take you through a series of simple steps which show how to create a report in *Enterprise Guide*, make into a Stored Process, run it in various ways, modify it, and finally build a simple web application using it. These directions will show how someone with almost no knowledge of SAS could actually make a web application using Stored Processes. The main features of SAS that make this possible are the ability to create a Stored Process using wizards in Enterprise Guide and the Stored Process Web Application which can run your Stored Process in a web browser.

The syntax and each idea used in this example are described fully in other sections of the book.

Step 1: Query Builder

In a windows environment, start up SAS Enterprise Guide. In Enterprise Guide, start the Query Builder from the Tasks menu by following the path shown in Figure 8-7.

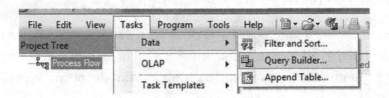

Figure 8-7. *Tasks ➤ Data ➤ Query Builder*

Now you can open some data to start building a query. As you can see in Figure 8-8, I picked a standard sample dataset from our SAS 9.3 installation – *sashelp.orsales*.

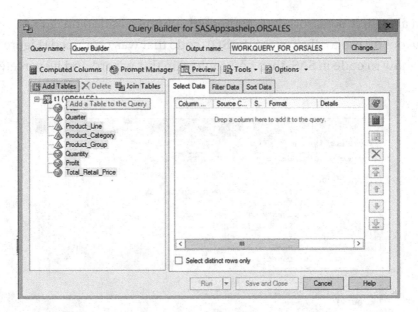

Figure 8-8. *Query Builder with sashelp.orsales*

Now you can add tables, variables, and join tables. In Figure 8-9, I just added them all in.

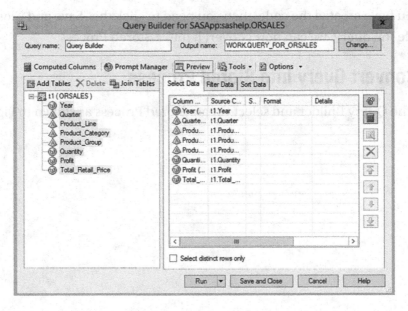

Figure 8-9. *Selecting data in Query Builder*

You can also filter data, sort data, computed columns, and so on. You can also click the *Preview* tool on the toolbar to see the SQL code that was produced (Figure 8-10). So, if you know how to code in SAS, then you could skip this wizard and just create the code yourself.

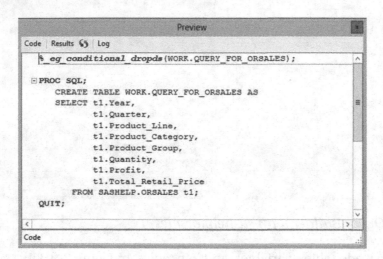

Figure 8-10. Preview of SAS code produced by Figure 8-9

Once you have created the code, then you need to click the "Save and Close" button. Having made the query, we can now convert it into a Stored Process.

Step 2: Convert Query into Stored Process

Right-click the Query Builder and select Create Stored Process as shown in Figure 8-11.

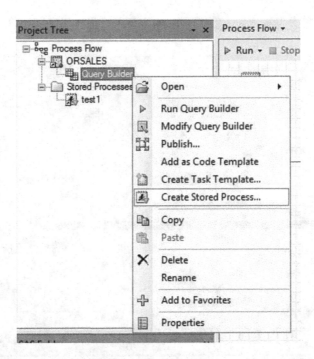

Figure 8-11. *Choosing to create a stored process from a query made with Query Builder*

Now use the wizard to create a Stored Process and give it a name. You can fill in the other fields although you can leave them to default (see Figure 8-12). The location defaults to the last one used; I am creating it in My Folder, which is a location set up by default that only I can use. If I wanted others to use this stored process, then I should pick a different location accessible by others.

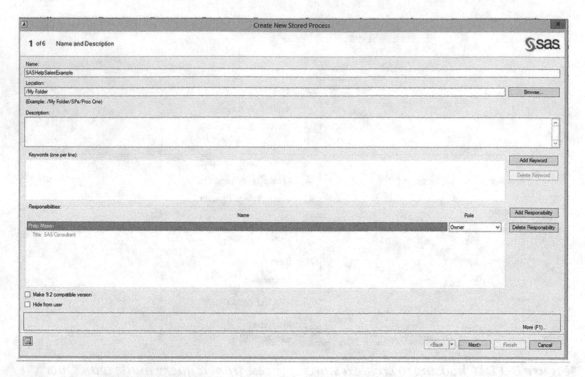

Figure 8-12.   *First page of stored process creation wizard*

Press Next to see the SAS code of the Stored Process being created (Figure 8-13).

Figure 8-13. *Second page of wizard showing SAS code produced*

Leave code and other settings as they are[8] and then press Next to see the execution options, which you *can* also just let default. It is advisable to choose the type of server you want the Stored Process to run on. If you stick with Default Server, then it may run on a workspace server or a Stored Process server. However, if you choose the type of server,

---

[8]Include code for has three things you can tick: Stored process macros, global macro variables, and Libname references. The first two are ticked by default.

then you will know where it will run and where to find the log for it (see Figure 8-14). You might need to modify the source code repository field so that you can ensure the SAS code is stored where you want it to be.

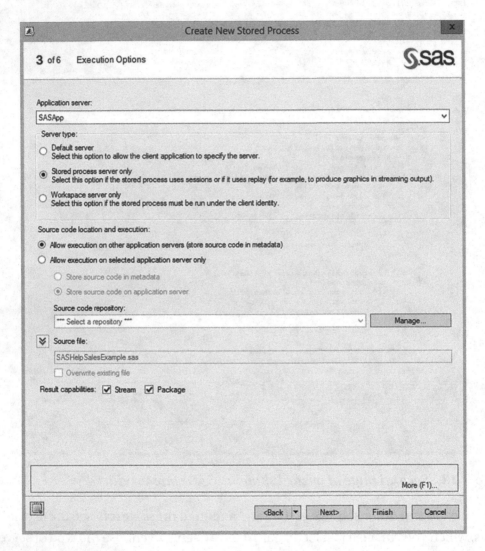

Figure 8-14. *Third page of stored process creation wizard*

Hit Next and you see a screen where you can define prompts, which can be used to prompt the user for values when a Stored Process is run (Figure 8-15). The values can then be passed through to the Stored Process code as macro variables. We are not defining any prompts at this stage.

Figure 8-15. *Screen to define prompts for a Stored Process*

Hit Next and you see the page where we can define input and output streams for the Stored Process (Figure 8-16). Our simple Stored Process won't need any of these.

Figure 8-16. *Data sources and targets screen*

Finally, hit Next and you will see a summary page showing key information about the Stored Process you have created (Figure 8-17).

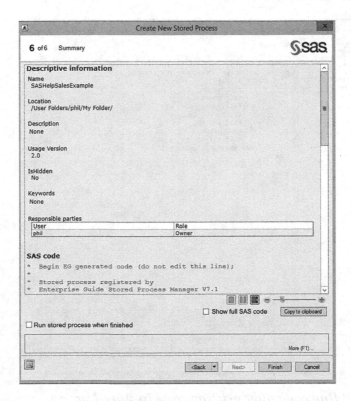

Figure 8-17. *Summary page of wizard*

Hit Finish and the Stored Process is created. This Stored Process can then be run, and it creates a dataset based on the query that we built. However, we want to see that dataset on the screen, so we will modify the Stored Process to do that.

Step 3: Modify Stored Process

Now we need to right-click the Stored Process and modify it, as shown in Figure 8-18.

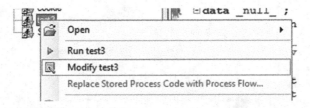

Figure 8-18. *Context menu when right-clicking stored process*

We can add a proc print or similar to show the data at the end (see Figure 8-19). Save it and run it to test.

Figure 8-19. *Adding code after existing code in stored process*

Step 4: Access Stored Process Web Application

Now you will need to find how to access your Stored Process Web Application. To open the Stored Process Web Application at my site, we use this link: **http://my-sas-server/SASStoredProcess/**. This will show us the Stored Process Web Application home page (Figure 8-20).

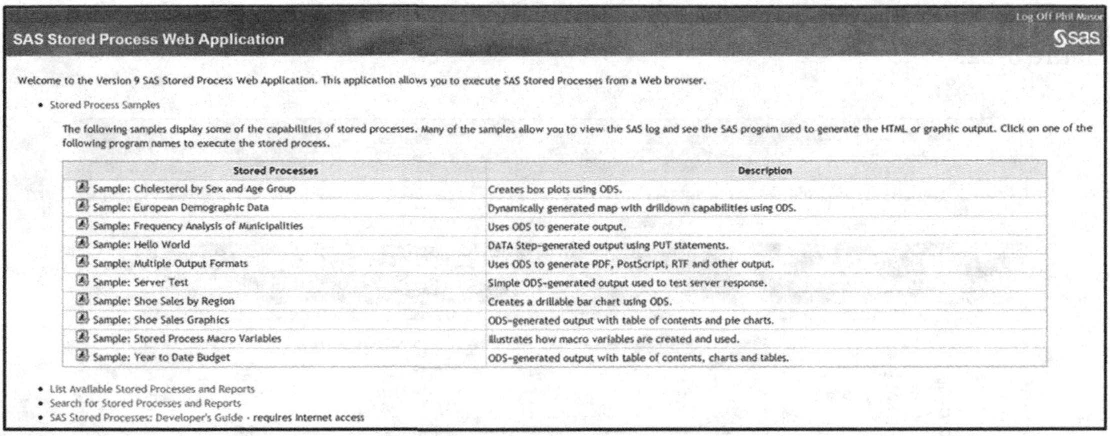

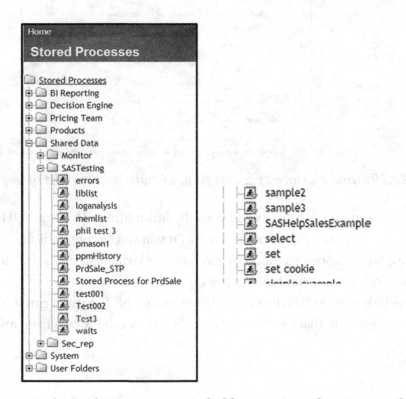

Figure 8-20. *Stored Process Web Application home page*

Select "List Available Stored Processes and Reports". Then drill down through tree to show your Stored Process from the location in the metadata that you saved it, as shown in Figure 8-21.

Figure 8-21. *List of stored processes provided by SAS Stored Process Web Application*

Click your Stored Process to run it. The results show up on the page, as shown in Figure 8-22.

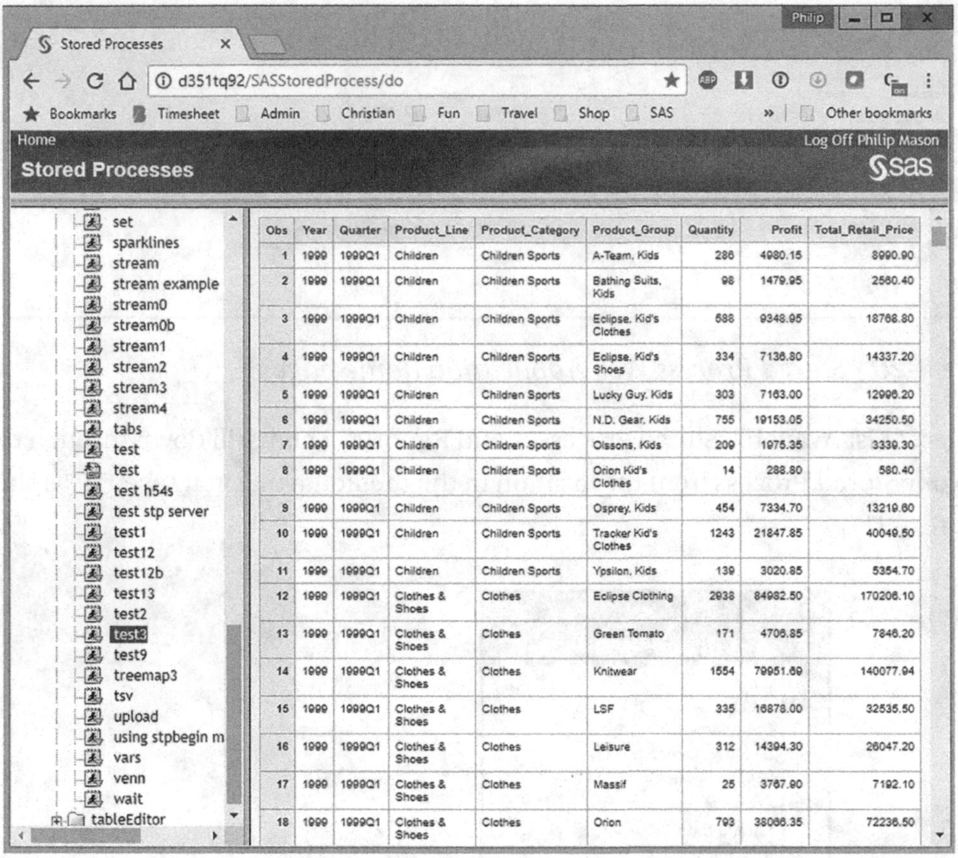

Figure 8-22. *Running a stored process shows results on the right of page*

Right-click your Stored Process and copy the link address. This link will let us run the Stored Process from a number of other places. Or you can simply right-click and select "Open in new tab/window" so that the Stored Process will be opened and run in another tab/window. The URL will be shown at the top of that window.

Paste the link into the URL box in the browser, and hit Return to run it. You now have the complete URL that can be used to call your Stored Process from anywhere (Figure 8-23).

Obs	Year	Quarter	Product_Line	Product_Category	Product_Group	Quantity	Profit	Total_Retail_Price
1	1999	1999Q1	Children	Children Sports	A-Team, Kids	286	4980.15	8990.90
2	1999	1999Q1	Children	Children Sports	Bathing Suits, Kids	98	1479.95	2560.40
3	1999	1999Q1	Children	Children Sports	Eclipse, Kid's Clothes	588	9348.95	18768.80
4	1999	1999Q1	Children	Children Sports	Eclipse, Kid's Shoes	334	7136.80	14337.20

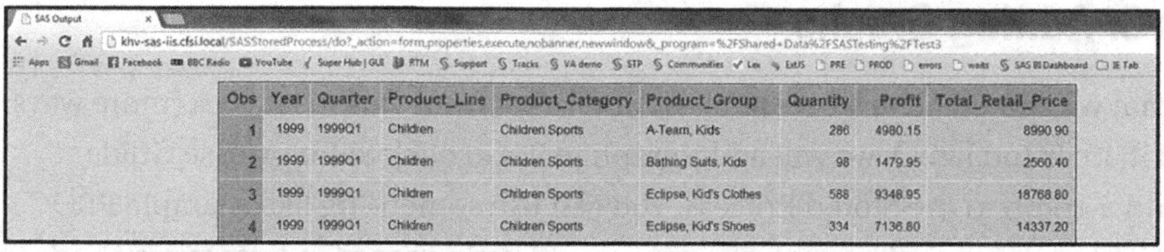

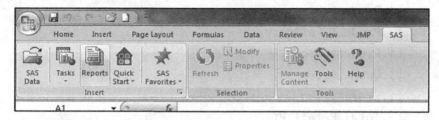

Figure 8-23. *Result of stored process shown in a separate tab*

Step 5: Run Stored Process from Excel

To show how flexible this is, we will run the Stored Process from EXCEL. This assumes you have the Microsoft Office SAS Add-in installed. Open EXCEL. Select SAS menu item and then click Reports as shown in Figure 8-24.

Figure 8-24. *SAS tab in EXCEL*

Navigate to your Stored Process and open it.

The Stored Process will run. A little progress bar is displayed while it runs.

When the Stored Process finishes running, then the table that it produces will be imported into EXCEL. You now have the results of the Stored Process in EXCEL (Figure 8-25).

Obs	Year	Quarter	Product_Line	Product_Category	Product_Group	Quantity	Profit	Total_Retail_Price
1	1999	1999Q1	Children	Children Sports	A-Team, Kids	286	4980.15	8990.90
2	1999	1999Q1	Children	Children Sports	Bathing Suits, Kids	98	1479.95	2560.40
3	1999	1999Q1	Children	Children Sports	Eclipse, Kid's Clothes	588	9348.95	18768.80
4	1999	1999Q1	Children	Children Sports	Eclipse, Kid's Shoes	334	7136.80	14337.20
5	1999	1999Q1	Children	Children Sports	Lucky Guy, Kids	303	7163.00	12996.20
6	1999	1999Q1	Children	Children Sports	N.D. Gear, Kids	755	19153.05	34250.50
7	1999	1999Q1	Children	Children Sports	Olssons, Kids	209	1975.35	3339.30
8	1999	1999Q1	Children	Children Sports	Orion Kid's Clothes	14	288.80	580.40
9	1999	1999Q1	Children	Children Sports	Osprey, Kids	454	7334.70	13219.60

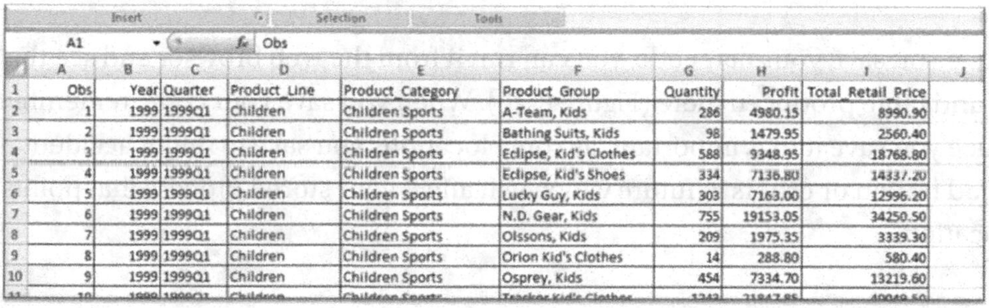

Figure 8-25. *Excel results*

Step 6: Adding Graphs

Now that we can create a Stored Process and run it from various places (more ways
to run it are listed later), we will add a graph to it. Go back to Enterprise Guide
and add a graph to the Stored Process. You can use something like a simple PROC
GCHART (as shown in Listing 8-1), or you could use a wizard in Enterprise Guide to
help you with this.

Listing 8-1. Code in stored process that has been modified to add a graph

```
PROC SQL;
   CREATE TABLE WORK.QUERY_FOR_ORSALES AS
      SELECT t1.Year,
             t1.Quarter,
             t1.Product_Line,
             t1.Product_Category,
             t1.Product_Group,
             t1.Quantity,
             t1.Profit,
             ti.Total_Retail_Price
      FROM SASHELP.ORSALES t1;
QUIT;
/* --- End of code for "Query Builder" --- */
proc gchart ;
   hbar product_category / subgroup=year sumvar=profit ;
run ;
proc print ;
run ;
```

Once you save your new code, you can run it from the web browser and see the
graph and table produced there (Figure 8-26). When you save your code, remember that
the place you save it to is important, as some locations you save to might accidentally be
modified by you or others in future which will affect your stored process that points to
that location.

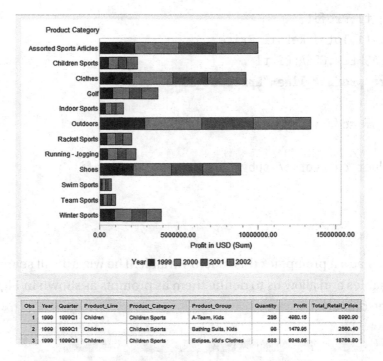

Figure 8-26. *Output from the code that had a graph added*

Step 7: Apply a Parameter

We might like to add a filter to our Stored Process, so let's go back to EG. We will add
a parameter to let us filter on a variable (e.g., product_line). You can then use a macro
variable for the value of the that variable (e.g., where product_line="&product_line";) as
shown in Listing 8-2. This means that by changing the value of the macro variable, we
can apply a different filter.

Listing 8-2. *Code for stored process that has a where clause added*

```
PROC SQL;
  CREATE TABLE WORK.QUERY_FOR_ORSALES AS
    SELECT t1.Year,
           t1.Quarter,
           t1.Product_Line,
           t1.Product_Category,
           t1.Product_Group,
           t1.Quantity,
```

```
            t1.Profit,
            t1.Total_Retail_Price
      FROM SASHELP.ORSALES t1
        where product_line="&product_line" ;
QUIT;
/* ---- End of code for "Query Builder". --- */
proc gchart ;
   hbar product_category / subgroup=year sumvar=profit ;
run ;
proc print ;
run ;
```

Now we can add a prompt for this macro variable. The wizard will search our code for macro variables and allow us to define them as prompts as shown in Figure 8-27. We can just use the defaults.

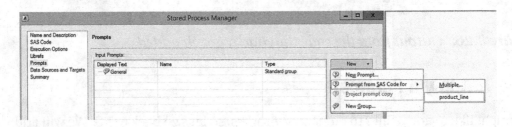

Figure 8-27. *Prompt created for stored process to pass a value for macro variable to where clause*

Run the Stored Process again. You will be prompted for a value, so enter one (Figure 8-28). Make sure your value matches one of the values from the data; otherwise, you won't find anything. Then click Run to execute the Stored Process using the value you entered.

General
product_line
Children

Run

Figure 8-28. *Specifying a value to be passed to program as macro variable value*

You now see the Stored Process with your parameter applied (Figure 8-29).

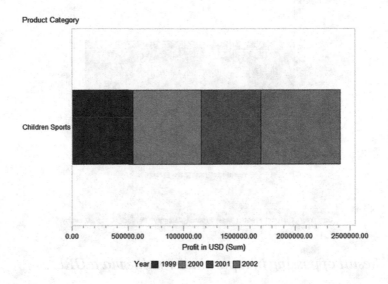

Figure 8-29. *Resulting graph when we pass in a value that is used in where clause*

If you want to use a URL to pass your parameter to your Stored Process, you can do so by making use of one of the key features of the Stored Process Web Application. Any parameter/value pairs like &parameter=value will be passed into the SAS code as macro variables. They don't even have to be predefined in the SAS code. So that means that I can call our Stored Process using the following URL to pass the **value** in, and then I can see that the results are shown correctly in the graph shown next (Figure 8-30). This is the URL that was used:

```
http://d351tq92/SASStoredProcess/do?_program=%2FShared+Data%2FSASTesting%2F
Test3&product_line=Sports
```

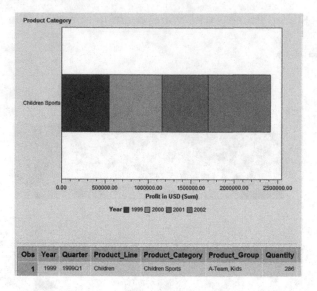

Figure 8-30. *Result of passing in a parameter value via a URL*

A Note About Authentication

Sometimes you might find that you get an unexpected error message that says that your application server has timed out (Figure 8-31). This will happen if you stop using the Stored Process Web Application for a while, so that your authentication times out. You will just need to re-authenticate to SAS, and then it should be OK again. This can usually be done just by running your stored process again via the Stored Process Web Application, and it should prompt you to authenticate and then it should work.

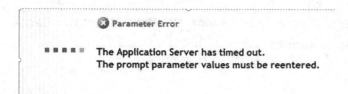

Figure 8-31. *Error message when authentication in browser has timed out*

Creating an HTML Menu for Our Stored Process

We can make a simple HTML file which allows us to select the report we want to run from a menu. So, the following code simply calls our Stored Process and passes a different value for product_line each time:

```
<HTML> <body>
<h1>Pick a report to run</h1>
<a href="http://my.server/SASStoredProcess/do?
_program=%2FShared+Data%2FSASTesting%2FTest3
&product_line=Children"> Children</a><p>
<a href="http://my.server/SASStoredProcess/do?
_program=%2FShared+Data%2FSASTesting%2FTest3
&product_line=Clothes+%26+Shoes">Clothes & Shoes</a><p>
<a href="http://my.server/SASStoredProcess/do?
_program=%2FShared+Data%2FSASTesting%2FTest3
&product_line=Outdoors">Outdoors</a><p>
<a href="http://my.server/SASStoredProcess/do?_program=%2FShared+Data%2FSAS
Testing%2FTest3
&product_line=Sports">Sports</a><p>
</body> </HTML>
```

This displays the menu shown in Figure 8-32.

Figure 8-32. *Menu displayed by the previous HTML code*

Selecting a value (e.g., Sports) runs the Stored Process with the appropriate parameter to display the required report. So, you can see in Figure 8-33 that I now have a graph and table reflecting my selection of "Sports". You can also see this reflected in the URL which shows &product_linc=Sports:

```
/SASStoredProcess/do?_program=%2FShared+Data%2FSASTesting%2FTest3&produ
ct_line=Sports
```

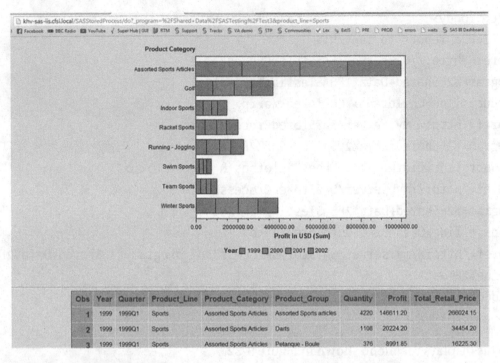

Figure 8-33. *Result in browser from passing in a parameter value via URL to web application*

Step 8: Use HTML Forms to Run Stored Processes

With a little basic HTML knowledge, we can modify the HTML to make a better menu. This introduces another useful technique of using HTML forms to run Stored Processes. The key points in using this technique are

The form tag has two elements:

- Action element which defines the start of the URL to use when calling your Stored Process

- Method element

The form uses other tags which are form elements defining what will be on the form. These include Input and Select tags.

Input tags define name/value pairs which will be passed to the Stored Process as parameters. Some of these tags simply define a field where the user can type in a value, but others such as **Hidden** and **Submit** have special characteristics.

Input tags with a type of **Hidden** won't be displayed on the form but will be passed to the Stored Process as a parameter. In the following example, we are passing the name of the Stored Process with its parameter _program. You must always have this pointing to your Stored Process when using this technique.

Input tags with a type of **Submit** will display a Submit button which can be pressed to run the Stored Process and pass any values from the form to it.

Select tags will create a drop-down box of options. This allows the user to choose an option and then the selected value will be passed to the Stored Process. The value from the "value=" attribute is passed from the form to the Stored Process we are calling. The text between the tags (e.g., "Clothes & Shoes") is what is displayed in the drop-down box, as shown in Listing 8-3.

Listing 8-3. HTML code to produce a drop-down menu of choices to pass as a parameter

```
<html>
<body>
<h1>Pick a report to run</h1>
<form method="get" action='http://khv-sas-iis.cfsi.local/SASStoredProcess/
do?'>
<input type="hidden" name="_program" value="/Shared Data/SASTesting/Test3">
<select name="product_line">
<option value="Children">Children</option>
<option value="Clothes+&+Shoes">Clothes & Shoes</option>
<option value="Outdoors">Outdoors</option>
<option value="Sports">Sports</option>
</select>
<input type="submit" value="Run">
</form>
</body>
</html>
```

Our menu in Figure 8-34 now has a drop-down menu of choices. You select one and click Run which then adds your selection onto the URL as a parameter.

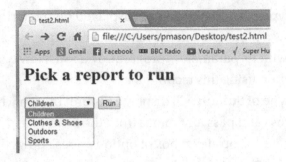

Figure 8-34. *Web browser menu displayed using HTML from Listing 8-3*

To automate this application a little more, we can automatically generate the drop-down list of options. Create a new Stored Process which will create our HTML menu for us. This can be done by using a Stored Process that will write the HTML directly into the web browser. To do this, you need to write to a `fileref` called `_webout` which is predefined for the Stored Process to use. You also need to turn off the automatically generated Stored Process macros by using the *Include Code For* button. These macros usually allocate the `_webout fileref` for their own use, which means that we can't use it from a data step.

The program in Listing 8-4 first runs some SQL code which gets the different values of product_line and puts them into option tags, then concatenates them together, and puts the result into a macro variable called options.

You have to be careful as you can run up against the 32K limit for a macro variable when creating macro variables like this. If you reach the limit, then the value will be truncated. You can get around this problem by using PROC STREAM and generating values with a macro program which will write directly into the stream and has no practical limits.

The program then runs a data step which basically just gets lines from the cards4 area and writes them out to the `_webout` file ref. After reading a line in, we then run it through a resolve() function, which is very important. The resolve() function will resolve any macro language in the line that was read, which means that our options' macro variable is resolved and the option lines that were made by our PROC SQL are inserted.

The SAS code for the stored process is as shown in Listing 8-4.

Listing 8-4. SAS code for the stored processes

```
proc sql ;
    select distinct '<option value="' || strip(product_line) || '">'
                        || strip(product_line) || '</option>'
    into :options separated by ' '
    from sashelp.orsales ;
quit ;
data _null_ ;
    file _webout ;
    input ;
    line=resolve(_infile_) ;
    put line ;
    cards4 ;
<html>
<body>
<h1>Pick a report to run</h1>
<form method="get" action="http://d351tq92/SASStoredProcess/do?"
target="content">
<input type="hidden" name="_program" value="/User Folders/phil/My Folder/
test">
<select name="product_line">
&options
</select>
<input type="submit" value="Run">
</form>
</body>
</html>
;;;;
run ;
```

This generates the same web page that we made before, but now it is data driven and flexible. So, if we added another product_line to our data, then we would get another option in our drop-down list as shown in Figure 8-35.

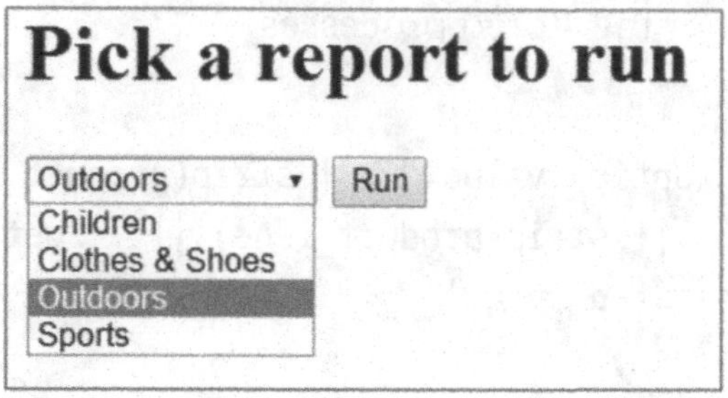

Figure 8-35. *Menu shown in web browser*

We can further improve this by combining the menu and output onto a single page. To do this, we add an IFRAME to our web page, specifying the size so it doesn't default to something too small. Then we must add TARGET= to the FORM tag, specifying a name which matches the one for the IFRAME (see Listing 8-5). This means the URL for our Stored Process will be opened in the IFRAME.

Listing 8-5. Improving the SAS program that generates the HTML

```
proc sql ;
    select distinct '<option value="'||strip(product_line)||'">'||
                    strip(product_line)||'</option>'
    into :options separated by ' '
    from sashelp.orsales ;
quit ;
data _null_ ;
    file _webout ;
    input ;
    line=resolve(_infile_) ;
    put line ;
    cards4 ;
<html>
<body>
<h1>Pick a report to run</h1>
<form method="get" action="http://d351tq92/SASStoredProcess/do?"
target="content">
<input type="hidden" name="_program" value="/User Folders/phil/My Folder/
test">
```

```
<select name="product_line">
&options
</select>
<input type="submit" value="Run">
</form>
<iframe name="content" height="100%" width="100%">
</iframe>
</body>
</html>
;;;;
run ;
```

Now we have a simple web application that takes some input and updates the page with output based on that (Figure 8-36).

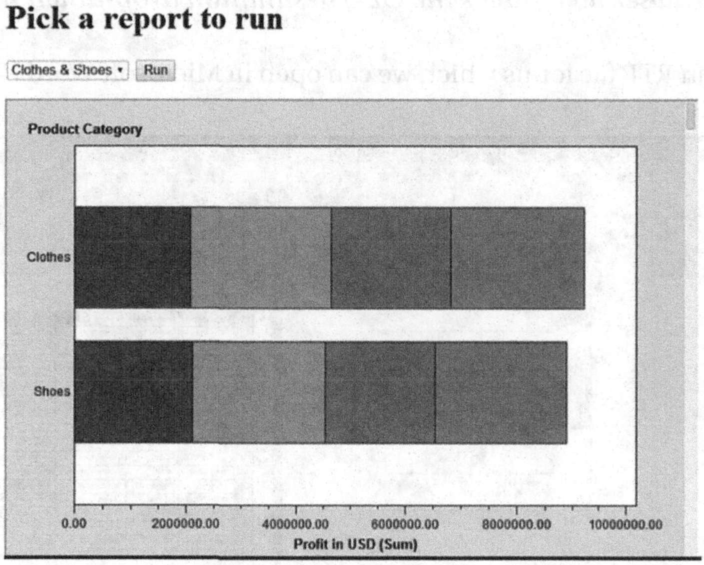

Figure 8-36. *Web browser displays graphs after making selection and clicking the Run button*

We can use _ODSDEST to produce output in various formats, rather than the default HTML format. We could add a drop-down for _ODSDEST to our web page. You can use the HTML select tag to make this as shown in Figure 8-37. Then, we could run it and select RTF, for example (see Listing 8-6). That would call the Stored Process passing _ODSDEST=RTF to it.

Listing 8-6. HTML to create a drop-down menu to select an ODS destination

```
<select name="_odsdest">
<option value="html">html</option>
<option value="pdf">pdf</option>
<option value="csv">csv</option>
<option value="rtf">rtf</option>
</select>
```

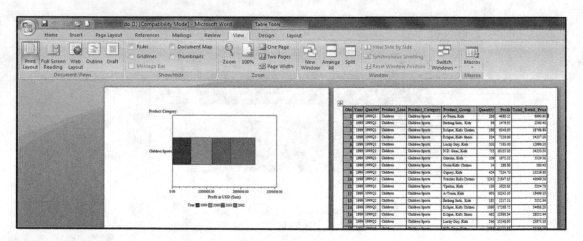

Figure 8-37. *Browser now shows the ODS destination drop-down menu*

This makes an RTF file for us which we can open in Microsoft Word (Figure 8-38).

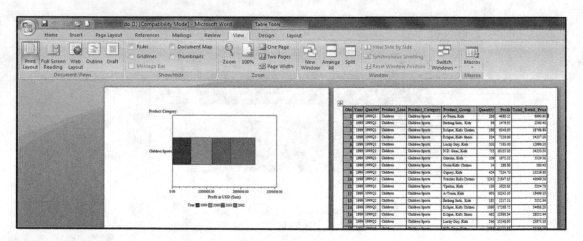

Figure 8-38. *Choosing RTF from the drop-down and pressing Run button generates report seen here in Microsoft Word*

Remember that this is a simple example where we are not handling headers in an ideal way.

We can enhance our web app again using _ODSSTYLE to choose different ODS styles which control colors, fonts, and so on. So, we can add a drop-down with a select tag for _ODSSTYLE as shown in Listing 8-7.

Listing 8-7. HTML to create drop-down menu for choosing an ODS style

```
<select name="_odsstyle">
<option value="meadow">meadow</option>
<option value="seaside">seaside</option>
<option value="statistical">statistical</option>
</select>
```

Then if we select seaside and run it, then it will produce output using that style. This is because it will have passed _ODSSTYLE=SEASIDE to the Stored Process. Running it and selecting statistical will produce output using that style (Figure 8-39).

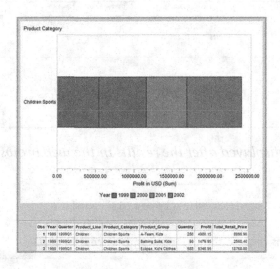

Figure 8-39. *Output using _ODSSTYLE=SEASIDE*

We can further enhance our web app by using the _debug parameter to get various debug information. So we add check boxes for each debug option, since there are several that can be specified concurrently, such as log and time, as shown in Listing 8-8 and Figure 8-40.

Listing 8-8. HTML to add two check boxes

```
<input type="checkbox" name="_debug" value="log">Show log<nbsp>
<input type="checkbox" name="_debug" value="time">Show time taken
```

Pick a report to run

Children ▾ | html ▾ | meadow ▾ | ☑ Show log
☑ Show time taken
[Run]

Figure 8-40. *Check boxes being displayed for choosing to show log and time taken*

Now if we select the check boxes, it will pass parameters for those selected, for example, &_debug=log&_debug=time. This will let us see the log (Figure 8-41) and time it took for the Stored Process to run (Figure 8-42).

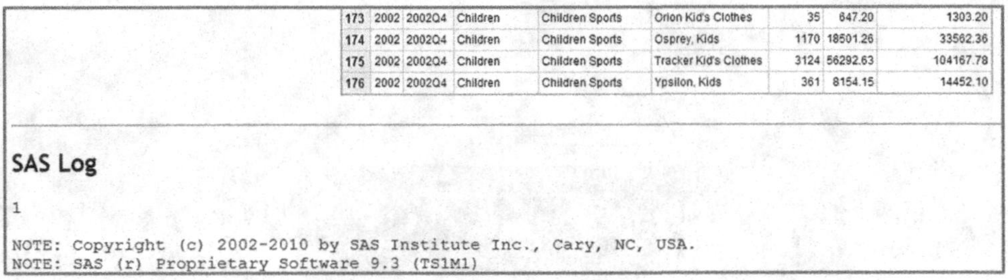

173	2002	2002Q4	Children	Children Sports	Orion Kid's Clothes	35	647.20	1303.20
174	2002	2002Q4	Children	Children Sports	Osprey, Kids	1170	18501.26	33562.36
175	2002	2002Q4	Children	Children Sports	Tracker Kid's Clothes	3124	56292.63	104167.78
176	2002	2002Q4	Children	Children Sports	Ypsilon, Kids	361	8154.15	14452.10

SAS Log

```
1

NOTE: Copyright (c) 2002-2010 by SAS Institute Inc., Cary, NC, USA.
NOTE: SAS (r) Proprietary Software 9.3 (TS1M1)
```

Figure 8-41. *Log is displayed after the results in the web browser*

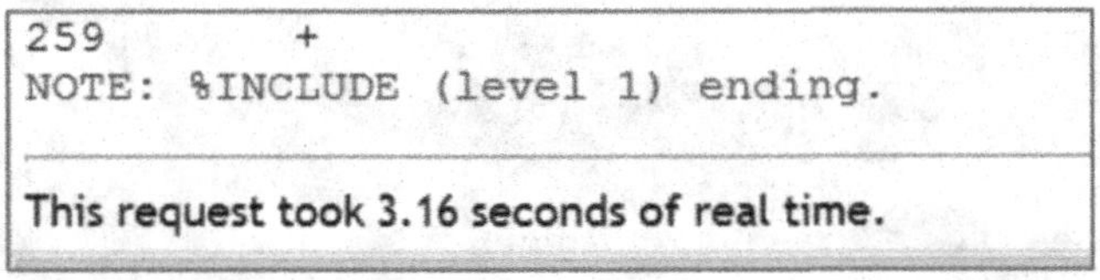

```
259       +
NOTE: %INCLUDE (level 1) ending.
```
This request took 3.16 seconds of real time.

Figure 8-42. *Time taken appears after the results and log in web browser*

It's interesting to look at the URL that has been generated by our web app to run this. It is

http://my-sas-server/SASStoredProcess/do?_program=%2FShared+Data%2FSAS
Testing%2FTest3&product_line=Children&_ODSDEST=HTML&_ODSSTYLE=meadow&_
debug=log&_debug=time

You can break this URL up into sections to understand what the HTML has generated:

http://**your-server**/SASStoredProcess/**do?**
_program=%2FShared+Data%2FSASTesting%2FTest3

```
&product_line=Children
&_ODSDEST=HTML
&_ODSSTYLE=meadow
&_Debug=log
&_debug=time
```

An interesting thing we can see from the log of the Stored Process is that there are various macro variables which could be used to reconstruct the URL of the Stored Process call, such as _program, _srvname, _srvport, and _url (see Figure 8-43). These macro variables are generated when calling a stored process using the Stored Process Web Application. You won't see them if you just run a stored process in Enterprise Guide though.

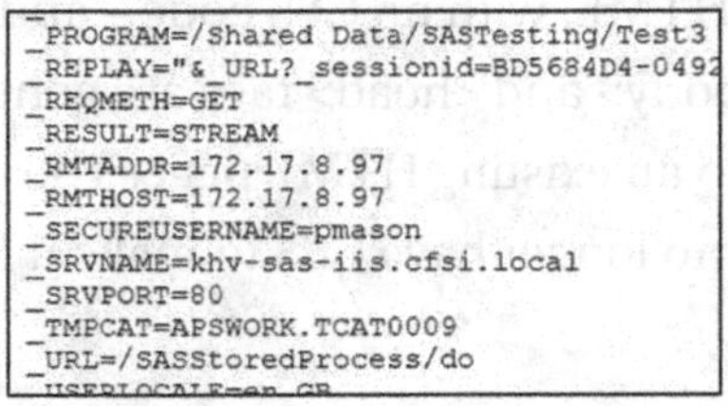

```
_PROGRAM=/Shared Data/SASTesting/Test3
_REPLAY="&_URL?_sessionid=BD5684D4-0492
_REQMETH=GET
_RESULT=STREAM
_RMTADDR=172.17.8.97
_RMTHOST=172.17.8.97
_SECUREUSERNAME=pmason
_SRVNAME=khv-sas-iis.cfsi.local
_SRVPORT=80
_TMPCAT=APSWORK.TCAT0009
_URL=/SASStoredProcess/do
_USERLOCALE=en_GB
```

Figure 8-43. *Automatic macro variables we can see in the log in web browser*

Using these automatically generated macro variables, we can change the hard-coded URL in the Stored Process to use them. This will mean that if the Stored Process name changes or the Stored Process is moved to another place in the metadata, then it will still work as expected. So

```
http://your-server/SASStoredProcess/do?
```

would become

```
http://&_srvname.:&_srvport/&_url.?
```

We should always do this when possible as it is best practice. The reason is that we can then move the Stored Process to other places, and it will still work. Or other things could potentially change such as the name of our server, and the code would still work as it is without need for modification (see Listing 8-9).

Listing 8-9. Rewriting the action to use macro variables

```
<form method="get" action="http://&_srvname:&_srvport/&_url?"
target="content">
```

When the Stored Process runs, the resolve function will resolve these macro variables. So, looking at the HTML code that the Stored Process has generated, we can see how it has substituted the right values to create the HTML.

Another very useful parameter which we can pass to the Stored Process Web Application is _RESULT. It can be used to determine how complex your HTML generated will be. For instance, using _RESULT=stream (which is the default) for our current example, we would generate 3998 lines of HTML, including almost 2000 lines of CSS code. This is quite a lot for a quite simple report. Using _RESULT=STREAMFRAGMENT would generate 1989 lines of HTML, with no CSS code – and the lines are shorter as they don't use the CSS. Also, no <body> and <head> tags are generated which makes it easier to insert generated HTML into an existing HTML page. The downside is that your results won't look as good since you no longer have CSS to make it look nice.

Uploading Files with a Stored Process

You can use the SAS Stored Process Web Application to upload files for use with a Stored Process. This is done by using a custom input form which specifies a field on an HTML form with a type of file. For instance, the following HTML would achieve this:

```
<input name='order_file' type='file'>
```

You would be prompted to enter or browse for the file you want to upload, and when the form is submitted, then the file would be uploaded to the server that your Stored Process is running on. You also get a collection of macro variables populated, so that in your Stored Process code, you will be able to know where the file has been put in order for you to use it.

The file is put into a temporary location when uploaded, and it is only available for the life of the Stored Process. So, if you want to keep it permanently, then you need to copy it to a permanent location from your Stored Process. Although, you might want to process it in some way and then save the processed information. For example, you might upload a CSV file, read it into SAS to produce a SAS table, and then save that table permanently.

You can upload any number of files at one time; you just need an input field for each of the files to be uploaded. You get useful macro variables that give you all the information you need to handle many files. The reserved SAS macro variables that are associated with uploading files all start with **_WEBIN_**. For instance, _webin_file_count tells you how many files were uploaded.

The macro variables involved in the upload process are as follows:

_WEBIN_CONTENT_LENGTH specifies the length, in bytes, of the file that was uploaded.

_WEBIN_CONTENT_TYPE specifies the content type that is associated with the file.

_WEBIN_FILE_COUNT specifies the number of files that were uploaded. If no files were uploaded, then the value of this variable is set to zero.

_WEBIN_FILEEXT specifies the extension of the file that was uploaded.

_WEBIN_FILENAME specifies the original location of the file.

_WEBIN_FILEREF specifies the SAS `fileref` that is automatically assigned to the uploaded file. You can use this `fileref` to access the file. The uploaded file is stored in a temporary location on the Stored Process server or workspace server and is deleted when the request is completed. Be sure to copy the file to a permanent location if you need to access it at a later date.

_WEBIN_NAME specifies the value that is specified in the NAME attribute of the INPUT tag.

_WEBIN_SASNAME specifies a unique name for the SAS table, view, or catalog that was uploaded. A value is set for this macro variable only if a SAS table, view, or catalog was uploaded. All SAS data types are stored in the Work library. The type of SAS file that was uploaded is stored in the _WEBIN_SASTYPE macro variable. See also _WEBIN_SASNAME_ORI.

_WEBIN_SASNAME_ORI specifies the original name of the SAS table, view, or catalog that was uploaded. If a SAS table named **mydata.sas7bdat** was uploaded, then _WEBIN_SASNAME_ORI contains the value **mydata**. A value is set for this macro variable only if a SAS table, view, or catalog was uploaded. All SAS data types are stored in the Work library. The type of SAS file that was uploaded is stored in the _WEBIN_SASTYPE macro variable. See also _WEBIN_SASNAME.

_WEBIN_SASTYPE specifies the type of SAS file that was uploaded: DATA for SAS tables, VIEW for SAS views, and CATALOG for SAS catalogs. A value is set for this macro variable only if a SAS table, view, or catalog was uploaded. The name of the uploaded file is stored in the _WEBIN_SASNAME macro variable.

_WEBIN_STREAM specifies the name of the data source that was used to upload the file.

_WEBIN_STREAM_COUNT specifies the number of files that were uploaded. If no files were uploaded, then the value of this variable is set to zero.

If you are uploading more than one file, then unique macro variables are created for each file. This applies to all of the previous reserved macro variables, except _WEBIN_FILE_COUNT and _WEBIN_STREAM_COUNT.

Note   For z/OS, the SAS server must be invoked with the FILESYSTEM=HFS option in order to be able to upload SAS file types.

One last thing is that when uploading a file, you need to specify **enctype="multipart/form-data"** on the FORM tag, for example:

```
<form action="http://your.server.name:8080/SASStoredProcess/do"
method="post" enctype="multipart/form-data">
```

Example: Uploading Three Files

The following code prompts for three files to upload and then calls the Stored Process **upload** which takes care of uploading those files. If you are going to try any of this HTML code out, it is best to have a good text editor to do it such as Notepad++, which is one of the best free editors there is. It will highlight the syntax you use and has powerful find/replace features and many other things.

```
<HTML>
<form method="post" action="http://d351tq92/SASStoredProcess/do?"
enctype="multipart/form-data">
①   <input type="hidden" name="_program" value="/User Folders/phil/My
Folder/upload">
Enter CSV to upload and import <input name="file1" type="file"><p>
Enter CSV to upload and import <input name="file2" type="file"><p>
Enter CSV to upload and import <input name="file3" type="file"><p>
Show this many rows <input name="obs" type="text" value="10"><p>
Debug options <input name='_debug' type='text'><p>
<input type="submit" value="Run">
</form>
</HTML>
```

This displays the following web page (Figure 8-44).

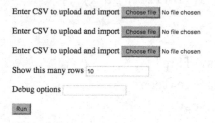

Figure 8-44. *Web browser displays menu produced by HTML*

On entering some files to upload, the Stored Process (code as follows) is called. First, this shows the values of the parameters passed in to do with the upload. These all start with _WEBIN. The Stored Process takes care of uploading the CSV files, imports them, and shows the first ten rows of each one. You can call it anything you like, but you must point to the stored process where you specify the value of _program in the HTML (shown

249

in the previous code marked by ①). The SAS code for the stored process is shown as follows. And the other settings in the stored process can be defaults.

```
* display values of the _webin macro variables passed in ;
proc sql ;
    select * from dictionary.macros
    where name like '_WEBIN_%' ;
quit ;

filename temp temp ;
%macro read_loop ;
    %if &_webin_file_count=1 %then %do ;
        %let _webin_fileref1=&_webin_fileref ;
        %let _webin_filename1=&_webin_filename ;
        %end ;
    %do i=1 %to &_webin_file_count ;
        %let csv_file=%sysfunc(pathname(&&_webin_fileref&i));
        %put &=csv_file ;
        * fix the end of line character for Proc Import ;
        data _null_ ;
            infile "&csv_file" sharebuffers termstr=cr ;
            file temp  termstr=crlf  ;
            input ;
            line=compress(_infile_,'1a'x) ;
            put line ;
        run ;
        filename in "&csv_file"  ;
        proc import datafile=temp
                    dbms=csv
                    replace
                    out=file&i ;
            getnames=yes ;
        run ;
        %let dsid=%sysfunc(open(file&i)) ;
        title "%sysfunc(attrn(&dsid,nobs),comma12.) rows imported from CSV
        file: &&_webin_filename&i" ;
```

```
        %let dsid=%sysfunc(close(&dsid)) ;
        title2 "Table produced: file&i" ;
        proc print data=file&i(obs=&obs) ;
        run ;
        %end ;
%mend read_loop ;
%read_loop
```

Figures 8-45 and 8-46 show what is displayed after uploading some files.

Macro Scope	Macro Variable Name	Offset into Macro Variable	Macro Variable Value
GLOBAL	_WEBIN_CONTENT_LENGTH	0	170351
GLOBAL	_WEBIN_CONTENT_LENGTH0	0	3
GLOBAL	_WEBIN_CONTENT_LENGTH1	0	170351
GLOBAL	_WEBIN_CONTENT_LENGTH2	0	40419
GLOBAL	_WEBIN_CONTENT_LENGTH3	0	549
GLOBAL	_WEBIN_CONTENT_LENGTH_COUNT	0	3
GLOBAL	_WEBIN_CONTENT_TYPE	0	text/csv
GLOBAL	_WEBIN_CONTENT_TYPE0	0	3
GLOBAL	_WEBIN_CONTENT_TYPE1	0	text/csv
GLOBAL	_WEBIN_CONTENT_TYPE2	0	text/csv
GLOBAL	_WEBIN_CONTENT_TYPE3	0	text/csv
GLOBAL	_WEBIN_CONTENT_TYPE_COUNT	0	3
GLOBAL	_WEBIN_FILEEXT	0	csv
GLOBAL	_WEBIN_FILEEXT0	0	3
GLOBAL	_WEBIN_FILEEXT1	0	csv
GLOBAL	_WEBIN_FILEEXT2	0	csv
GLOBAL	_WEBIN_FILEEXT3	0	csv
GLOBAL	_WEBIN_FILENAME	0	API_SP.POP.TOTL_DS2_en_csv_v2.csv
GLOBAL	_WEBIN_FILENAME0	0	3
GLOBAL	_WEBIN_FILENAME1	0	API_SP.POP.TOTL_DS2_en_csv_v2.csv
GLOBAL	_WEBIN_FILENAME2	0	Metadata_Country_API_SP.POP.TOTL_DS2_en_csv_v2.csv
GLOBAL	_WEBIN_FILENAME3	0	Metadata_Indicator_API_SP.POP.TOTL_DS2_en_csv_v2.csv
GLOBAL	_WEBIN_FILENAME_COUNT	0	3
GLOBAL	_WEBIN_FILEREF	0	#LN01070
GLOBAL	_WEBIN_FILEREF0	0	3
GLOBAL	_WEBIN_FILEREF1	0	#LN01070
GLOBAL	_WEBIN_FILEREF2	0	#LN01072
GLOBAL	_WEBIN_FILEREF3	0	#LN01074
GLOBAL	_WEBIN_FILE_COUNT	0	3
GLOBAL	_WEBIN_NAME	0	file1
GLOBAL	_WEBIN_NAME0	0	3
GLOBAL	_WEBIN_NAME1	0	file1
GLOBAL	_WEBIN_NAME2	0	file2
GLOBAL	_WEBIN_NAME3	0	file3
GLOBAL	_WEBIN_NAME_COUNT	0	0
GLOBAL	_WEBIN_STREAM	0	_in1
GLOBAL	_WEBIN_STREAM0	0	3
GLOBAL	_WEBIN_STREAM1	0	_in1
GLOBAL	_WEBIN_STREAM2	0	_in2
GLOBAL	_WEBIN_STREAM3	0	_in3
GLOBAL	_WEBIN_STREAM_COUNT	0	3

Figure 8-45. *Macro variables and values related to file upload*

528 rows imported from CSV file: Metadata_Country_API_SP.POP.TOTL_DS2_en_csv_v2.csv
Table produced: file1

Obs	Country_Code	Region	IncomeGroup	SpecialNotes	TableName	VAR6
1						
2	ABW	Latin America & Caribbean	High income	SNA data for 2000-2011 are updated from official government statistics; 1994-1999 from UN databases. Base year has changed from 1995 to 2000.	Aruba	
3						
4	AFG	South Asia	Low income	Fiscal year end: March 20; reporting period for national accounts data is calendar year, estimated to insure consistency between national accounts and fiscal data. National accounts data are sourced from the IMF and differ from the Central Statistics Organization numbers due to exclusion of the opium economy.	Afghanistan	
5						
6	AGO	Sub-Saharan Africa	Lower middle income		Angola	
7						
8	ALB	Europe & Central Asia	Upper middle income		Albania	
9						
10	AND	Europe & Central Asia	High income	WB-3 code changed from ADO to AND to align with ISO code.	Andorra	

538 rows imported from CSV file: API_SP.POP.TOTL_DS2_en_csv_v2.csv
Table produced: file2

Obs	Data_Source	World_Development_Indicators	VAR3	VAR4	VAR5	VAR6	VAR7	VAR8	VAR9	VAR10	VAR11	VAR12	VAR13	VAR14	VAR15	VAR16	VAR17	VAR18	VAR19
1																			
2																			
3																			
4	Last Updated Date	2017-10-30																	
5																			
6																			
7																			
8	Country Name	Country Code	Indicator Name	Indicator Code	1960	1961	1962	1963	1964	1965	1966	1967	1968	1969	1970	1971	1972	1973	1974
9																			
10	Aruba	ABW	Population, total	SP.POP.TOTL	54211	55438	56225	56695	57032	57360	57715	58055	58386	58726	59063	59440	59840	60243	60528

4 rows imported from CSV file: Metadata_Indicator_API_SP.POP.TOTL_DS2_en_csv_v2.csv
Table produced: file3

Obs	INDICATOR_CODE	INDICATOR_NAME	SOURCE_NOTE	SOURCE_ORGANIZATION	VAR5
1					
2	SP.POP.TOTL	Population, total	Total population is based on the de facto definition of population, which counts all residents regardless of legal status or citizenship. The values shown are midyear estimates.	(1) United Nations Population Division. World Population Prospects, (2) Census reports and other statistical publications from national statistical offices, (3) Eurostat: Demographic Statistics, (4) United Nations Statistical Division. Population and Vita	
3					
4					

Figure 8-46. *Listings of data to browser from SAS code in stored process*

Passing Multiple Parameters of the Same Name

Often when you are making selections from a list of values in HTML, you will have the option choosing multiple values. As we know, parameters are passed on to the URL as name/value pairs. In the following Stored Process shown in Listing 8-10, we have a select list called "pick" and have specified that the user can make multiple selections.

Listing 8-10. SAS code to create HTML menu

```
%macro logic ;
%if %symexist(pick) %then %do ;
    %put _global_ ;
    %end ;
%else %do ;
    data _null_ ;
        set menu ;
        file _webout ;
        put line ;
    run ;
    %end ;
%mend logic ;
data menu ;
    input ;
    line=_infile_ ;
    datalines ;
    <html>
    <form action="http://d351tq92/SASStoredProcess/do?">
    <input name="_program" value="/User Folders/phil/My Folder/test13"
    type="hidden">
    <select name="pick" multiple>
    <option value="A">A</option>
    <option value="B">B</option>
    <option value="C">C</option>
    </select>
    <input type="submit">
    </form>
    </html>
    ;;
run ;
%logic
```

When this is run, we can make multiple selections and then press Submit
(Figure 8-47).

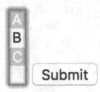

Figure 8-47. *HTML menu displayed in web browser allowing multiple selections*

Looking at the URL in Figure 8-48, you can see how it was constructed and the two selections that were passed from the form to the Stored Process.

ⓘ **d351tq92**/SASStoredProcess/do?_program=%2FUser+Folders%2Fphil%2FMy+Folder%2Ftest13&pick=A&pick=C

Figure 8-48. *URL generated when Submit button is pressed in web browser*

After this has run, we can look at the SAS log to see the macro variables defined. We see that our selection resulted in creating five macro variables:

&pick is the first value that was selected.

&pick0 shows how many selections were made.

&pick1 shows the first value selected.

&pick2 shows the second value selected.

&pick_count also shows how many selections were made.

```
·>> SAS Macro Variables:

PICK=A
PICK0=2
PICK1=A
PICK2=C
PICK_COUNT=2
```

Figure 8-49. *Macro variables available to stored process code*

It's easy to make a macro to construct a macro variable for use with an IN operator, for instance, you could simply assign a macro variable like this:

```
%let picks="a","b" ;
```

The following code shows an example where we use the SAS macro variables that are created when passing multiple values in with a form to a Stored Process. We can use a macro program to automatically create a list of quoted values separated by commas which can then be used in a where clause:

```
data sample ;
   input key $ 1 ;
   cards ;
A
B
C
D
E
;;
run ;

%let pick0=2;
%let pick1=A;
%let pick2=C;
%let pick_count=2;
%macro make_where_clause(var) ;
   %do i=1 %to &pick_count ;
      "&&pick&i"
      %if &i ne &pick_count %then , ;
   %end ;
%mend make_where_clause ;

proc print ;
   where key in (%make_where_clause(pick)) ;
run ;
```

The SAS log for this shows the where clause that was created and used:

```
161   options nosymbolgen nomlogic nomprint ;
162   data sample ;
163      input key $ 1 ;
164      cards ;

NOTE: The data set WORK.SAMPLE has 5 observations and 1 variables.
NOTE: DATA statement used (Total process time):
      real time           0.00 seconds
      cpu time            0.01 seconds
```

```
170  ;;
171  run ;
172
173  %let pick0=2;
174  %let pick1=A;
175  %let pick2=C;
176  %let pick_count=2;
177  %macro make_where_clause(var) ;
178      %do i=1 %to &pick_count ;
179          "&&pick&i"
180          %if &i ne &pick_count %then , ;
181      %end ;
182  %mend make_where_clause ;
183
184  proc print ;
NOTE: Writing HTML Body file: sasHTML1.htm
185      where key in (%make_where_clause(pick)) ;
186  run ;

NOTE: There were 2 observations read from the data set WORK.SAMPLE.
      WHERE key in ('A', 'C');
NOTE: PROCEDURE PRINT used (Total process time):
      real time            0.51 seconds
      cpu time             0.32 seconds
```

How to Use Sessions

The Web is a stateless environment, which means that when you open a page, the next page starts with a clean slate having nothing remaining from the previous one. This simplifies many things and makes them potentially more stable. If you are building web applications, then you need to maintain the state of some things between one request and the next. You can use cookies to store some text and retrieve it again, as many web applications do. But another way to maintain state is to use SAS sessions.

Sessions enable storing macro variable values which start their name with "SAVE_". They also save tables and catalogs stored in the SAVE library. This means that you are able to pass macro variables, tables, and so on from one Stored Process to another. The data stored in a session generally expires after 15 minutes, but this is long enough to be quite useful when developing applications constructed from a number of Stored Processes which need to pass information between each other. You can increase the session timeout from 15 minutes to a higher value by using the stpsrvset function, for example:

```
%LET rc=%sysfunc(stpsrvset(session timeout,1800));
```

To use a session, you have to create one in the Stored Process. You can use some code like this to create a session:

```
%let rc=%sysfunc(stpsrv_session(create));
```

The following Stored Process code creates a session using the stpsrv_session function. Then it creates a macro variable starting with "save_" and puts a table into the save library. These will then both be available when used through another Stored Process that is started up using the sessionid. It creates a little piece of HTML that will call another Stored Process using the same sessionid, making the macro variable and table available to it:

```
* here is some code with macro variable and table I want to save ;
%let name=Phil Mason ;
data x ;
    set sashelp.class ;
run ;

%* create a session, so we can save macro/table for later ;
%let rc=%sysfunc(stpsrv_session(create));
%put _SESSIONID=&_SESSIONID;
%put _THISSESSION=&_THISSESSION;

%* save them to session ;
%let save_name=&name ;
data save.x ;
    set x ;
run ;

* make HTML to link to another Stored Process where we will use session
data ;
 data _null;
```

```
file _webout;
put '<HTML>';
put '<body>';
put '<h1>test use of sessions</h1>';
put '<a href="' "&_thissession"
    '&_program=/User Folders/phil/My Folder/use session">Call next Stored
  Process</a>';
put '</body>';
put '</HTML>';
run;
```

Running this Stored Process through the web application displays the following (Figure 8-50).

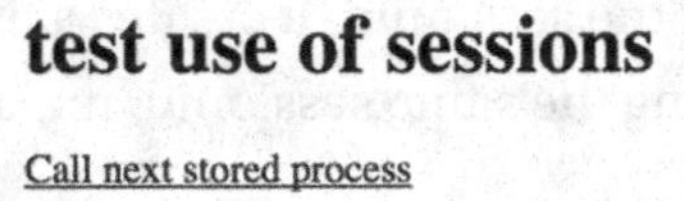

test use of sessions

Call next stored process

Figure 8-50. *Web browser displays this from the previous Stored Process*

The following code is for the Stored Process ("use session") which the previous code will call when the link is clicked. It uses the saved macro in a title and prints out the saved table.

```
title 'Table x, created in previous Stored Process' ;
title "Macro variable from previous Stored Process - &save_name" ;
proc print data=save.x ;
run ;
```

The output produced by this Stored Process is shown in Figure 8-51.

Macro variable from previous stored process - Phil Mason

Obs	Name	Sex	Age	Height	Weight
1	Alfred	M	14	69.0	112.5
2	Alice	F	13	56.5	84.0
3	Barbara	F	13	65.3	98.0
4	Carol	F	14	62.8	102.5
5	Henry	M	14	63.5	102.5
6	James	M	12	57.3	83.0
7	Jane	F	12	59.8	84.5
8	Janet	F	15	62.5	112.5
9	Jeffrey	M	13	62.5	84.0
10	John	M	12	59.0	99.5
11	Joyce	F	11	51.3	50.5
12	Judy	F	14	64.3	90.0
13	Louise	F	12	56.3	77.0
14	Mary	F	15	66.5	112.0
15	Philip	M	16	72.0	150.0
16	Robert	M	12	64.8	128.0
17	Ronald	M	15	67.0	133.0
18	Thomas	M	11	57.5	85.0
19	William	M	15	66.5	112.0

Figure 8-51. *Web browser showing macro variable from previous session in title*

If you wait too long and the session expires, then the saved macro variables and tables are discarded. You will then get this message displayed in Figure 8-52.

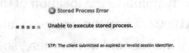

Figure 8-52. *Stored process error when session has expired*

Sessions with Graphs

When you create a graph in a Stored Process through the Stored Process Web Application, it creates a session and stores the graph image in a catalog within that session. Here is some SAS code I used to create a graph:

```
Proc gchart data=sashelp.class ;
  Vbar sex / group=age ;
Run ;
```

Running this through the Stored Process Web Application shows this image on the web page (Figure 8-53).

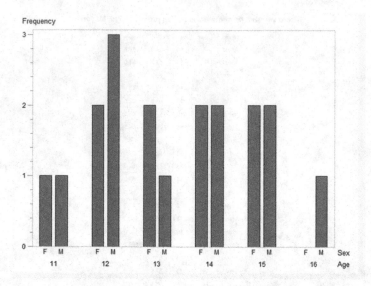

Figure 8-53. *Displaying a graph in browser with stored process*

If I view the source for the page, I can see the HTML tag that displays the graph. I have highlighted the session id ⓪ which is used to point to the session in which the created image is stored. The _program value is replay ① which is used to display the image on the web page. The value of _entry points to the location of the actual image, which is in a catalog called APSWORK.TCAT0002 ②, and the image is called gchart.png ②. Note: I have inserted line feeds in the URL which should not be there, so that it is more easily read.

```
<img alt="Bar chart of Sex" src="/SASStoredProcess/do?
_sessionid=57B00B1A-E808-44C5-AB98-D454D16988F9      ⓪
&_program=replay                                     ①
&_entry=APSWORK.TCAT0002.gchart.png"                 ②
style=" border-width: 0px; height: 480px; width: 640px;" border="0"
usemap="#LN00102" class="c graph">
```

You can read all about sessions and how to use them in the SAS documentation.[9]

---

[9]SAS Stored Processes – Sessions – http://support.sas.com/rnd/itech/doc9/dev_guide/
  stprocess/sessions.HTML

Logs That Record Information About Stored Processes

There are many logs recorded for various programs within SAS. When using Stored Processes, the most interesting ones are as follows.

Stored Process Server Logs

These store a copy of the SAS logs from any Stored Processes that run on the Stored Process servers. There will be a separate log for each Stored Process server, so if you have the standard three defined, you will have three logs. On my system, this is located in C:\SAS\Config\Lev1\SASApp\StoredProcessServer\Logs. Here are some sample lines from a log:

```
Host: 'D351TQ92', OS: 'WIN', Release: '6.2', SAS Version: '9.04.01M3P06242015',
Command: '"C:\Program Files\SASHome\SASFoundation\9.4\sas.exe" -config
"C:\SAS\Config\Lev1\SASApp\StoredProcessServer\sasv9.cfg" /nologo /noterminal
/noxcmd /netencryptalgorithm SASProprietary /metaserver d351tq92 /metaport
8561 /metarepository Foundation /objectserver /objectserverparms "protocol=
bridge spawned spp=49263 cid=41 dnsmatch=d351tq92 pb classfactory=15931E31-
667F-11D5-8804-00C04F35AC8C server=OMSOBJ:SERVERCOMPONENT/A5GU5YZJ.AY000008
cel=credentials lb multiuser port=8611 saslangrunas=client"'
Log continued from C:\SAS\Config\Lev1\SASApp\StoredProcessServer\Logs\
SASApp_STPServer_2016-01-29_D351TQ92_18056.log
2016-01-31T15:52:09,183 INFO  [00017309] :Administrator@D351TQ92 - New out
call client connection (41) for user phil@D351TQ92.  Encryption level is
Credentials using encryption algorithm SASPROPRIETARY.  Peer IP address and
port are [fe80::7d53:808:9a3c:a7b1%12]:8561.
2016-01-31T15:52:09,184 INFO  [00017309] :phil@D351TQ92 - New client
connection (40) accepted from server port 8611 for SAS token user
phil@D351TQ92.  Encryption level is Credentials using encryption algorithm
SASPROPRIETARY.  Peer IP address and port are [::ffff:192.168.0.48]:49476
for APPNAME=Stored Process Web App 9.4.
2016-01-31T15:52:09,186 INFO  [00017317] 40:phil@D351TQ92 - STP: 27:
Creating New Context, sessionID=
```

```
2016-01-31T15:52:09,233 INFO  [00017317] 40:phil@D351TQ92 - STP: Sending
cost=101 to Load Balancer. Context Cost=100 STP Session Cost=1
2016-01-31T15:52:09,299 INFO  [00017407] 40:phil@D351TQ92 - STP: 27:
Executing Client Source code from Metadata for /User Folders/phil/
My Folder/proc_stream
2016-01-31T15:52:09,299 INFO  [00000003] :Administrator@D351TQ92 -
[00000027] STPXUTL Execute using SAS stmts directly.
2016-01-31T15:52:09,635 INFO  [00017407] 40:phil@D351TQ92 - STP: 27:
Execution Complete.  Status=0
2016-01-31T15:52:09,637 ERROR [00017407] 40:phil@D351TQ92 - STP: 27:
Fileref Deassign Failure for _WEBOUT
2016-01-31T15:52:09,639 INFO  [00017650] 40:phil@D351TQ92 - STP: 27:
Context Close
2016-01-31T15:52:09,656 INFO  [00017650] 40:phil@D351TQ92 - STP: Sending
cost=0 to Load Balancer. Context Cost=0 STP Session Cost=0
```

Workspace Server Logs

These store a copy of the SAS logs from any Stored Processes that run on the workspace servers. It also stores logs from any other clients that use workspace servers such as the Office Add-in, Enterprise Guide, Data Integration Studio, and so on.

Pooled Workspace Server Logs

These store a copy of SAS logs from any Stored Processes that run on the Stored Process servers. It also stores logs from any other clients that use pooled workspace servers. On my system, logs are stored here: C:\SAS\Config\Lev1\SASApp\PooledWorkspaceServer\Logs. Here's a sample of some lines from a log:

```
Host: 'D351TQ92', OS: 'WIN', Release: '6.2', SAS Version:
'9.04.01M4P11092016', Command: '"C:\Program Files\SASHome\
SASFoundation\9.4\sas.exe" -config "C:\SAS\Config\Lev1\SASApp\
PooledWorkspaceServer\sasv9.cfg" /nologo /noterminal /noxcmd /
netencryptalgorithm SASProprietary /metaserver d351tq92 /metaport 8561 /
metarepository Foundation /objectserver /objectserverparms "protocol=bridge
spawned spp=49286 cid=14 dnsmatch=d351tq92 pb classfactory=620963ee-32bf-
```

4128-bf5f-4b0df8ff90eb server=OMSOBJ:SERVERCOMPONENT/A5GU5YZJ.AY000007 cel=credentials lb sspool saslangrunas=client"'
2017-11-02T09:43:02,620 INFO [00000003] :Administrator@D351TQ92 - NOTE: Unable to open SASUSER.PROFILE. WORK.PROFILE will be opened instead.
2017-11-02T09:43:02,620 INFO [00000003] :Administrator@D351TQ92 - NOTE: All profile changes will be lost at the end of the session.
2017-11-02T09:43:02,620 INFO [00000003] :Administrator@D351TQ92 -
2017-11-02T09:43:02,689 INFO [00000007] :Administrator@D351TQ92 - Server is executing on host D351TQ92 (fe80::7d53:808:9a3c:a7b1%12).
2017-11-02T09:43:02,689 INFO [00000007] :Administrator@D351TQ92 - Also known as:
2017-11-02T09:43:02,689 INFO [00000007] :Administrator@D351TQ92 - localhost
2017-11-02T09:43:02,689 INFO [00000007] :Administrator@D351TQ92 - fe80::7d53:808:9a3c:a7b1%12
2017-11-02T09:43:02,689 INFO [00000007] :Administrator@D351TQ92 - 192.168.0.46
2017-11-02T09:43:02,689 INFO [00000007] :Administrator@D351TQ92 - ::1
2017-11-02T09:43:02,689 INFO [00000007] :Administrator@D351TQ92 - 127.0.0.1
2017-11-02T09:43:02,694 INFO [00000007] :Administrator@D351TQ92 - New out call client connection (1) for user Administrator@D351TQ92. Encryption level is Credentials using encryption algorithm SASPROPRIETARY. Peer IP address and port are [fe80::7d53:808:9a3c:a7b1%12]:8561.
2017-11-02T09:43:02,760 INFO [00000010] :Administrator@D351TQ92 - NOTE: Libref SASDATA successfully assigned from logical server.
2017-11-02T09:43:02,760 INFO [00000010] :Administrator@D351TQ92 - NOTE: Libref WRSDIST successfully assigned from logical server.
2017-11-02T09:43:02,760 INFO [00000010] :Administrator@D351TQ92 - NOTE: Libref WRSTEMP successfully assigned from logical server.
2017-11-02T09:43:02,760 INFO [00000010] :Administrator@D351TQ92 - NOTE: Libref STPSAMP successfully assigned from logical server.
2017-11-02T09:43:02,770 INFO [00000009] :Administrator@D351TQ92 -

2017-11-02T09:43:02,770 INFO [00000009] :Administrator@D351TQ92 -
NOTE: AUTOEXEC processing beginning; file is C:\SAS\Config\Lev1\SASApp\
PooledWorkspaceServer\autoexec.sas.
2017-11-02T09:43:02,770 INFO [00000009] :Administrator@D351TQ92 -
2017-11-02T09:43:02,771 INFO [00000009] :Administrator@D351TQ92 -
2017-11-02T09:43:02,771 INFO [00000009] :Administrator@D351TQ92 - NOTE:
AUTOEXEC processing completed.
2017-11-02T09:43:02,771 INFO [00000009] :Administrator@D351TQ92 -
2017-11-02T09:43:02,777 INFO [00000188] :Administrator@D351TQ92 - New
client connection (2) to the object spawner daemon. Peer IP address and
port are [fe80::7d53:808:9a3c:a7b1%12]:49286.
2017-11-02T09:43:02,783 INFO [00000197] 2:Administrator@D351TQ92 -
Reserved IPv6 port 8811 for server listen (connection 3).
2017-11-02T09:43:02,784 INFO [00000197] 2:Administrator@D351TQ92 -
Activated listen on IPv6 port 8811 (connection 3).
2017-11-02T09:43:02,788 INFO [00000203] :Administrator@D351TQ92 - New out
call client connection (5) for user phil@D351TQ92. Encryption level is
Credentials using encryption algorithm SASPROPRIETARY. Peer IP address and
port are [fe80::7d53:808:9a3c:a7b1%12]:8561.
2017-11-02T09:43:02,788 INFO [00000203] :phil@D351TQ92 - New client
connection (4) accepted from server port 8811 for SAS token user phil@
D351TQ92. Encryption level is Credentials using encryption algorithm
SASPROPRIETARY. Peer IP address and port are [::ffff:192.168.0.46]:58599
for APPNAME=Stored Process Web App 9.4.
2017-11-02T09:43:02,958 ERROR [00000011] :phil@D351TQ92 - ERROR: The SAS
system library SASHELP may not be reassigned.
2017-11-02T09:43:02,958 ERROR [00000011] :phil@D351TQ92 - ERROR: Error in
the LIBNAME statement.
2017-11-02T09:43:03,048 ERROR [00000011] :Administrator@D351TQ92 - ERROR:
Errors printed on page 1.

Metadata Server Logs

These keep a record of things that happen in the metadata server. In relation to Stored
Processes, you can look at when people authenticate to the system before running

a Stored Process. On my system, this is stored in C:\SAS\Config\Lev1\SASMeta\
MetadataServer\Logs. Here is a sample of a log:

```
017-11-15T18:26:33,100 INFO  [00057488] :sasevs@saspw - Redirect client in
cluster SASMeta - Logical Metadata Server (A5GU5YZJ.AW000001) to server
SASMeta - Metadata Server (A5GU5YZJ.AY000001) at d351tq92:8561.
2017-11-15T18:26:33,134 INFO  [00057516] 6042:SYSTEM@D351TQ92 - Client
connection 6042 for user sasevs@saspw closed.
2017-11-15T18:26:33,135 INFO  [00057479] 5996:SYSTEM@D351TQ92 - Client
connection 5996 for user sastrust@saspw closed.
2017-11-15T18:26:33,142 INFO  [00057519] :sastrust@saspw - New client
connection (5128) accepted from server port 8561 for user sastrust@
saspw. Encryption level is Credentials using encryption algorithm
SASPROPRIETARY. Peer IP address and port are [::ffff:192.168.0.55]:63626
for APPNAME=Web Infra Platform Identity Services 9.4.
2017-11-15T18:26:33,142 INFO  [00057519] :sastrust@saspw - Request made to
cluster SASMeta - Logical Metadata Server (A5GU5YZJ.AW000001).
2017-11-15T18:26:33,144 INFO  [00057519] :sastrust@saspw - Redirect client
in cluster SASMeta - Logical Metadata Server (A5GU5YZJ.AW000001) to server
SASMeta - Metadata Server (A5GU5YZJ.AY000001) at d351tq92:8561.
2017-11-15T18:26:33,146 INFO  [00057524] :sasevs@saspw - New client
connection (5962) accepted from server port 8561 for SAS token user
sasevs@saspw.  Encryption level is Credentials using encryption algorithm
SASPROPRIETARY.  Peer IP address and port are [::ffff:192.168.0.55]:63627
for APPNAME=Web Infra Platform Identity Services 9.4.
2017-11-15T18:26:33,146 INFO  [00057524] :sasevs@saspw - Request made to
cluster SASMeta - Logical Metadata Server (A5GU5YZJ.AW000001).
2017-11-15T18:26:33,146 INFO  [00057524] :sasevs@saspw - Redirect client
in cluster SASMeta - Logical Metadata Server (A5GU5YZJ.AW000001) to server
SASMeta - Metadata Server (A5GU5YZJ.AY000001) at d351tq92:8561.
2017-11-15T18:26:33,152 INFO  [00057535] 5128:SYSTEM@D351TQ92 - Client
connection 5128 for user sastrust@saspw closed.
2017-11-15T18:26:33,156 INFO  [00057539] 5962:SYSTEM@D351TQ92 - Client
connection 5962 for user sasevs@saspw closed.
```

Object Spawner Logs

These keep a record of things happening to the object spawner. The object spawner starts up Stored Process, workspace, and pooled workspace servers. On my system, the logs are located here:

```
Host: 'D351TQ92', OS: 'WIN', Release: '6.2', Command: '"C:\Program Files\
SASHome\SASFoundation\9.4\objspawn" -name "SAS [Config-Lev1] Object
Spawner"'
Log continued from C:\SAS\Config\Lev1\ObjectSpawner\Logs\
ObjectSpawner_2017-11-16_D351TQ92_8768.log
2017-11-17T00:00:00,097 INFO  [00035160] :SYSTEM@D351TQ92 - New out call
client connection (2942) for user sasevs@saspw.  Encryption level is
Credentials using encryption algorithm SASPROPRIETARY.  Peer IP address and
port are [fe80::7d53:808:9a3c:a7b1%12]:8561.
2017-11-17T00:00:00,100 INFO  [00035160] :SYSTEM@D351TQ92 - Client
connection 2942 for user sasevs@saspw closed.
2017-11-17T00:00:00,100 INFO  [00035160] :sasevs@saspw - New client
connection (2939) accepted from server port 8581 for user sasevs@
saspw. Encryption level is Credentials using encryption algorithm
SASPROPRIETARY. Peer IP address and port are [::ffff:192.168.0.55]:57843
for APPNAME=Environment Manager 904400.
2017-11-17T00:00:00,111 INFO  [00035183] 2939:SYSTEM@D351TQ92 - Client
connection 2939 for user sasevs@saspw closed.
```

Remember that most things in a SAS configuration can be customized, so you should make sure your server options are set so you get the log info written that you want.

Linking Stored Processes

In Chapter 4, we discussed the utility of JavaScript, JavaScript and JQuery libraries, and where to store them. One of the goals of this book is to help you see the utility of bringing this functionality to your Stored Processes. Now we will talk about how to implement them as part of your Stored Process Web Application.

Often as part of an application, you will want to run a Stored Process which will then run other Stored Processes for you. You can link Stored Processes together in a number of ways. You can use the window.open method mentioned in the previous section to enable a JavaScript program to open other pages, which can be Stored Processes if run via the Stored Process Web Application. Sometimes you might want to run a Stored Process when a web page opens, so that you can do some processing needed for that web page before it is used.

The best way I have found to do this is by using the body onload method. The following code would execute the alert before loading the rest of the web page:

```
<HTML>
<body onload="alert('hello')">
<h1>Hello World!</h1>
</body>
</HTML>
```

To run a Stored Process before loading the page, you could use something like this:

```
<HTML>
<body onload="window.open('http://d351tq92/SASStoredProcess/do?_program=%2F
User+Folders%2Fphil%2FMy+Folder%2FpreProcess')">
<h1>Pre-Processing has completed.</h1>
</body>
</HTML>
```

With JavaScript, you can detect all kinds of events in the page, on forms, and in drag and drop events, print events, mouse events, and many others. Any of those can be used to trigger the running of a Stored Process. Since a Stored Process can write any JavaScript code out, you can use logic from your SAS programs to decide when you need to link to another Stored Process and then write out the appropriate JavaScript code to do that. Easy.

Stored Process Example

The following Stored Process generates an input form that does client-side validation of an input field, by checking that the user has entered something for a table name. If the user doesn't enter something, then the JavaScript displays an alert and aborts the submit. When it passes the validation, then the same Stored Process is resubmitted, but it detects the presence of the table macro variable which indicates that this is the second call of the Stored Process with a table name being passed in. The server-side validates that the table exists, and if it doesn't, then it uses JavaScript to display an alert and then uses JavaScript to go back one page to display the original form again. If the table does exist, then it does a proc print of it.

All this functionality effectively results in a single-page application with some validation done in the browser by JavaScript and some done on the server by SAS. You don't need to enter any values for prompts as you create this stored process.

Here is the Stored Process code:

```
data lines ;
    input ;
    line=resolve(_infile_) ;
    cards4 ;
<HTML>
<head>
<script>
function validateForm() {
    var x = document.forms["myForm"]["table"].value;
    if (x == "") {
        alert("You have to enter a table");
        return false;
    }
}
</script>
</head>
<body>
<form method="get" action="http://&_srvname:&_srvport/&_url?"
    name="myForm" onsubmit="return validateForm()">
<input type="hidden" name="_program" value="&_program">
Enter the name of a table: <input type="text" name="table">
<input type="submit" value="Run">
</form>
<p>Try using sashelp.orsales as the table</p>
</body>
</HTML>
;;;;
run ;
```

```
%macro logic ;
    %if %symexist(table) %then %do ;
        %if %sysfunc(exist(&table)) %then %do ;
            %stpbegin
            proc print data=&table ;
            run ;
            %stpend
        %end ;
        %else %do ;
            data _null_ ;
                file _webout ;
                put "<script>alert('Table &table does not exist!');" ;
                put "window.history.back()</script>" ;
            run ;
        %end ;
    %end ;
    %else %do ;
        data _null_ ;
            file _webout ;
            set lines ;
            put line ;
        run ;
    %end ;
%mend logic ;
%logic
```

Figure 8-54 is what is displayed when it is run.

Enter the name of a table: [   ] [Run]

Figure 8-54. *Prompt in browser*

If this is run without entering a table name, then this alert is displayed (Figure 8-55).

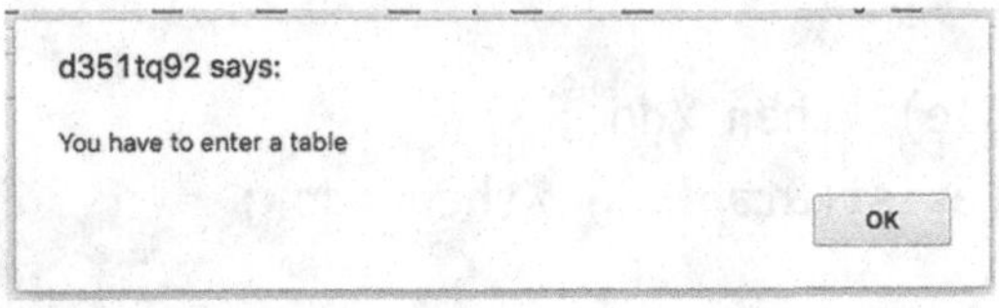

Figure 8-55. *Alert displayed in browser if you don't enter a table*

If a table name is entered and the Run button pressed, but the table does not exist, then the message in Figure 8-56 is displayed.

Figure 8-56. *Alert displayed in browser if you enter a table that can't be found*

When a table that does exist is entered and Run pressed, then the table in Figure 8-57 is displayed.

Obs	Name	Sex	Age	Height	Weight
1	Alfred	M	14	69.0	112.5
2	Alice	F	13	56.5	84.0
3	Barbara	F	13	65.3	98.0
4	Carol	F	14	62.8	102.5
5	Henry	M	14	63.5	102.5
6	James	M	12	57.3	83.0
7	Jane	F	12	59.8	84.5
8	Janet	F	15	62.5	112.5
9	Jeffrey	M	13	62.5	84.0
10	John	M	12	59.0	99.5
11	Joyce	F	11	51.3	50.5
12	Judy	F	14	64.3	90.0
13	Louise	F	12	56.3	77.0
14	Mary	F	15	66.5	112.0
15	Philip	M	16	72.0	150.0
16	Robert	M	12	64.8	128.0
17	Ronald	M	15	67.0	133.0
18	Thomas	M	11	57.5	85.0
19	William	M	15	66.5	112.0

Figure 8-57. *Report produced in browser when valid table is entered*

Loading a Stored Process into Part of a Web Page

Here is a piece of HTML which will run a Stored Process ① and load its output into **part of a web page** when a button is pressed. This technique can form the basis of a web application as you can prompt the user for things in one part of the screen and then run a Stored Process to load the results into another part of the screen.

The text shown in **bold** shows the Stored Process that is being run. Whatever output that this Stored Process produces will be returned and loaded into the div section called div1.

The text shown in *italics* shows the id for the part of the HTML page that will be populated with the output of the Stored Process. It is a div section, which is generally a great tag to use to populate with things since it is basically a container for other things. I have some text in the div section which will be displayed first, but will then be replaced once the Stored Process has run and its results loaded into the div:

```
<!DOCTYPE HTML>
<HTML>
<head>
<script src="https://ajax.googleapis.com/ajax/libs/jquery/1.12.0/jquery.
min.js"></script>
<script>
$(document).ready(function(){
  $("button").click(function(){
    $("#div1").load("http://my_server/SASStoredProcess/do?_program=%2FUser
    +Folders%2Fphil%2FMy+Folder%2FExercise+2"); ①
  });
});
</script>
</head>
<body>
<h1>This is how we can load something to this web page</h2>
<hr>
<div id="div1"><h2>Let jQuery AJAX Change This Text</h2></div>
<button>Get External Content</button>
</body>
</HTML>
```

This produces the following page as shown in Figure 8-58.

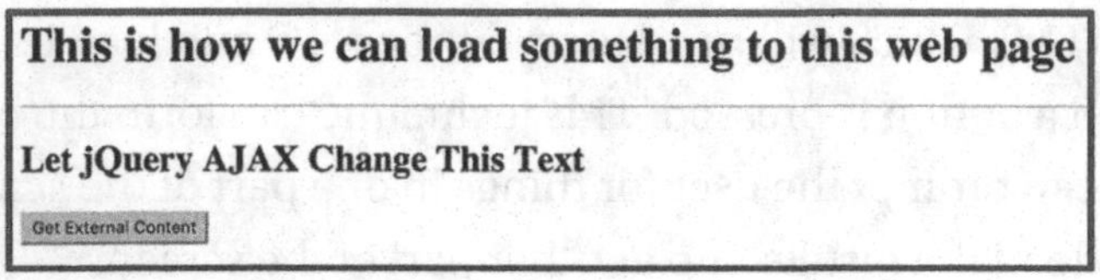

Figure 8-58. *Displayed in browser using previous code*

Other Recommended JavaScript Libraries

I have used many libraries over the years and have found some to be great ones that I use over and over again. Here is a list of some libraries to get you started. There are bound to be other great ones I don't know about, so you shouldn't use this as a definitive list but keep looking and seeing what people are using. A good place to see what people are using is to search for a list of top JavaScript libraries and read one of the many reviews. Or you can go to a Content Delivery Network and look at a list of how many times a library has been used.[10]

Grids

If you are unfamiliar with web technology, you may wonder what exactly a grid is – it's just a table displayed on a web page. We can make a table in HTML and display that; however, when we scroll down a big table, we leave behind the column headings at the top and can be left wondering what we are looking at. Same goes for when we scroll to the right across a wide table and lose row titles. Grids work a bit like EXCEL keeping row and column titles in place, so we avoid this problem. They can also add a lot of functionality along the lines of what something like EXCEL can do. So, they might let us use traffic lighting, create calculated columns, pop up menus of functionality with the right mouse button, and so on. We can do some of this with a standard HTML table and by using some CSS with it, but it is limited and quickly becomes overly complex. But grids can make all this very simple, and if we choose the right one, it can work in a similar/compatible way as jQuery.

---

[10]Top 200 link on https://cdnjs.com/

jqGrid

jqGrid (jQuery grid plug-in) is a JavaScript library which enables creating data grids on web pages quite easily.

You can see demos and learn all about jqgrid at www.guriddo.net/demo/guriddojs/. Their website shows many examples of grids you can display on a web page and the huge amount of functionality available.

The following code shows an example of using a grid like this in conjunction with a **Stored Process** ①, which produces JSON-formatted data that is then displayed by the JavaScript object as a grid:

```
<!DOCTYPE HTML>

<HTML lang="en">
<head>
    <!-- The jQuery library is a prerequisite for all jqSuite products -->
    <script type="text/ecmascript" src="http://code.jquery.com/jquery--
    2.2.4.min.js"></script>
    <!-- This is the JavaScript file of jqGrid -->
    <script type="text/ecmascript" src="http://www.guriddo.net/demo/js/
    trirand/jquery.jqGrid.min.js"></script>
    <!-- This is the localization file of the grid controlling messages,
    labels, etc. -->
    <!-- We support more than 40 localizations -->
    <script type="text/ecmascript" src="http://www.guriddo.net/demo/js/
    trirand/i18n/grid.locale-en.js"></script>
    <!-- A link to a jQuery UI ThemeRoller theme, more than 22 built-in and
    many more custom -->
    <link rel="stylesheet" type="text/css" media="screen" href="http://www.
    guriddo.net/demo/css/jquery-ui.css" />
    <!-- The link to the CSS that the grid needs -->
    <link rel="stylesheet" type="text/css" media="screen" href="http://www.
    guriddo.net/demo/css/trirand/ui.jqgrid.css" />
    <meta charset="utf-8" />
    <title>jqGrid Loading Data - JSON</title>
</head>
<body>
```

```
    <table id="jqGrid"></table>
    <div id="jqGridPager"></div>
<script type="text/JavaScript">

$(document).ready(function () {

        $("#jqGrid").jqGrid({
①         url: 'http://my_server/SASStoredProcess/do?_program=%2FUser+Folders%2F
                phil%2FMy+Folder%2Fjson',
        datatype: "json",
         colModel: [
            { label: 'Year', name: 'Year', width: 75 },
            { label: 'Quarter', name: 'Quarter', width: 90 },
            { label: 'Product_Line', name: 'Product_Line', width: 100 },
            { label: 'Product_Category', name: 'Product_Category', width: 100 },
            { label: 'Product_Group', name: 'Product_Group', width: 100 },
            { label: 'Profit', name: 'Profit', width: 80, sorttype: 'integer' },
            { label: 'Total_Retail_Price', name: 'Total_Retail_Price',
                      width: 80, sorttype: 'integer' },
            // sorttype is used only if the data is loaded locally or loadonce
            is set to true
            { label: 'Quantity', name: 'Quantity', width: 80, sorttype:
                      'number' }
        ],
        viewrecords: true, // show the current page, data range and total
                           records on the toolbar
        width: 780,
        height: 400,
        rowNum: 30,
        loadonce: true, // this is just for the demo
        pager: "#jqGridPager"
    });
});

 </script>
</body>
</HTML>
```

The following SAS code is for the Stored Process (JSON) that delivers the data to this grid. Here I have looked at the format of the JSON data that the grid needs and used some nice options available from SAS 9.4 onward that allows me to customize my JSON data to match what is required exactly:

```
* create a JSON version of the SAS table ;
proc json out=_webout pretty nosastags ;
   write open object ;
   write values "rows" ;
   write open array ;
   export sashelp.orsales ;
   write close ;
   write close ;
run ;
```

The grid that this makes will look like Figure 8-59, and you can sort the columns. The drawback to using this specific technique on large tables is that I am loading the entire table first and then using the grid to display it.

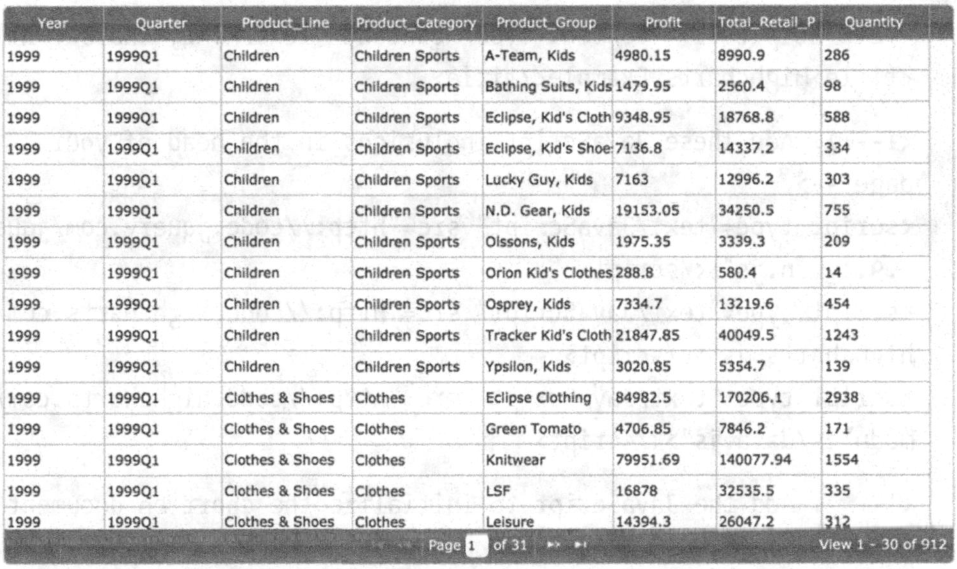

Year	Quarter	Product_Line	Product_Category	Product_Group	Profit	Total_Retail_P	Quantity
1999	1999Q1	Children	Children Sports	A-Team, Kids	4980.15	8990.9	286
1999	1999Q1	Children	Children Sports	Bathing Suits, Kids	1479.95	2560.4	98
1999	1999Q1	Children	Children Sports	Eclipse, Kid's Cloth	9348.95	18768.8	588
1999	1999Q1	Children	Children Sports	Eclipse, Kid's Shoe	7136.8	14337.2	334
1999	1999Q1	Children	Children Sports	Lucky Guy, Kids	7163	12996.2	303
1999	1999Q1	Children	Children Sports	N.D. Gear, Kids	19153.05	34250.5	755
1999	1999Q1	Children	Children Sports	Olssons, Kids	1975.35	3339.3	209
1999	1999Q1	Children	Children Sports	Orion Kid's Clothes	288.8	580.4	14
1999	1999Q1	Children	Children Sports	Osprey, Kids	7334.7	13219.6	454
1999	1999Q1	Children	Children Sports	Tracker Kid's Cloth	21847.85	40049.5	1243
1999	1999Q1	Children	Children Sports	Ypsilon, Kids	3020.85	5354.7	139
1999	1999Q1	Clothes & Shoes	Clothes	Eclipse Clothing	84982.5	170206.1	2938
1999	1999Q1	Clothes & Shoes	Clothes	Green Tomato	4706.85	7846.2	171
1999	1999Q1	Clothes & Shoes	Clothes	Knitwear	79951.69	140077.94	1554
1999	1999Q1	Clothes & Shoes	Clothes	LSF	16878	32535.5	335
1999	1999Q1	Clothes & Shoes	Clothes	Leisure	14394.3	26047.2	312

Page **1** of 31 ▶▶ ▶▮   View 1 - 30 of 912

Figure 8-59. *Resulting grid*

There are other features that can be used with this JavaScript object to change the behavior of the grid. For instance, if you have a very large number of rows, then you can specify a pager, rownum, and page parameter. When data is requested, it will pass these parameters on the URL call to the Stored Process, which will enable you to modify your Stored Process to just return the rows that are required for that page, rather than all the rows in the table. This can make it very efficient to view very large tables.

Highcharts

Highcharts is a JavaScript library which enables you to create powerful charts quite easily with a relatively small amount of JavaScript. You can feed the graphs with data from a Stored Process, like all other JavaScript objects we will look at. Many examples are shown on their website – www.highcharts.com.

Here is some sample code which provides the data for the graph using a **Stored Process** ①. Note that I am using a CSV file as input here, although Highcharts supports a lot of different data formats.

```
<HTML>
  <head>
        <meta http-equiv="Content-Type" content="text/HTML; charset=utf-8">
        <title>Highcharts Example</title>

        <!-- 1. Add these JavaScript inclusions in the head of your
        page -->
        <script type="text/JavaScript" src="http://code.jquery.com/jquery--
        1.9.1.min.js"></script>
        <script type="text/JavaScript" src="http://code.highcharts.com/
        highcharts.js"></script>
        <script type="text/JavaScript" src="http://code.highcharts.com/
        modules/data.js"></script>

        <!-- 2. Add the JavaScript to initialize the chart on document
        ready -->
        <script type="text/JavaScript">
```

```
      $(document).ready(function() {
①    $.get('http://d351tq92/SASStoredProcess/do?_program=%2FUser+Folders%2
      Fphil%2FMy+Folder%2Fcsv', function(csv) {
            $('#container').highcharts({
                  chart: { type: 'column' },
                  data: { csv: csv },
                  title: { text: 'Sales Data' },
                  yAxis: {  title: { text: 'USD' } }
            });
         });
      });
      </script>
   </head>
   <body>
      <!-- 3. Add the container -->
      <div id="container" style="width: 800px; height: 400px; margin: 0
      auto"></div>
   </body>
</HTML>
```

The following SAS code is the Stored Process (csv) which delivers the data to the Highcharts object:

```
proc summary data=sashelp.orsales nway ;
   class Quarter  ;
   var Total_Retail_Price Quantity Profit ;
   output out=sum_orsales(drop=_type_ _freq_) sum= ;
run ;

* create a CSV version of the summary ;
proc export data=sum_orsales outfile=_webout dbms=csv replace ;
run ;
```

This code produces a nice vertical bar chart which looks great and has some built-in functionality. One simple thing you can do is to click the legend and eliminate bars from the graph or click again to include them.

277

D3

D3 is a very powerful and hugely popular JavaScript visualization library. It is reasonably easy to make use of but is capable of quite complex usage to visualize in almost any way you can think of. They have many great examples on their website – https://d3js.org.

This code uses the D3 library together with the DC and Crossfilter libraries which allows you to link objects to create a very powerful visualization. Data is provided using the **Stored Process** ①.

```
<!DOCTYPE HTML>
<HTML lang="en">
<head>
    <title>dc.js - Number Display Example</title>
    <meta charset="UTF-8">
    <link rel="stylesheet" type="text/css" href="http://dc-js.github.io/
    dc.js/css/dc.css"/>
</head>
<body>
<h1>Stored Process with simple crossfilter</h1>
<div id="chart-ring-Year"></div>
<div id="chart-hist-spend"></div>
<div id="chart-row-spenders"></div>

<script type="text/JavaScript" src="http://dc-js.github.io/dc.js/js/
d3.js"></script>
<script type="text/JavaScript" src="http://dc-js.github.io/dc.js/js/
crossfilter.js"></script>
<script type="text/JavaScript" src="http://dc-js.github.io/dc.js/js/
dc.js"></script>
<script type="text/JavaScript">

var YearRingChart    = dc.pieChart("#chart-ring-Year"),
    spendHistChart   = dc.barChart("#chart-hist-spend"),
    spenderRowChart  = dc.rowChart("#chart-row-spenders");
```

① d3.csv(**"http://d351tq92/SASStoredProcess/do?_program=%2FUser+Folders%2Fp hil%2FMy+Folder%2Fcsv2&table=sashelp.orsales"**, function(spendData) {

```
// normalize/parse data
spendData.forEach(function(d) {
    d.Quantity = d.Quantity.match(/\d+/);
});

// set crossfilter
var ndx = crossfilter(spendData),
    YearDim  = ndx.dimension(function(d) {return +d.Year;}),
    spendDim = ndx.dimension(function(d) {return Math.floor(d.
    Quantity/1000);}),
    Product_CategoryDim  = ndx.dimension(function(d) {return d.Product_
    Category;}),
    spendPerYear = YearDim.group().reduceSum(function(d) {return
    +d.Quantity;}),
    spendPerProduct_Category = Product_CategoryDim.group().
    reduceSum(function(d) {return +d.Quantity;}),
    spendHist    = spendDim.group().reduceCount();

YearRingChart
    .width(300).height(300)
    .dimension(YearDim)
    .group(spendPerYear)
    .innerRadius(50);

spendHistChart
    .width(400).height(300)
    .dimension(spendDim)
    .group(spendHist)
    .x(d3.scale.linear().domain([0,10]))
    .elasticY(true);

spendHistChart.xAxis().tickFormat(function(d) {return d*1000}); // convert
back to base unit
spendHistChart.yAxis().ticks(2);

spenderRowChart
    .width(700).height(300)
    .dimension(Product_CategoryDim)
```

```
    .group(spendPerProduct_Category)
    .elasticX(true);

dc.renderAll();
});

</script>
</body>
</HTML>
```

The SAS code in the Stored Process (csv2) which delivers the data is very simple, as follows:

```
proc export data=&table outfile=_webout dbms=csv replace ;
run ;
```

The following output in Figure 8-60 is produced by the preceding code. The three graphs displayed are linked together so that if you click any bar or pie segment, then that is selected, and the other graphs change to reflect your selection. This enables some interactive data exploration to be done.

Stored Process with simple crossfilter

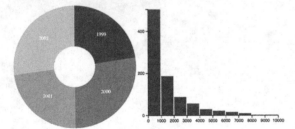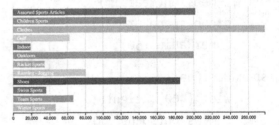

Figure 8-60. *Output graphs*

Summary

In this chapter, we look at the incredibly useful SAS Stored Process Web Application. This is provided by SAS to enable stored processes to execute through a web browser and other RESTful applications. We looked at some of these topics:

- Index page that allows browsing through stored processes available and running them

- Sample stored processes available with a SAS installation

- Lots of macro variables that can be used with %stpbegin to affect what the web application returns, for example, _debug=log to return a SAS log

- Using automatic SAS macro variables to detect things about the environment that the stored process is executing in, for example, &_metaperson holds the name of the user from metadata

- How to use HTML forms to run stored processes from a web page

- Process of creating a simple SAS program and converting it into a stored process–based web application providing flexibility and some powerful features by using the macro variables available

- How to upload files to a server with a stored process

- How to use sessions for sharing information between stored processes

- Logs that are available for help with understanding the execution of stored processes

- Linking stored processes so that one will run after another

- Some very useful JavaScript libraries that can provide useful functionality to web applications

CHAPTER 9

SAS Procedures

You can use all the power of SAS as you develop Stored Processes, including the many procedures that provide so much functionality in an easy-to-use package. There are several procedures that are particularly helpful with developing Stored Processes. In this chapter, we will cover

- PROC STP, which allows you to run a Stored Process from other SAS code.

- PROC JSON, which lets you produce JSON-formatted data that is used extensively by JavaScript objects used in building web pages.

- PROC STREAM, which will take some text, resolve any macro variables in it, and send the output on to somewhere, which could be a file or web page.

- PROC HTTP, which can issue HTTP requests and get the response for use in SAS.

- PROC EXPORT, which will export SAS data in various formats including CSV and tab-separated formats.

- PROC IMPORT, which will import data from various supported formats into a SAS table. This is useful to read CSV and other formats of data.

PROC STP

This procedure allows Stored Processes to be executed from a SAS program. This opens up a lot more flexibility and power for the use of Stored Processes. You can execute them in batch, interactively or on servers. It can run locally or on a server, but with its own execution environment, so it has its own work library and so on. If you want to run it on a server, then it needs some additional configuration to work that way.

© Philip Mason 2020

P. Mason, *SAS Stored Processes*, https://doi.org/10.1007/978-1-4842-5925-2_9

The following example code in Listings 9-1 and 9-2 shows how to run a stored process from a normal SAS program. This could be run in batch overnight or in fact from anywhere you can execute SAS code.

Listing 9-1. SAS Program to run a stored process from a regular SAS program

```
* connect to metadata server ;
options metaserver=d351tq92 metaport=8561 metauser=phil metapass=goodnight_
for_president ;
* close any open ODS destinations ;
ods _all_ close;
* run Stored Process and put the ODS results into an ODS Item Store ;
proc stp program='/Products/SAS Intelligence Platform/Samples/Sample:
Cholesterol by Sex and Age Group'
        odsout=store;
run;
* set the format for graphics we will produce ;
goptions device=png;
* Open an HTML destination ;
ods HTML path="%sysfunc(pathname(work))" file='test.htm' style=HTMLBlue;
* Send  the output to the current ODS destination ;
proc document name=&_ODSDOC (read);
   replay / levels=all;
run;
quit ;
ods HTML close;
%put _ODSDOC: %superq(_ODSDOC) ;
%put Output has been put into %sysfunc(pathname(work)) ;
```

Listing 9-2. SAS Log produced from running the program

```
1    * connect to metadata server ;
2    options metaserver=d351tq92 metaport=8561 metauser=phil
     metapass=XXXXXXXXX;

3    * close any open ODS destinations ;
4    ods _all_ close;
```

```
5    * run Stored Process and put the ODS results into an ODS Item Store ;
6    proc stp program='/Products/SAS Intelligence Platform/Samples/Sample:
     Cholesterol by Sex and Age
6  ! Group'
7              odsout=store;
8    run;
```

NOTE: The Stored Process will execute locally.
NOTE: PROC_STP: ====== Proc STP Execution Starting ======
NOTE: PROC_STP: ====== Stored Process: /Products/SAS Intelligence
Platform/Samples/Sample:
     Cholesterol by Sex and Age Group ======

>>> SAS Macro Variables:

```
 _CLIENT=PROCSTP TKESTP Windows X64_SRV12 X86_64 6.2
 _METAPERSON=phil
 _METAUSER=phil@!*(generatedpassworddomain)*!
 _ODSDEST=DOCUMENT
 _ODSDOC=APSWORK._odsdoc00000001
 _RESULT=STREAM

2    %STPBEGIN;
3
4    proc format;
5      value AgeAtStart low-35  = '< 36'
6                       36-45   = '36 - 45'
7                       46-55   = '46-55'
```
NOTE: Format AGEATSTART has been output.
```
8                       56-high = '> 55';
9    run;
```
NOTE: PROCEDURE FORMAT used (Total process time):
      real time   0.04 seconds
      cpu time   0.01 seconds
```
9  !     quit;
10
```

```
11   title 'Cholesterol by Sex and Age Group';
12   footnote "Generated %sysfunc(datetime(), datetime19.).";
13
14   proc sgpanel data=sashelp.heart;
15     panelby sex / columns=1
16                     novarname;
17     hbox Cholesterol / category=AgeAtStart;
18     format AgeAtStart AgeAtStart.;
19   run;
19 !     quit;
```

NOTE: There were 5209 observations read from the data set SASHELP.HEART.
NOTE: PROCEDURE SGPANEL used (Total process time):
      real time   0.16 seconds
      cpu time   0.11 seconds

```
20
21   %STPEND;
```

NOTE: PROC_STP: ====== Stored Process: /Products/SAS Intelligence Platform/
Samples/Sample:
      Cholesterol by Sex and Age Group Return Status = 0 ======
NOTE: PROC_STP: ====== Proc STP Execution Ending ======
NOTE: PROCEDURE STP used (Total process time):
      real time   0.60 seconds
      cpu time   0.35 seconds

```
9    * set the format for graphics we will produce ;
10   goptions device=png;
11   * Open an HTML destination ;
12   ods HTML path="%sysfunc(pathname(work))" file='test.htm'
     style=HTMLBlue;
```

NOTE: Writing HTML Body file: test.htm

```
13   * Send  the output to the current ODS destination ;
14   proc document name=&_ODSDOC (read);
15     replay / levels=all;
16   run;
```

NOTE: The data set WORK.DATA1 has 4 observations and 21 variables.
NOTE: Format AGEATSTART has been output.
NOTE: There were 4 observations read from the data set WORK.DATA1.
NOTE: PROCEDURE FORMAT used (Total process time):
        real time   0.03 seconds
        cpu time   0.00 seconds

17   quit ;

NOTE: PROCEDURE DOCUMENT used (Total process time):
        real time   1.59 seconds
        cpu time   0.37 seconds

18   ods HTML close;
19   %put _ODSDOC: %superq(_ODSDOC) ;
_ODSDOC: APSWORK._odsdoc00000001
20   %put Output has been put into %sysfunc(pathname(work)) ;

    Output has been put into

C:\Users\phil\AppData\Local\Temp\2\SAS Temporary Files_TD11484_D351TQ92_

    The SAS Output is written to the location shown in the log, and the directory listing of where PROC STP wrote the output to is also listed in the log. Notice that the PROC DOCUMENT created a graphic file (Figure 9-1) called SGPanel.png (Figure 9-2). The type was set by device= on the goptions statement, and the name defaults to the procedure that was used to produce the graphic. If we have multiple graphics, then they get a sequence number on the end, for example, SGPanel.png, SGPanel1.png, SGPanel2. png, and so on.

Cholesterol by Sex and Age Group
Female
Male
< 36
36 - 45
46-55
> 55
Age at Start
100
200
300
400
500
Cholesterol
Generated 04NOV2017:09:25:48.

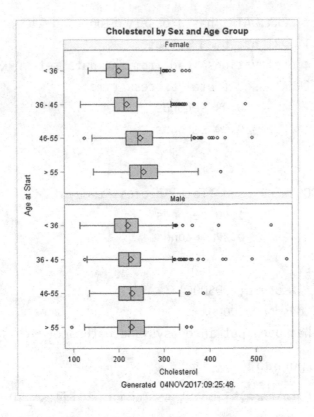

***Figure 9-1.** Output produced by the previous program*

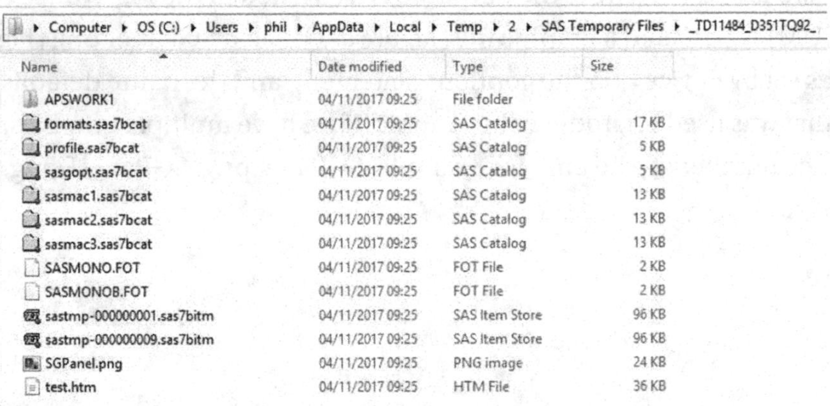

Computer ▸ OS (C:) ▸ Users ▸ phil ▸ AppData ▸ Local ▸ Temp ▸ 2 ▸ SAS Temporary Files ▸ _TD11484_D351TQ92_
Name | Date modified | Type | Size
APSWORK1 | 04/11/2017 09:25 | File folder
formats.sas7bcat | 04/11/2017 09:25 | SAS Catalog | 17 KB
profile.sas7bcat | 04/11/2017 09:25 | SAS Catalog | 5 KB
sasgopt.sas7bcat | 04/11/2017 09:25 | SAS Catalog | 5 KB
sasmac1.sas7bcat | 04/11/2017 09:25 | SAS Catalog | 13 KB
sasmac2.sas7bcat | 04/11/2017 09:25 | SAS Catalog | 13 KB
sasmac3.sas7bcat | 04/11/2017 09:25 | SAS Catalog | 13 KB
SASMONO.FOT | 04/11/2017 09:25 | FOT File | 2 KB
SASMONOB.FOT | 04/11/2017 09:25 | FOT File | 2 KB
sastmp-000000001.sas7bitm | 04/11/2017 09:25 | SAS Item Store | 96 KB
sastmp-000000009.sas7bitm | 04/11/2017 09:25 | SAS Item Store | 96 KB
SGPanel.png | 04/11/2017 09:25 | PNG image | 24 KB
test.htm | 04/11/2017 09:25 | HTM File | 36 KB

***Figure 9-2.** Temporary files in work area used by the program run*

To read more about the STP procedure in SAS 9.4, you can use this link: `http://support.sas.com/documentation/cdl/en/stpug/68399/HTML/default/ p0yy4kd3k4dc03n1mcd76hog6y2u.htm`. Remember that Proc STP is only available from SAS 9.3 onward.

PROC JSON

In SAS 9.4, there is a new procedure called PROC JSON which will create data in JSON format from any data that SAS can read. This enables us to create JSON output to be used in JavaScript objects from virtually any other data source. Some options are provided to customize the JSON produced, which enables very flexible JSON output to be created.

Figure 9-3 shows a table we will use in an example.

	Name	Sex	Age	Height	Weight
1	Alfred	M	14	69	112.5
2	Alice	F	13	56.5	84
3	Barbara	F	13	65.3	98
4	Carol	F	14	62.8	102.5
5	Henry	M	14	63.5	102.5
6	James	M	12	57.3	83
7	Jane	F	12	59.8	84.5
8	Janet	F	15	62.5	112.5
9	Jeffrey	M	13	62.5	84
10	John	M	12	59	99.5
11	Joyce	F	11	51.3	50.5
12	Judy	F	14	64.3	90
13	Louise	F	12	56.3	77
14	Mary	F	15	66.5	112
15	Philip	M	16	72	150
16	Robert	M	12	64.8	128
17	Ronald	M	15	67	133
18	Thomas	M	11	57.5	85
19	William	M	15	66.5	112

Figure 9-3. *sashelp.class table to use in the following example*

Here is the Stored Process code to create some JSON:

```
proc json out=_webout;
    export &table / tablename="&table";
run;
```

Here is some of the JSON that is produced by it, when I feed in a parameter of &table=sashelp.class:

{"SASJSONExport":"1.0","SASTableData+sashelp.class":[{"Name":"Alfred","Sex":"M","Age":14,"Height":69,"Weight":112.5},{"Name":"Alice","Sex":"F","Age":13,"Height":56.5,"Weight":84},{"Name":"Barbara","Sex":"F","Age":13,"Height":65.3,"Weight":98},{"Name":"Carol","Sex":"F","Age":14,"Height":62.8,"Weight":102.5},{"Name":"Henry","Sex":"M","Age":14,"Height":63.5,"Weight":102.5},{"Name":"James","Sex":"M","Age":12,"Height":57.3,"Weight":83},{"Name":"Jane","Sex":"F","Age":12,"Height":59.8,"Weight":84.5},{"Name":"Janet","Sex":"F","Age":15,"Height":62.5,"Weight":112.5},{"Name":"Jeffrey","Sex":"M","Age":13,"Height":62.5,"Weight":84},{"Name":"John","Sex":"M","Age":12,"Height":59,"Weight":99.5},{"Name":"Joyce","Sex":"F","Age":11,"Height":51.3,"Weight":50.5},{"Name":"Judy","Sex":"F","Age":14,"Height":64.3,"Weight":90},{"Name":"Louise","Sex":"F","Age":12,"Height":56.3,"Weight":77},{"Name":"Mary","Sex":"F","Age":15,"Height":66.5,"Weight":112},{"Name":"Philip","Sex":"M","Age":16,"Height":72,"Weight":150},{"Name":"Robert","Sex":"M","Age":12,"Height":64.8,"Weight":128},{"Name":"Ronald","Sex":"M","Age":15,"Height":67,"Weight":133},{"Name":"Thomas","Sex":"M","Age":11,"Height":57.5,"Weight":85},{"Name":"William","Sex":"M","Age":15,"Height":66.5,"Weight":112**}]}**

You can trim some extraneous information from the JSON using the **nosastags** option on PROC JSON. Here is the output we get if we use NOSASTAGS. Note: In the previous output, I have **bolded** what is dropped by using NOSASTAGS.

[{"Name":"Alfred","Sex":"M","Age":14,"Height":69,"Weight":112.5},{"Name":"Alice","Sex":"F","Age":13,"Height":56.5,"Weight":84},{"Name":"Barbara","Sex":"F","Age":13,"Height":65.3,"Weight":98},{"Name":"Carol","Sex":"F","Age":14,"Height":62.8,"Weight":102.5},{"Name":"Henry","Sex":"M","Age":14,"Height":63.5,"Weight":102.5},{"Name":"James","Sex":"M","Age":12,"Height":57.3,"Weight":83},{"Name":"Jane","Sex":"F","Age":12,"Height":59.8,"Weight":84.5},{"Name":"Janet","Sex":"F","Age":15,"Height":62.5,"Weight":112.5},

```
{"Name":"Jeffrey","Sex":"M","Age":13,"Height":62.5,"Weight":84},{"Name":
"John","Sex":"M","Age":12,"Height":59,"Weight":99.5},{"Name":"Joyce","Sex":
"F","Age":11,"Height":51.3,"Weight":50.5},{"Name":"Judy","Sex":"F","Age":
14,"Height":64.3,"Weight":90},{"Name":"Louise","Sex":"F","Age":12,"Height":
56.3,"Weight":77},{"Name":"Mary","Sex":"F","Age":15,"Height":66.5,"Weight":
112},{"Name":"Philip","Sex":"M","Age":16,"Height":72,"Weight":150},{"Name":
"Robert","Sex":"M","Age":12,"Height":64.8,"Weight":128},{"Name":"Ronald",
"Sex":"M","Age":15,"Height":67,"Weight":133},{"Name":"Thomas","Sex":"M",
"Age":11,"Height":57.5,"Weight":85},{"Name":"William","Sex":"M","Age":15,
"Height":66.5,"Weight":112}]
```

You can also lay out the JSON produced in an easier to read form using the **pretty** option on PROC JSON. This makes it far easier to read. Here is the first part of the output produced:

```
{
    "SASJSONExport": "1.0 PRETTY",
    "SASTableData+class": [
      {
        "Name": "Alfred",
        "Sex": "M",
        "Age": 14,
        "Height": 69,
        "Weight": 112.5
      },
      {
        "Name": "Alice",
        "Sex": "F",
        "Age": 13,
        "Height": 56.5,
        "Weight": 84
      },
```

If we use the PRETTY and NOSASTAGS options, then here is the first part of the output produced:

```
[
   {
     "Name": "Alfred",
     "Sex": "M",
     "Age": 14,
     "Height": 69,
     "Weight": 112.5
   },
   {
     "Name": "Alice",
     "Sex": "F",
     "Age": 13,
     "Height": 56.5,
     "Weight": 84
   },
```

As we know, PROC JSON can produce JSON data, and there are many JavaScript objects that can use JSON data as input. There is an object called jqGrid which has a URL parameter which lets you point to a data source that is in JSON format. Here is a JavaScript snippet of code which would be used to define where the data is for that object. In this case, I can point the object to the SAS Stored Process Web Application, which will call a Stored Process to provide the JSON data:

```
url: 'http://localhost/SASStoredProcess/do?_program=%2FUser+Folders%2Fphil%
2FMy+Folder%2Fjson',
```

In that Stored Process, I can use PROC JSON to produce the JSON data which is needed to feed the object. If you need to customize the standard JSON in order to fit some specific requirements for a JavaScript object, then you are able to use the write statement to write out extra structure to your JSON. In the case of using the jqGrid object, it needs a slightly different JSON layout to standard. I used the code here to get my JSON in the right format for using with the jqGrid object:

```
proc json out=_webout pretty nosastags;
    write open object;
    write values "rows";
    write open array;
    export sashelp.orsales;
    write close;
    write close;
run;
```

Notice in the preceding code that we write to _webout, which when used in a Stored Process with the Stored Process Web Application will stream data directly to the browser.

Another useful thing you might do with PROC JSON is that when you are using some kind of static HTML, you might want to get a list of variables that exist in the data table you are using, so you can automatically generate the menus (for instance). The following code in a stored process would get variable name, type, and label from a table, and then send it back to the browser where JavaScript could make use of that data:

```
proc contents data=sashelp.class out=contents noprint;
run;

filename _webout temp;

proc json out=_webout nosastags pretty;
    export contents(keep=name type memlabel) ;
run;
```

The JSON that would be generated is as follows in Listing 9-3.

Listing 9-3. Generated JSON

```
[
  {
    "MEMLABEL": "Student Data",
    "NAME": "Age",
    "TYPE": 1
  },
  {
    "MEMLABEL": "Student Data",
    "NAME": "Height",
```

```
    "TYPE": 1
  },
  {
    "MEMLABEL": "Student Data",
    "NAME": "Name",
    "TYPE": 2
  },
  {
    "MEMLABEL": "Student Data",
    "NAME": "Sex",
    "TYPE": 2
  },
  {
    "MEMLABEL": "Student Data",
    "NAME": "Weight",
    "TYPE": 1
  }
]
```

Here is a full working example in Listing 9-4.

Listing 9-4. Full example

```
var myfilter = "http://<server>/SASStoredProcess/do?_program=<program>%2F
<stored process name>";

<!DOCTYPE html PUBLIC "-//W3C//DTD XHTML 1.0 Strict//EN" "http://www.
w3.org/TR/xhtml1/DTD/xhtml1-strict.dtd">
<html xmlns="http://www.w3.org/1999/xhtml" xmlns:mso="urn:schemas-
microsoft-com:office:office" xmlns:msdt="uuid:C2F41010-65B3-11d1-A29F-
00AA00C14882">

<head>
<meta http-equiv="Content-Type" content="text/html; charset=utf-8" />
<meta http-equiv="X-UA-Compatible" content="IE=edge" />

<script type="text/javascript" charset="utf8" src="../../webres/jquery--
3.2.1.min.js"></script>
```

```
<script type="text/javascript" charset="utf8" src="../../webres/jquery-
ui-1.12.1/jquery-ui.js"></script>
<link rel="stylesheet" type="text/css" href="../../webres/jquery-ui-
themes-1.9.2/base/jquery-ui.css" />
<link rel="stylesheet" type="text/css" href="../../webres/DT4/datatables.
min.css"/>
<script type="text/javascript" src="../../webres/DT4/datatables.min.js">
</script>

<script type="text/javascript">
var myfilter = "http://<server>/SASStoredProcess/do?_program=<program>%2F
<stored process name>";
var call = $.ajax({ url: myfilter,
    type: "GET",
    dataType: "json",
});
call.done(function (data,textStatus, jqXHR){
    $('#example2 tbody').off('click', 'tr');
    table2 = $('#example2').DataTable({
        dom: 'l<B>frtip', //'Bfrtip', /*dtsettings,*/
        bLengthChange: true,
        buttons: [
            'excelHtml5'
        ],
        "orderCellsTop": true,
        "bDestroy": true,
        "bProcessing": true,
        "lengthMenu": [[10, 25, 50, -1], [10, 25, 50, "All"]],
        "aaData": data,
        "scrollX": true,
        "aoColumns": [
            { 'sTitle': 'Year','mData': 'Year',  'sClass': 'center_column' }
            ,{ 'sTitle': 'Quarter','mData': 'Quarter',  'sClass': 'center_
            column' }
            ,{ 'sTitle': 'Product_Line','mData': 'Product_Line',  'sClass':
            'center_column' }
```

```
            ,{ 'sTitle': 'Product_Category','mData': 'Product_
            Category',  'sClass': 'center_column' }
            ,{ 'sTitle': 'Product_Group','mData': 'Product_
            Group',  'sClass': 'center_column' }
            ,{ 'sTitle': 'Quantity','mData': 'Quantity',  'sClass':
            'center_column' }
            ,{ 'sTitle': 'Profit','mData': 'Profit',  'sClass': 'center_
            column' }
            ,{ 'sTitle': 'Total_Retail_Price','mData': 'Total_Retail_
            Price',  'sClass': 'center_column' }
        ]
        ,"oLanguage": {
            "sSearch": "Search All Columns: "
        }
    });
});
call.fail(function (jqXHR,textStatus,errorThrown){
    alert('unable to obtain data from SAS');
});
</script>
</head>
<body>
<table id='example2' class='display' width='100%'><tfoot><tr></tr>
</tfoot></table>
</body>
</html>
```

PROC STREAM

There are various ways that we can get code into a web browser. We could just write a simple file and then load that into the web browser, such as by creating a file report. HTML and opening it. Usually a better way to do this is to use SAS/Intrnet or a Stored Process to stream code to the browser. From a Stored Process, you can do this by writing lines to the _webout fileref. This could be done by writing to it from a data step, but you can also use PROC STREAM to do this.

Streaming with a Data Step

The data step can be used to stream by writing to **_webout**, when used from a Stored Process in the SAS Stored Process Web Application. If you use any macro language in what is streamed, then it would not be resolved. For example, the following Stored Process

```
%let name=Phil Mason ;
data _null_ ;
    file _webout ;
    input ;
    put _infile_ ;
    cards ;
<HTML>
<h1>Hello &name</h1>
</HTML>
;;
run ;
```

Listing 9-5 would produce this output (Figure 9-4), when run through the SAS Stored Process Web Application.

Hello &name

Figure 9-4. *This is displayed when we view the HTML generated from Listing 9-1*

If you want to resolve the macro language before streaming the HTML code out, then you can use something like the resolve() function. You would then change your Stored Process code to be like this:

```
%let name=Phil Mason ;
data _null_ ;
    file _webout ;
    input ;
    line=resolve(_infile_) ;
    put line ;
    cards ;
<HTML>
```

```
<h1>Hello &name</h1>
</HTML>
;;
run ;
```

This will produce the following output (Figure 9-5) in the web browser.

Hello Phil Mason

Figure 9-5. *Using resolve function means we see this from the HTML generated*

There are some problems using the resolve function in the data step, particularly that there is a limitation on size. So the text for each line can only ever fit into the size of a variable, which is 32K maximum. If macro language expands to take more space than that, then it will be truncated. This can lead to unexpected results and errors. There can be additional issues with escaped HTML characters such as & which is not a SAS macro variable, although SAS will think it is.

Streaming with PROC STREAM

Another way to stream data is to use PROC STREAM. The program would look like this:

```
proc stream outfile=_webout;
    BEGIN
<HTML>
<h1>Hello &name</h1>
</HTML>
;;;;
run;
```

PROC STREAM reads text that appears after the BEGIN statements up to the four semi-colons which indicate the end of input. It then writes the lines to the _webout filreref. As the lines are written, any macro references are resolved, and unlike the RESOLVE() function, there is no limit of data size. This is a hugely powerful facility. In the simplest example, we could have an HTML file where we have a macro variable for the title, which would be replaced as the HTML is streamed to the browser.

A more complex example shows how macro variables and other macro language such as macro functions are all resolved when used within PROC STREAM:

```
%let name=Phil Mason ;
proc stream outfile=_webout ;
BEGIN
<HTML>
<h1>Hello &name</h1>
The time is %sysfunc(time(),time.)
</HTML>
;;;;
run ;
```

The output produced by this is displayed in Figure 9-6.

Hello Phil Mason

The time is 15:48:30

Figure 9-6. *Output with text resolved from macro function call*

An even more complex example shows how all macro language is resolved by PROC STREAM, so even if you use macro programs, they will resolve and what they produce will be included into the stream. If you have a Stored Process with the following code

```
%let name=Phil Mason ;
%macro loop(n) ;
    %do i=1 %to &n ;
        Counting: &i <br>
    %end ;
%mend loop ;
proc stream outfile=_webout ;
BEGIN
<HTML>
<h1>Hello &name</h1>
The time is %sysfunc(time(),time.)
```

```
<p>
%loop(5)
</HTML>
;;;;
run ;
```

it produces the following output (Figure 9-7).

Hello Phil Mason

The time is 15:55:52

Counting: 1
Counting: 2
Counting: 3
Counting: 4
Counting: 5

Figure 9-7. *HTML produced by macro program looping and generating text*

Streaming RTF Files with PROC STREAM

PROC STREAM also works well with other kinds of text files, such as RTF files. You could make a letter and save it as RTF and replace certain parts with macro variables, and then by using PROC STREAM, you could effectively carry out a mail merge to produce a customized letter for a set of macro variables.

So if I go into Microsoft Word and make a document like the one shown in Figure 9-8

Dear Sir,

The date is %sysfunc(date(),date.).

Yours sincerely,
&name

Figure 9-8. *Document in Microsoft Word with some macro code*

I can then save that as an RTF file. This file will have many lines of RTF code, but the lines of interest to use are the ones with the macro statements on them. These are

```
\par The date is %sysfunc(date(),date.).
\par
\par Yours sincerely,
\par &name
```

The following code can be used to read the RTF file in, resolve any macro language, and write it to a new RTF file: "&streamdelim;"

```
%let name=Phil Mason ;
filename oldrtf "F:\letter.rtf" recfm=v lrecl=32767;
filename newrtf "F:\letter1.rtf" recfm=v lrecl=32767;
proc stream outfile=newrtf quoting=both asis;
begin
&streamdelim;
%include oldrtf;
;;;;
```

DOSUB

We can also run SAS code while processing the PROC STREAM by using the dosub function with a %sysfunc. SAS code to be run is pointed to by a `fileref`, and then the dosub uses that `fileref`. If you have some code that you want to run during PROC STREAM, such as this

```
filename myHTML "temp.txt";
data _null_;
    file myHTML;
    set sashelp.class end=end ;
    if _n_=1 then put '<h1>This is my heading</h1><table>';
    put '<tr><td>' name '</td>' '<td>' age '</td></tr>' ;
    if end then put '</table>' ;
run;
```

you can run the preceding code by pointing to the file it is in (dosub.sas) and using the dosub function to run it in PROC STREAM as follows:

```
filename makeHTML 'c:\test\dosub.sas' ;
filename myHTML "temp.txt";
filename report "report.HTML";

proc stream outfile=report ;
begin
%let abc=%sysfunc(dosub(makeHTML));
%include myHTML;
;;;;
```

This runs dosub.sas, which writes HTML to temp.txt. Then in PROC STREAM, we include temp.txt which writes the HTML that the data step generated out to report. HTML. Being able to run code on the fly from within PROC STREAM adds a huge amount of power and flexibility to the use of PROC STREAM.

If you wanted to read a file in to be streamed, without having any macro language resolved, then you can use the readfile keyword. Often this might be used to get some content and put it between PRE tags in HTML, since they are used for pre-formatted content. If you had a log you wanted shown as is in a non-proportional font, then that would be easily done as shown in the code that follows.

For example, the following code uses readfile to read in some text using the exact formatting it had in the file. We then use the PRE HTML tags to enclose that text which indicates that it is pre-formatted text. You can also see that the *&name* which is inside the pre-formatted text is not resolved. However, the **&name** which is inside the text of PROC STREAM is resolved.

```
%let name=Phil ;
filename text temp ;
data _null_;
   file text ;
   input ;
   put _infile_;
   cards4 ;
Here is a line
And here is the next line
```

```
Here is a macro variable - &name
;;;;
run ;

filename dest temp ;
proc stream outfile=dest ;
begin
<PRE>
&streamdelim readfile text ;
</PRE>
My name is &name
;;;;

data _null_;
   infile dest ;
   input ;
   put _infile_ ;
run;
```

The code produces the following output in the log:

```
341   %let name=Phil ;
342   filename text temp ;
343   data _null_;
344      file text ;
345      input ;
346      put _infile_;
347      cards4 ;

NOTE: The file TEXT is:
      Filename=C:\Users\phil\AppData\Local\Temp\2\SAS Temporary
      Files\_TD10384_D351TQ92_\#LN00216,
      RECFM=V,LRECL-32767,File Size (bytes)=0,
      Last Modified=28 September 2017 21:46:30 o'clock,
      Create Time=28 September 2017 21:46:30 o'clock

NOTE: 4 records were written to the file TEXT.
      The minimum record length was 80.
      The maximum record length was 80.
```

```
NOTE: DATA statement used (Total process time):
      real time            0.01 seconds
      cpu time             0.01 seconds

352  ;;;;
353  run ;
354
355  filename dest temp ;
356  proc stream outfile=dest ;
357  begin
358  <PRE>
359  &streamdelim readfile text ;
NOTE: PROCEDURE STREAM used (Total process time):
      real time            0.00 seconds
      cpu time             0.00 seconds

360  </PRE>
361  My name is &name
362  ;;;;

363
364  data _null_;
365     infile dest ;
366     input ;
367     put _infile_ ;
368  run;

NOTE: The infile DEST is:
      Filename=C:\Users\phil\AppData\Local\Temp\2\SAS Temporary
      Files\_TD10384_D351TQ92_\#LN00217,
      RECFM=V,LRECL=32767,File Size (bytes)=358,
      Last Modified=28 September 2017 21:46:30 o'clock,
      Create Time=28 September 2017 21:46:30 o'clock

<PRE>
Here is a line
And here is the next line
Here is a macro variable - &name
```

```
</PRE>My name is Phil
NOTE: 6 records were read from the infile DEST.
      The minimum record length was 5.
      The maximum record length was 80.
NOTE: DATA statement used (Total process time):
      real time           0.01 seconds
      cpu time            0.01 seconds
```

You can force a new line in the streamed output by using newline. You must have the stream delimiter followed by newline in order to do this. There is no other way to be absolutely sure of having a line break in a particular place.

For example, the following code redefines the stream delimiter to be _delim_ and then uses that with newline to make it go to a new line in the output.

```
filename sample temp ;
proc stream outfile=sample resetdelim='_delim_'; begin
Line 1
_delim_ newline;
Line 2

;;;;data _null_ ;
   infile sample ;
   input ;
   put _infile_ ;
run ;
```

The log for this is as follows.

```
393  filename sample temp ;
394  proc stream outfile=sample resetdelim='_delim_'; begin
395  Line 1
NOTE: PROCEDURE STREAM used (Total process time):
      real time           0.00 seconds
      cpu time            0.00 seconds

396  _delim_ newline;
397  Line 2
398  ;;;;
```

```
399
400  data _null_ ;
401     infile sample ;
402     input ;
403     put _infile_ ;
404  run ;
```

```
NOTE: The infile SAMPLE is:
      Filename=C:\Users\phil\AppData\Local\Temp\2\SAS Temporary
      Files\_TD10384_D351TQ92_\#LN00220,
      RECFM=V,LRECL=32767,File Size (bytes)=16,
      Last Modified=28 September 2017 21:59:28 o'clock,
      Create Time=28 September 2017 21:59:28 o'clock
```

```
Line 1
Line 2
NOTE: 2 records were read from the infile SAMPLE.
      The minimum record length was 6.
      The maximum record length was 6.
NOTE: DATA statement used (Total process time):
      real time              0.00 seconds
          cpu time               0.00 seconds
```

If we didn't redefine the delimiter, then the code would have been like the following and produced the same result:

```
filename sample temp ;
proc stream outfile=sample ; begin
Line 1
&streamdelim newline;
Line 2
;;;;

data _null_ ;
   infile sample ;
   input ;
   put _infile_ ;
run ;
```

If we remove the line which forces the newline, then the code will be as follows:

```
filename sample temp ;
proc stream outfile=sample ; begin
Line 1
Line 2
;;;;

data _null_ ;
   infile sample ;
   input ;
   put _infile_ ;
run ;
```

And this produces the following result:

```
451   filename sample temp ;
452   proc stream outfile=sample ; begin
NOTE: PROCEDURE STREAM used (Total process time):
         real time              0.00 seconds
         cpu time               0.00 seconds
453   Line 1
454   Line 2
455   ;;;;

456
457   data _null_ ;
458      infile sample ;
459      input ;
460      put _infile_ ;
461   run ;

NOTE: The infile SAMPLE is:
      Filename=C:\Users\phil\AppData\Local\Temp\2\SAS Temporary
      Files\_TD10384_D351TQ92_\#LN00225,
      RECFM=V,LRECL=32767,File Size (bytes)=14,
      Last Modified=28 September 2017 22:07:29 o'clock,
      Create Time=28 September 2017 22:07:29 o'clock
```

```
Line 1Line 2
NOTE: 1 record was read from the infile SAMPLE.
      The minimum record length was 12.
      The maximum record length was 12.
NOTE: DATA statement used (Total process time):
      real time              0.00 seconds
      cpu time               0.01 seconds
```
You should always check the performance of code using features like dosub, as it can be quite inefficient in some cases and may require some tuning or careful design. Read more about PROC STREAM in the SAS 9.4 documentation here: http://documentation.sas.com/?docsetId=proc&docsetTarget =p06pqn7v5nkz02n0zkpq7832j1yp.htm&docset Version=9.4&locale=en.

PROC HTTP

The HTTP procedure lets you issue HTTP requests. This means that you can make GET or POST requests as well as other kinds of requests. You send data in the request and can receive a response. Then you'll be able to effectively make a call to a URL using PROC HTTP and get the results of it. You can parse the output returned and extract data from it or do something else with that output. You could call a web service, Stored Process, or virtually any web page.

Example Accessing a Web Page

The simplest usage of PROC HTTP is simply to open a web page and receive the response, which will usually be the HTML. The following code in Listings 9-5 and 9-6 opens the SAS home page and collects the HTML into a temporary file under the `fileref` resp.

Listing 9-5. SAS Program that opens a web page and writes out response

```
filename resp TEMP;
proc http
    url="http://www.sas.com"
    out=resp;
run;
```

Listing 9-6. SAS Log of Listing 9-5

```
73    filename resp TEMP;
74    proc http
75        url="http://www.sas.com"
76        out=resp;
77    run;

NOTE: PROCEDURE HTTP used (Total process time):
      real time             1.87 seconds
      cpu time              0.01 seconds

NOTE: 200 OK
```

Example Using a Web Service

The following code in Listing 9-7 allocates two temporary files, one which is used as input to a web service and Listing 9-8 is used to receive the output.

Listing 9-7. SAS Program that opens a web service passing in a value

```
dm 'log;clear' ;
filename in temp ;
filename out temp ;
data _null_;
   file in;
   input;
   put _infile_;
   datalines4;
Celsius=0
;;;;

 proc http
    in=in
    out=out
    url="https://www.w3schools.com/xml/tempconvert.asmx/CelsiusToFahrenheit"
    method="post"
```

```
    ct="application/x-www-form-urlencoded"
    verbose
    ;
run;

data _null_ ;
    infile out ;
    input ;
    put _infile_ ;
run ;
```

Listing 9-8. SAS Log from Listing 9-7 that uses a web service

```
84    dm 'log;clear' ;
85
86    filename in temp ;
87    filename out temp ;
88    data _null_;
89        file in;
90        input;
91        put _infile_;
92        datalines4;
```

```
NOTE: The file IN is:
      Filename=C:\Users\phil\AppData\Local\Temp\2\SAS Temporary Files\_
      TD15020_D351TQ92_\#LN00044,
      RECFM=V,LRECL=32767,File Size (bytes)=0,
      Last Modified=05 September 2017 21:45:59 o'clock,
      Create Time=05 September 2017 21:45:59 o'clock

NOTE: 1 record was written to the file IN.
      The minimum record length was 80.
      The maximum record length was 80.
NOTE: DATA statement used (Total process time):
      real time          0.00 seconds
      cpu time           0.01 seconds
```

```
94    ;;;;
95
96    proc http
97       in=in
98       out=out
99       url="https://www.w3schools.com/xml/tempconvert.asmx/
         CelsiusToFahrenheit"
100      method="post"
101      ct="application/x-www-form-urlencoded"
102      verbose
103      ;
URL                     = https://www.w3schools.com/xml/tempconvert.asmx/
                          CelsiusToFahrenheit
METHOD                  = post
CT                      = application/x-www-form-urlencoded
In                      = C:\Users\phil\AppData\Local\Temp\2\SAS Temporary
Files\_TD15020_D351TQ92_\#LN00044
Out                     = C:\Users\phil\AppData\Local\Temp\2\SAS Temporary
Files\_TD15020_D351TQ92_\#LN00045

104  run;

NOTE: PROCEDURE HTTP used (Total process time):
      real time             0.30 seconds
      cpu time              0.03 seconds

NOTE: 200 OK

105
106  data _null_ ;
107     infile out ;
108     input ;
109     put _infile_ ;
110  run ;
```

```
NOTE: The infile OUT is:
      Filename=C:\Users\phil\AppData\Local\Temp\2\SAS Temporary Files\_
      TD15020_D351TQ92_\#LN00045,
      RECFM=V,LRECL=32767,File Size (bytes)=98,
      Last Modified=05 September 2017 21:45:59 o'clock,
      Create Time=05 September 2017 21:45:59 o'clock

<?xml version="1.0" encoding="utf-8"?>
<string xmlns="https://www.w3schools.com/xml/">32</string>
NOTE: 2 records were read from the infile OUT.
      The minimum record length was 38.
      The maximum record length was 58.
NOTE: DATA statement used (Total process time):
      real time           0.01 seconds
      cpu time            0.01 seconds
```

Note   The URL access method on the FILENAME statement provides quite similar functionality to PROC HTTP. It might be a better option if you are considering PROC HTTP. You can read about PROC HTTP in SAS 9.4 here: `https://support.sas.com/documentation/cdl/en/proc/68954/HTML/default/viewer.htm#n0bdg5vmrpyi7jn1pbgbje2atoov.htm`.

PROC EXPORT

PROC EXPORT takes a SAS table and converts to another format supported. The converted formats could be

- CSV

- EXCEL

- JMP

These are delimited files, like a CSV, but with another delimiter.

The file produced is written to a `fileref` specified using OUTFILE. From a Stored Process running through the Stored Process Web Application, we could specify this as _webout in order to send the exported data directly back to the browser. The REPLACE parameter can be specified in order to replace any file which is there already. When streaming to the browser, we always need to specify this. For example, to stream CSV data from a specific table back to the browser, we could use a PROC EXPORT like this:

```
proc export data=sashelp.orsales outfile=_webout dbms=csv replace;
run;
```

Use Code with a Macro Variable for the Table Name

To generalize this code so it can be used for different tables, we can replace the table name with a macro variable. Here is that code:

```
proc export data=&table outfile=_webout dbms=csv replace;
run;
```

Call Stored Process Passing Parameter for Table

If we now create a Stored Process containing the previous SAS code, then we will be able to call that by using the SAS Stored Process Web Application as follows, remembering to specify a value for the table to be exported. This will then send the table converted to a CSV back to the web browser:

```
http://localhost/SASStoredProcess/do?_program=/User+Folders/phil/My+Folder/
csv&table=sashelp.class
```

Use Code in JavaScript to Feed Objects

If you needed CSV data to feed to a JavaScript object, then you could use a line of JavaScript like the following:

```
$.get('http://localhost/SASStoredProcess/do?_program=/User+Folders/phil/
My+Folder/csv&table=sashelp.class', function(csv)
```

PROC IMPORT

This can be used to read data of various formats into SAS tables. When used with Stored Processes, you could use this to import the data from files uploaded to the server.

Here is some HTML code which will prompt the user for some files to upload to the server. Note that we set the *method* to **POST**, so that we can handle the files being posted in the HTTP request; the alternative would be **GET** but that would not work in all cases. The <u>enctype</u> is set so that we can send multiple files in the upload.

```
<HTML>
<form method="post" action="http://d351tq92/SASStoredProcess/do?"
enctype="multipart/form-data">
<input type="hidden" name="_program" value="/User Folders/phil/My Folder/
upload">
Enter CSV to upload and import <input name="file1" type="file"><p>
Enter CSV to upload and import <input name="file2" type="file"><p>
Enter CSV to upload and import <input name="file3" type="file"><p>
Show this many rows <input name="obs" type="text" value="10"><p>
Debug options <input name='_debug' type='text'><p>
<input type="submit" value="Run">
</form>
</HTML>
```

Figure 9-9 is what is displayed when the HTML is used. Notice that when you specify a type of "file", you get a button which opens a dialog and lets you browse the file system and select a file. When files are uploaded, we get a bunch of automatic macro variables populated which all start with _WEBIN_.

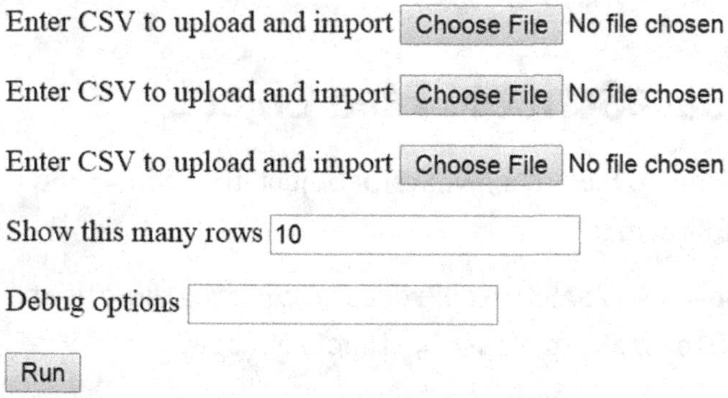

Enter CSV to upload and import [Choose File] No file chosen

Enter CSV to upload and import [Choose File] No file chosen

Enter CSV to upload and import [Choose File] No file chosen

Show this many rows [10]

Debug options [   ]

[Run]

Figure 9-9. *Displayed in browser from previous HTML*

Here is the Stored Process code which the HTML form calls. The PROC SQL at the start of the code lets us look at the values of the *_WEBIN_* macro variables. We get a count of the number of files uploaded which is in _webin_file_count, and we use that to look through each filename to carry out an import on it. We have some **code** ① to fix up the file format of the CSV so it is ready for PROC IMPORT. PROC IMPORT imports each CSV in and assigns it a table name.

```
proc sql ;
    select * from dictionary.macros
    where name like '_WEBIN_%' ;
quit ;
filename temp temp ;
%macro read_loop ;
    %if &_webin_file_count=1 %then %do ;
        %let _webin_fileref1=&_webin_fileref ;
        %let _webin_filename1=&_webin_filename ;
        %end ;
    %do i=1 %to &_webin_file_count ;
        %let csv_file=%sysfunc(pathname(&&_webin_fileref&i));
        %put &=csv_file ;
        * fix the end of line character for Proc Import ;
        data _null_ ; ①
            infile "&csv_file" sharebuffers termstr=cr ;
            file temp  termstr=crlf  ;
            input ;
            line=compress(_infile_,'1a'x) ;
            put line ;
        run ;
        filename in "&csv_file"  ;
        proc import datafile=temp
                    dbms=csv
                    replace
                    out=file&i ;
            getnames=yes ;
        run ;
        %let dsid=%sysfunc(open(file&i)) ;
        title "%sysfunc(attrn(&dsid,nobs),comma12.) rows imported from CSV
        file: &&_webin_filename&i" ;
```

```
        %let dsid=%sysfunc(close(&dsid)) ;
        title2 "Table produced: file&i" ;
        proc print data=file&i(obs=&obs) ;
        run ;
    %end ;
%mend read_loop ;
%read_loop
```

Figure 9-10 is the kind of output you get from the PROC SQL, which shows the automatic variables that describe the file being uploaded.

Macro Scope	Macro Variable Name	Offset into Macro Variable	Macro Variable Value
GLOBAL	_WEBIN_CONTENT_LENGTH	0	2597
GLOBAL	_WEBIN_CONTENT_TYPE	0	text/csv
GLOBAL	_WEBIN_FILEEXT	0	csv
GLOBAL	_WEBIN_FILENAME	0	Barclays 2017-10.csv
GLOBAL	_WEBIN_FILEREF	0	#LN00631
GLOBAL	_WEBIN_FILE_COUNT	0	1
GLOBAL	_WEBIN_NAME	0	file1
GLOBAL	_WEBIN_STREAM	0	_in1
GLOBAL	_WEBIN_STREAM_COUNT	0	1

Figure 9-10. *Automatic macro variables available relating to reading files into stored processes from a web browser*

As this section is about using PROC IMPORT, let me describe its use in this instance. PROC IMPORT specifies the file that is being read in by using the *datafile* option which in our case points to a `fileref`, although it can also point directly at a file. The *dbms* option specifies what the file format is, and several formats are supported such as delimited files, EXCEL, and more. The *out* option specifies what SAS table to create when the file is imported. The *replace* option specifies that a file should be overwritten if it exists already. You can read about the procedure and options in depth in the documentation.[1]

---

[1] http://documentation.sas.com/?docsetId=proc&docsetTarget=n18jyszn33umngn14czw2qfw7 thc.htm&docsetVersion=9.4&locale=en

Summary

In this chapter, we look at some of the most useful SAS procedures for using with stored processes and building web applications:

- Proc STP allows us to run a stored process from a regular SAS program, meaning it could be run in the background or batch, or we could run several stored processes from a single SAS program.

- Proc JSON allows us to access any data that SAS can access and write JSON data out. There is quite a lot of flexibility available so we can even build quite complex JSON structures.

- Proc STREAM allows us to take a "stream" of text and send it to a destination (e.g., the web browser) and resolve all macro variables and programs as it goes. You can stream all kinds of text, such as HTML, JavaScript, CSS, RTF, CSV, and so on.

- You can use DOSUB to run SAS code while streaming text.

- Proc HTTP lets you issue HTTP GET or POST requests and capture the response for further processing.

- Proc EXPORT will convert data the SAS can access into another format such as CSV or EXCEL.

- Proc IMPORT will read in a range of different data and convert it into a SAS-supported format.

Index

A

Action element, 236
_ACTION parameter
    background, 207, 208
    combining values, 209
    data, 208
    FORM, 209
    INDEX, 208
    JSP, 209, 210
Agile approach, 13
Anchor tag, 79
Application programming
        interface (API), 81
Architectural concepts, 14, 15
Asynchronous JavaScript and
        XML (AJAX), 85
Authentication
    error message, 234
    HTML Menu, creation
        code, 235
        parameter value, 236
Automatic macro variables, 245, 316

B

Bespoke tools, 20
Beyond Compare, 26, 27
Body onload method, 267
Browser support, 81

C

CDN jQuery, 84
Client-side validation, 77
Code comparison tools
    Beyond Compare, 26, 27
    FC command, 28, 29
    WinMerge, 28
Color prompt, 188
Comma-separated values (CSV)
    consecutive commas, 105
    data step, 106–110
    list of values, 105
    PROC EXPORT, 110, 111
    SASHELP.SAS, 111
    spreadsheet program, 105
Common Development
        (CDEV), 18
Component integration
        testing (CIT), 18
Concurrent versions
        system (CVS), 17
Content delivery
        networks (CDNs), 84, 85
Cookies, 60, 61
Crossfilter, 84
Cross-platform support, 81
Custom HTML, 37, 38
    macro variables, 46
    _webout fileref, 39

© Philip Mason 2020
P. Mason, *SAS Stored Processes*, https://doi.org/10.1007/978-1-4842-5925-2

D

D3, 278, 280
Data, *See also* Dynamic data; Static data
    JavaScript objects, 101, 104
        nosastags, 104
        Stored process code, 102, 103
Datafile option, 316
Data Integration Studio, 19, 129
Data Library Manager, 193
Data library prompt, 189
Data source item prompt, 184–186
Data structures, 72
Date prompt, 173, 175
Date range prompt, 175–179
_debug flags, 210, 211
Debugging JavaScript, 68, 69
Dependencies
    name prompt, 193
    prompt defining, sex, 191
    SAS code, 191
    stored process, 196
    user selects values, 193
    values for sex, 192
Developing web applications
    environments
        SAS, 19
        tools, SAS, 19
        write our own tools, 20
    IDE tools, 23, 24
    JavaScript IDE, 24–26
    Lint tools, 22, 23
    multiple environment system flow, 18
    techniques, stored processes, 21, 22
Development models
    Agile approach, 13
    architectural concepts, 14, 15
    documents production, 15
    freestyle approach, 11, 12
    source control systems (*see* Source
        control systems)
    V-model, 12, 13
Document Object Model (DOM), 70
dosub function, 301, 302, 304–308
Drop-down menu of choices, 237
Dynamic data
    creation, Stored Processes, 100
    JSON data, 99
    SAS program, 99

E

ECMAScript, 65
End-user documentation, 15
Enterprise Guide, 19, 21, 39
    context menu, Stored Process, 156
    data sources and targets, 153, 154
    execution options, 152
    icon, Stored Process, 155
    labelling and saving, Stored
        Process, 148
    location to run code, 150–152
    log, Stored Process run, 157
    modifying stored process
        context menu, 159
        general tab, add new
          prompt, 161, 162
        menu in left pane, 160
        new prompt, creation, 160
        prompt type, choosing (*see* Prompt
          types)
    new Stored Process wizard, 149
    process prompts, 152, 153
    prompting system, 157–159
    results tab, 156
    SAS code, 149, 150
    stored process creation, 148
    summary page, wizard, 155

Event-handler attributes, 72
Event handlers, 70
eXtensible Markup Language (XML)
    create SASHELP.CLASS, 113–115
    Proc Print, 113
    reading XML data into SAS, 112, 113
    text file, 112

F

File/directory prompt, 186–188
fileref, 117
Form attributes
    autocomplete, 58
    enctype, 58
    get, 58
    method, 58
    name, 58
    post, 59
    target, 58
FORM tag, 34–36, 236
Freestyle approach, 11, 12
Functionality, 82

G

GitHub, 17
_GOPT_DEVICE, 211
_GOPT_HSIZE, 211
_GOPTIONS, 212
_GOPT_VSIZE, 211
_GOPT_XPIXELS, 211
_GOPT_YPIXELS, 212

H

Handsontable, 84
Hide at runtime box, 162

Highcharts, 84, 276, 277
Highmaps, 84
Highstocks, 84
HTDOCS directory, 73, 74
HTML
    add HTML to web page
        HTML forms, 51–53
        macro variables, 46–51
        multiple data, 45
        template, 44
    CSS, 33
    form attributes (*see* Form attributes)
    FORM tag, 34–36
    generate HTML, stored process
        basic ODS, 37
        custom HTML, 37, 38
        PROC STREAM, 39
        STPBEGIN and STPEND
            macros, 39–44
    head section, 33
    menus, Stored Process, 54–57
    persistence (*see* Persistence)
    SAS library, 63
    simple HTML code, 32
    structure, 33
HTML5, 31
HTML form, 51–53
Hyperlink prompt, 167, 168

I

Index page
    context menu, 206
    link, Stored Process, 205
    metadata folder structure, 204
    run stored processes, 204
    Stored Processes, list of, 204
INPUT/PUT statements, 38

Input streams, 196

Interactive Development
    Environment (IDE), 23, 24

J, K

JavaScript
  debugging, 68, 69
  description, 65
  ECMAScript, 65
  event handlers, 70
  functions, 77
  generate, Stored Processes
    feed data to object, 72, 73
    load data, 72
    running SAS code, 71
  HTML
    attributes of tags, 69
    basic DOM, 70
  interactivity to web pages
    pop up window, 76, 77
    URLs, 79, 80
    validating form fields, 77–79
  libraries to HTML, 71
  limitations, 65
  program, 66, 67
  web server
    directories, 74
    libraries, 75
    relative paths, 74
  writing and testing, 67, 68

JavaScript debuggers
  Chrome developer tools, 25
  Firefox developer tools, 25
  Internet Explorer developer
    tools, 25
  Safari developer tools, 26

JavaScript dot notation, 88

JavaScript libraries
  benefits, 81, 82
  CDN, 84, 85
  cost, 83
  D3, 278, 280
  ease of use, 83
  functionality, 83
  grids, 272, 275
  Highcharts, 276, 277
  jqGrid, 273, 274
  jQuery (see jQuery)
  popularity, 82
  W3Schools, 83

JavaScript Lint tool, 23

JavaScript Object Notation (JSON)
  data source for JavaScript objects, 115
  data step, 122
  example, 116
  Lint, 121
  Proc Print output, 120
  reading, 117–121
  SAS data to produce, 122
  SASHELP.SAS, 123
  W3Schools website, 115

JavaServer Pages (JSP), 22

jqGrid, 83, 273, 274, 292

jQuery, 83
  actions, 94–96
  AJAX, 85
  code, 87
  elements selection, 92
    class, 91, 92
    ID, 90
    Tag Name, 89
  functionality, 87, 88
  function, single and double clicks, 95
  hello world program, 86
  HTML page, 93

methods, 94
script tag, 86
$ sign, 88
web applications, 85
jQuery JavaScript library, 75

L

Lint tool, 22, 23
Locking, 16
Logs
metadata server, 264, 265
object spawner, 266
pooled workspace server, 262–264
Stored Process Server Logs, 261, 262
workspace server, 262

M

Macro functions, 299
Macro programs, 49
Macro variables, 46–48, 50, 247, 248, 313
Management Console, 20
application server drop-down
menu, 134
connection profile, SAS metadata
server, 130
context menu, metadata folder, 132
context menu, stored process, 140
editing source code, 136
edit Source Code prompt, 137, 138
folders tab, 131
metadata folders, 131
New Stored Process wizard,
page, 132, 133
prompting, Stored Process
administered
folder icon, metadata folders, 145

general tab of properties window, 141
new prompt window, 143
parameters, Enterprise Guide
running, 146
parameters tab of properties
window, 142
prompt type and values window, 144
results tab, 146
screen showing parameter, 144
source code in Metadata, 145
result capabilities, 138
SAS Stored Process servers, 133
server type, selection, 134
source code location, 135
source code repository, 135
Stored Process creation, 139
storing code on disk, 135
Workspace servers, 134
Metadata, 3, 4
Metadata folder structure, 204
Metadata Server Logs, 264, 265
_METAPERSON, 214
_METAUSER, 214
Method element, 236

N

Non-blank value box, 162
Non-matching brackets and quotes, 121
Notepad++, 67
Numeric prompt, 168–172
Numeric range prompt, 172, 173

O

Object Spawner Logs, 266
_ODSDEST, 212, 241
_ODSOPTIONS, 212

_ODSSTYLE, 212
_ODSSTYLESHEET, 212
Output prompts, 196

P

Persistence
    cookies, 60, 61
    files/tables, 62
    storage, 60
    URL, 62
Personal Development (PDEV), 18
Platform differences, 15
Pooled Workspace Server
        Logs, 262–264
Procedures, SAS
    PROC EXPORT, 312, 313
    PROC HTTP, 308–312
    PROC IMPORT, 313, 314, 316
    PROC JSON, 289–296
    PROC STP, 283–289
Process prompts, 152, 153
PROC EXPORT, 110, 312, 313
PROC HTTP
    web page, accessing, 308, 309
    web service, 309–312
PROC IMPORT, 313, 314, 316
PROC JSON, 289–296
PROC PRINT statements, 120
PROC STP, 283–289
PROC STREAM, 39
    data step, 297, 298
    DOSUB, 301, 302, 304–308
    stream data, 298–300
    streaming RTF files, 300, 301
_program, 48, 52, 53
_PROGRAM, 214
Prompt manager, 158

Prompt types
    color, 188
    data library, 189
    data source, 184, 185
    data source item, 185, 186
    date, 173, 175
    date range, 175–179
    file/directory, 186–188
    hyperlink, 167, 168
    numeric, 168–172
    numeric range, 172, 173
    text (*see* Text prompt)
    text range, 167
    time, 179, 180
    time range, 180–182
    timestamp, 182, 183
    timestamp range, 183, 184
    variable, 189, 190

Q

Query Builder, 216

R

Read-only values box, 162
Release management, 17
REPLACE parameter, 313
Requirements documentation, 15
Reserved macro parameters
    automatic macro variables
        _METAPERSON, 214
        _METAUSER, 214
        _PROGRAM, 214
        _SRVNAME, 214
        _SRVPORT, 214
        stored process, 215
        _STPERROR, 214

_URL, 215
_USERNAME, 215
macro variables, %stpbegin
_ACTION (*see* _ACTION parameter)
_DEBUG, 210, 211
_GOPT_DEVICE, 211
_GOPT_HSIZE, 211
_GOPTIONS, 212
_GOPT_VSIZE, 211
_GOPT_XPIXELS, 211
_GOPT_YPIXELS, 212
_ODSDEST, 212
_ODSOPTIONS, 212
_ODSSTYLE, 212
_ODSSTYLESHEET, 212
_RESULT, 213
resolve() function, 238, 297, 298
_RESULT, 213
Revision control systems, 16

S

Sample stored processes, 206
SAS background, 1, 2
SAS/ACCESS, 2
SASHELP.CLASS, 114, 123
SAS/IntrNet, 1, 2
SAS Stored Process servers, 133
SAS Stored Process Web Application, 2, 47
HTML forms to run Stored Processes
automatic macro variables, 245
check boxes, 243, 244
drop-down menu of choices, 237
form tag, 236
graphs, display, 241
log, 244
macro variables, 246
menu in web browser, 240

ODS destination drop-down
menu, 242
_ODSSTYLE=SEASIDE, 243
resolve function, 246
RTF choosing, MS Word, 242
SAS code, 239, 240
time taken, 244
web browser menu, 238
reserved macro parameters (*see*
Reserved macro parameters)
upload files (*see* Uploading files)
SAS Studio, 19
SAS Workspace servers, 5
Scalability issues, 14
Script tags, 71
Sencha Ext JS, 84
Server-side validation, 77
Servlet container, 62
Sessions
data stored, 256
graphs, 259, 260
macro variable and table
available, 257, 259
Stored Process, 257
stored process error, 259
storing macro variable values, 256
stpsrv_session function, 257
web browser displays, 258
Source code repository, 135
Source control systems
archive and backup, 17
concurrent development, 16
configuration, 16
locking/branches, 16
release management, 17
tracking changes, 16
_SRVNAME, 214
_SRVPORT, 214

Static data
    CSV (*see* Comma-separated
        values (CSV))
    description, 104
    JSON (*see* JavaScript Object
        Notation (JSON))
    XML (*see* eXtensible Markup
        Language (XML))
Stored process
    benefits, 6, 7
    creation
        Enterprise Guide (*see* Enterprise
          Guide)
        management console (*see*
          Management Console)
    dependencies, 190–196
    description, 3
    features, 7, 8
    fileref, 8
    input streams and output
        prompts, 196–201
    loading, web page, 271, 272
    macros, 39, 40
    SAS code stored in metadata, 3
    SAS code stored on disk, 4
    SAS products requirement, 9
    SAS program, 3
    SAS program convertion, 128–131
    SAS Stored Process servers, 5
    server logs, 261, 262
    skills, 8
    techniques, building applications, 21, 22
    web application, 5
    vs. Workspace servers, 4, 5
STPBEGIN and STPEND macros, 8, 39–44
_STPERROR, 214
stpsrv_session function, 257

Subversion (SVN), 17
System Development Life
        Cycle (SDLC), 11, 12
System Integration Testing (SIT), 18

T

Team Foundation Server (TFS), 17
Technical documentation, 15
Text editors, 121
Text prompt
    getting values, 165
    options, populating values, 164
    sort order, dynamic prompt values, 166
    specifying number of values, 166
    user selects values, 164
Text range prompt, 167
Time prompt, 179, 180
Time range prompt, 180–182
Timestamp prompt, 182, 183
Timestamp range prompt type, 183, 184

U

UNIX system, 63
Uploading files
    code prompts, 249
    data, 252
    macro variables and
        values, 247, 248, 251
    passing multiple parameters, 252–256
    SAS code, 250, 251
    temporary location, 246
    web browser displays menu, 249
_URL, 215
User Acceptance Testing (UAT), 18
_USERNAME, 215

V

Variable prompt, 189, 190
Version control systems, 16
Virtual DOM frameworks, 70
Visual analytics, 2
V-model, 12, 13

W

w3.css CSS3 library, 75
W3Schools online tutorial website, 66
Waterfall model, 12
Web application building, Stored
    Processes
  access, 228–231
  adding graphs, 231, 232
  modify stored process, 225, 226

parameter, applying, 233–236
Query Builder, 216–218
run Stored Process from Excel, 229
stored process creation, 224–231
Web applications, 4
Web browser, 36, 121
WebDAV server, 101
WEBIN macro variables, 314
_WEBOUT fileref, 39, 40, 297, 298
window.open method, 267
WinMerge, 26, 28
Workspace Server Logs, 262
Workspace servers, 4, 5, 134

X, Y, Z

XML Mapper, 112
XMLMaps, 112

Printed in the United States
by Bookmasters

Printed in the United States
By Bookmasters